"*The Shattering* is a story of how God has made something beautiful out of Marty's life. A saved soul, not just from the pain of this life but a joy unspeakable due to the redemption power of her heavenly Father, Jesus Christ! She has been adopted into the family of God. No powers of darkness could thwart the healing power of the Holy Spirit. She is a soul white as snow with a compassion for others when the world would say 'she should curse God!' Just as Marty has kept her faith, keep reading, keep believing, and see the wonderful loving power of God."

—Larry D. Stewart, Jr.,
Family Preservation and Reunification Specialist

"For years, Marty has been inspiring and encouraging incarcerated women who know, as she does, the shattering effects of childhood sexual abuse. Her wit, humor, wisdom, and love will draw you in as she shares her compelling life story and offers hope and a way to find healing. She is living proof of the power of transformation—from the little 'hillbilly' girl in West Virginia to the powerful woman of faith that she is today. *The Shattering* is a must read book."

—Marilyn A. Nolte,
Chaplain Manager,
Lebanon County Correctional Facility

"Life-changing… Instead of presenting the victim mentality, *The Shattering* draws the reader into the joy of overcoming in victory"

—Nathaniel Johnson,
Executive Director and
Founder of Step into Life Ministries

THE SHATTERING

THE SHATTERING

A Child's Innocence Betrayed

MARSHA BARTH

TATE PUBLISHING
AND ENTERPRISES, LLC

Published by Tate Publishing & Enterprises, LLC
127 E. Trade Center Terrace | Mustang, Oklahoma 73064 USA
1.888.361.9473 | www.tatepublishing.com

Tate Publishing is committed to excellence in the publishing industry. The company reflects the philosophy established by the founders, based on Psalm 68:11,
"The Lord gave the word and great was the company of those who published it."

Published in the United States of America

ISBN: 978-1-62746-650-9
1. Biography & Autobiography / Personal Memoirs
2. Family & Relationships / Abuse / General
13.07.12

DEDICATION

I lovingly dedicate this book to my three precious heroes—my dear brothers, Donnie, Terry, and Pat.

ACKNOWLEDGMENTS

"In all your ways acknowledge Him and He shall direct your paths." I am ever grateful to my loving heavenly Father who was that thread of Hope. Thank you for making something beautiful out of my life.

My heart overflows with thankfulness and love to my beloved Mike, my soul mate, my best friend. You loved me always. You awakened my soul to what love truly is. You lead me into a new life and season. You were God's promise to me fulfilled. Your belief in me, support of my ministry, your endless hours of editing this work—to you, my love, thank you for our life. You are all my love. You are my heart.

To my dear momma—can you ever know the depth of love that you gave me? You inspired me to be more, to rise above my circumstances. You loved me and always believed in me. I honor you my dear Mom with the love you deserve.

To my dear big brothers—Donnie, Terry, and Pat. You loved me, protected me, and kept me in the shelter of your heart. I will forever love you. I dedicate this work to you.

To my family, my loved ones who are always in my heart, to those who sat with me at both of our grammas' dinners, who shared many of the same joys and sorrows, my aunts and uncles and cousins who played a loving part in my life at that time, thank you for your love. To my dear Shawna who shared with me the joy of this book being accepted, don't forget how special you are to me.

To my many friends and loved ones who have walked with me on this journey, I truly thank you. You know who you are and how very special you are to me. You have been there for me, supported and mentored me and urged me on every step of the way. Thank you for believing in me. I love you all dearly. Thank you Pammy and Vicki for being my faithful childhood and forever friends. You have encouraged me and loved me all of my life.

To my precious, precious children and grandchildren, you are my heritage. My dear Mike Jr., my only son, whose heart is as big as the love that engulfs everyone he meets, you are God's chosen one. To my daughter (Mike's wife) whose belief in me has always encouraged my heart, I love you, sweety. To my Jen, who will always be my baby girl, you are an inspiration to all who are around you. Your desire to help others is only surpassed by your love for those who struggle with life. You are so loved. To my precious grandsons—Ethan my philosopher, Jadon my little professor, Colin my entertainer, Benjamin my quiet thinker, and Baby Boy Barth to join us soon, you are Gramma's sunshine. You keep me young, playing ball, climbing trees, and filling my life with a laughter that never ends.

To Tate Publishing and all the staff that worked earnestly with me to make this book a success, thank you for giving me this opportunity.

PREFACE

I was born in the hills of Appalachia. Surrounded by the beautiful mountains, refreshing streams, and southern hospitality, it is a place so peaceful that it resounds of all that God intended for the beauty of His creation. It is an area where poverty has become a way of life, but there is a richness that supersedes the many troubles of life, a richness that comes from what God can do with just one thread of hope or even the faintest flicker of His light.

So often the beauty that God intended for a life is thwarted and darkness covers the soul in a blanket of pain and sorrow. The pain and sorrow of alcoholism, physical, verbal, and sexual abuse covers the child in a cloud of confusion. It is in this darkness that secrets are kept—secrets that can never be discussed or revealed, secrets that cause fear and shame and guilt and blame. It is for pure survival that the heart is kept locked and the key hidden deeply within the soul.

One cannot live the life that God intended when such secrets ravish the soul and destroy the heart. Through the devastation of abuse; hope, love, and innocence are shattered. The enemy of our soul desires to sift us as wheat, to steal, kill, and destroy, but God says, "No! I came to give you life and more abundantly." It is in these moments that hope flickers, and it is important that you know that God has not forsaken you, that He is not the cause of man's sins but the solution to our restoration.

In my heart, I have a passion to reach the brokenhearted and the crushed in spirit with the very knowledge of the reality of a God who is ever touched with our infirmities, who loves and cares for us despite the cruelty of a world that has chosen to live without Him and then to blame Him for the outcome of the very choices that they have imposed on others.

For many years, I had lived under the cloud of darkness and silence. It seemed proper for my secrets to remain hidden and to let the past be forgotten. A heart that is locked over a period will surely die. As it ceases to feel pain, it will also cease to feel love. It is in our silence that Satan holds his greatest shield of defense against us. When we let God tear down the veil of silence, the heart can begin to heal.

No longer silent, I speak out. I bring to you not only the many troubles and sorrows of my life but also the joy of what happens when there is one thread of hope or even the smallest flicker of His love. Sorrow is but for a season. Joy comes in the morning.

May you be blessed by the reading of this book. May your heart be opened to the joy of healing and to the laughter it brings, rather than the pain and suffering. May God heal your broken heart, give you a better understanding, and deliver you into a new life.

Now enter into my life. This is my story......

(circa 1980)

CHAPTER

1

A light breeze blew through the open door and blew the loose pictures off the end table. Julie bent down to pick them up. She leaned back in the chair and fingered the pictures tenderly, looking at them one by one. She paused, engulfed in the memories that they were stirring. A slight smile broke across her young face as she looked at the picture she now held in her hand. It was an old black and white picture. Julie remembered the little white house with the red shutters.

Julie shifted in the big chair. She tucked her legs up under her to get more comfortable. Slowly, she turned the pictures through her hands before stopping once again. The old photo with the pinked edges had caught her attention. Julie held the photo in her hand and placed the other photos down on the table beside her. She peered into the photo as if to glean some understanding from the young face that stared unknowingly back at her. The child in the picture looked to be six or seven years old. His straight, dark-brown hair hung to one side and swept over his small brow. Julie brought the picture closer and studied it in detail. The little boy did not smile, which saddened Julie. Even more disturbing was the lost look in his little eyes. They were void of laughter and appeared sorrowful. The innocence of childhood seemed all but gone. Julie sat puzzled, engulfed in the picture. There was something in his eyes that overshadowed the sorrow. She glanced away in an attempt to figure it out and then turned back to look at the picture once more. Again, she focused on the piercing sorrowful eyes. "It's anger," Julie said sadly to herself. She touched the child's face in the picture and rubbed his cheek as if to comfort the child and to erase his anger. Julie felt a gentle tug on her leg. She laid the picture aside and glanced down.

"Read me a story, Mommy."

Julie glanced down at the bright blue eyes that peered up at her. She reached down and tousled his blond hair.

"Come here, honey," she said and reached down to lift him up. He gathered his books tightly in his arms as she lifted him up onto her lap. "Which one do you want me to read, Mikey?" Julie asked.

Mikey laid his head on her shoulder and pulled out his favorite book. "Mikey wants the *Pokey Wittle Puppy*."

Julie took the book in her hand and began to read the book. "It's nap time, honey," Julie said to Mikey as she finished the story and closed the book. "You can bring some of your books with you if you want." Mikey slid off her lap to gather up his books. Julie knew that he would fall asleep looking at them. "You can lay on Mommy and Daddy's bed so that we don't wake up Jenny, okay?" Mikey gathered as many books as his three-year-old hands could carry and ran to the bedroom.

Julie tiptoed down the hallway and into the other bedroom where Jenny was asleep in her crib. Julie covered her with a light blanket. Blond ringlets surrounded the angelic face as she slept peacefully. Julie turned and left the room and closed the bedroom door quietly behind her as she left the room.

Mikey sat on the queen-sized bed surrounded by his books as Julie entered the room. Julie sat down beside him. "Time to go to sleep," she whispered.

"Okay," Mikey whispered back as he snuggled down into his little blanket. Julie bent down and kissed him. He smiled up at her and gave her an impish grin. Julie smiled back and tenderly touched his forehead and brushed the blond hair gently aside. She paused and peered at the little form nestled with his books and then tiptoed out of the room quietly and closed the door.

Julie went into the kitchen and made herself a cup of tea. She stirred the tea debating to herself on whether to do the wash or clean up the house.

Julie walked into the dining room and placed her tea on the dining table and then turned toward the stereo and lifted the wooden lid. She slid the records up and placed the metal arm to secure them in place before ejecting the first one to play. She would skip doing the cleaning, and the wash, she decided. She picked up her tea and went back into the living room to sit down.

She had no energy since she had returned home from West Virginia. Her grandma Emma's funeral had opened up a floodgate of memories, and Julie was struggling to sort through them. She had thought that looking at the pictures would help her. She knew it would take more than pictures to help her deal with her gramma's death. And she knew that it was more than her gramma's death that was bothering her. She was trying to cope with the past, a past that she had never understood. She felt that she had given it all to God years ago. But it continually crept up on Julie, unexpectedly at times. It would trouble her again and again, and Julie could not understand why. She felt that if she could just understand it all, even in part, that maybe then she could lay it to total rest. She felt tortured in her heart and spirit. She felt almost guilty for trying to understand it. *Everyone always says to put the past behind you*, Julie thought as she sipped her tea. People say "Don't dwell on the past," "Just block it out," "Go on with your life." Some even say cruelly, "Get over it" or "Get a life." Others say, "Well, just give it to God." *Well*, Julie thought to herself, *I've tried all of that, and I'm still troubled. I have so many unanswered questions that I need answered.*

Julie sat the tea down on the small end table beside the pictures and slipped slowly from the chair to her knees. She had learned a long time ago that there was someone she could share her every burden, someone, who cared, loved, and understood her. God had long ago become her refuge and guide. He comforted, encouraged, led, and guided her. Julie poured out her heart and asked Him to give her healing and resolve. After awhile, Julie pulled herself up and sat down in the chair. She propped her head on her hand and sat thinking. A gentle breeze blew through the screened door. Julie turned and glanced out the door. The giant blue spruce sprawled before the porch. She could hear the birds softly singing as she marveled at the beautiful fall foliage on the large sycamores that lined the street.

Julie heard the music playing softly from the stereo. The words seemed to settle into her heart. She curled up into the chair once more and tucked both of her legs beneath her. She reached for her tea and sipped it as she listened once again to the song that played. She had heard the song many times, but today, the words seemed to envelop her in a cloud of comfort. "Something beautiful, something good, all of my confusions, He understood. All I had to offer Him was brokenness and strife, but He made something beautiful out of my life." Julie sat peacefully. She clasped her cup between her hands and let the words from the song comfort her.

As the song ended, Julie sat the cup down and picked up the pictures that lay where she had placed them earlier. She knew what she had to do. God had been putting it on her heart for quite awhile. The trip to West Virginia had only confirmed it. She would deal with her past. Surely if God was big enough to bring her through it as a child, then surely He was big enough to help her to deal with it. Julie was convinced that she, like so many others that she knew, had not, as they said, put it under the blood but had only shoved it under the rug. People were trying to live in the present while stumbling over their past. They were tripping over the lumpy carpet of life where they had shoved everything rather than deal with the issues of the past that had affected them. What Julie could not understand was that if it was truly dealt with and people truly were over it, then why were so many people so quietly struggling and suffering.

"No!" Julie said out loud to herself, shaking her head gently. This was not the Jesus she had come to know. As God had begun to deal with her heart about her past, she had originally debated with Him. "But, God, she had implored, that is in the past." Slowly, over time, God had lovingly showed Julie that to truly heal, one must feel, and to feel, one must deal with their past and overcome it. "But I have dealt with it," Julie protested one day in prayer.

But lovingly, God had spoken to her heart, "I want to bring you higher, to heal you completely." Julie knew it would be painful to deal with her past. But she knew that she was still struggling. It was just that everything had been pent up for so long that Julie was afraid to let it out lest it would swallow her up and destroy her. She could not bear to speak of it. She feared speaking of it more than death itself. And then the still small voice would speak to her heart once more. "It is not that people cannot heal because they don't understand, people do not heal because they limit me. Fear not, lo I am with you, always."

Julie let out a long sigh and began to look at the aged pictures she held in her hands. She picked up the picture of the little boy once again and focused on it. His jaw was set rigid, his eyes stern and locked. The pain of a lost boy was overshadowed by anger. He looked ready to take on the world. His eyes were set in determination as if he could fend totally for himself.

Julie felt a tear come down her cheek. Where had the lost boy gone? What had caused his pain? What had broken his spirit at such a young age? Why was there no laughter or joy in his eyes?

Had he suffered the same pain as her own? Had his heart already hardened at such a young age? All of this she wondered as she looked at the picture of the little boy that would some day grow up to become her father.

Julie felt her cheek warm from the tears that continued to flow down unbidden. She put the picture back on the pile and picked up the cup of warm tea. She clasped the cup between her hands and laid her head against the back of the chair. Julie closed her eyes and let her thoughts run freely as a deluge of memories flooded over her and took her back to her past.

(circa 1950)

CHAPTER

2

The dirt road veered to the right off of the main highway. It began to incline slightly before it branched once again to the right. The incline now increased sharply and rounded a bend in the road. Here sat a little red insulbrick house. The narrow road continued upward to a dead end. At the very top of the hill was a little white house with red shutters; beside it and slightly down the hill sat a larger white clapboard house, and beneath that one, there was a small frame house painted sunshine yellow.

The little town of Cutters Ford lay in the valley below the narrow road. High on the mountainside, the houses lined this small country dirt lane. The sky seemed to reach endlessly like a blue stream of backdrop falling behind each house as the land disappeared leaving only a jutting edge of the steep cliff that was etched ages ago through the rugged mountains by the Potomac River. The river lay at the foot of the great mountain. Little islands peeked out of the river far below, the trees looking almost toy-like from atop the mountain.

It was a small quaint town, nestled in the southern Appalachians. Small houses speckled the hillsides throughout the valley. Dirt roads veered throughout the countryside connecting the houses one by one. Hills meandered in tiers, giving no distinction to where one ended and another began. Far in the distance, opposite the cliff, on another small hilltop stood a small country church. It stood as a pillar in the community and overshadowed the simple homes that were nestled in the foothills beneath it.

Cutters Ford was picturesque and reflected perfect serenity. There were no police stations or local governing bodies. The county seat was located nearly an hour's drive away. The closest hospitals were actually in nearby Grantville, the next nearest town.

Many houses did not have indoor plumbing and few had phones. Those who had indoor plumbing lived in the houses that lined the main highway.

It was a peaceful valley, a place where everyone knew everybody. There were no welfare or social services. Most people would have refused it anyway. They did not feel that they were poor and were much too proud to accept charity. People worked hard, asked for nothing, and just desired a simple and good life.

Ethel gave the porch swing a small push and then pulled her legs up quickly and let the swing sway freely. She loved the little house. They had moved so often during her fourteen years that she hoped that this would be home for a while. The small red insulbrick house had become home when her mom had married John. Ethel was glad to finally see her mom happy. Ethel had seen her mom work long hours for years at the laundry while trying to raise her family on just her meager earnings. Times had been tough; the Great Depression had hit the Appalachians the hardest.

Ethel was the next to the youngest of four girls. Her dad had left them when she was only six years old. Mary was seven, and Penny, the youngest, was only four. Sally, the oldest, was nearly fifteen when their parents had divorced and had left home shortly afterward to get married.

Ethel shifted on the swing, restlessly. She was fourteen years old and nearly grown up according to Appalachian standards. Ethel looked down the road and let her eyes rest on the big, white house that sat across the little stream on the opposite hillside. It was Tim O'Brian's home. She closed her eyes and let the wind blow through her hair as she dreamed of Tim. She heard her mom humming softly in the kitchen.

Winnie loved her girls and wanted the best for them. Winnie had very little schooling and insisted that her daughters would get a proper education. She continued to work at the laundry while still trying to supervise the girls. Winnie did not know whether to be relieved or troubled that they were growing up. Their interest in boys worried her. She did not know how to speak to them concerning the matters of womanhood or life.

Rocks spun up on the small porch that affronted the red insul-brick house as Ron spun his tires while breaking the bike. As he came to a quick halt, he brushed his hair to the side. Hearing the noise, Ethel sat up quickly.

"Hey," Ron called out to her, "when you goin' out with me?"

Ethel shrugged her shoulders uninterested. "Is Nancy home?" she called back, ignoring his question.

"Don't know," Ron answered quickly, not liking Ethel's brush off. "I'm off to work," he called back over his shoulder as he sped off.

Ethel sat on the porch swing and let her legs dangle aimlessly. She peered down the road and watched Ron's bike disappear around the curve. *Ron was nice*, Ethel thought, *but she just wasn't interested in him that way*. Her mind went to Tim O'Brian, and she felt her heart flutter with excitement at the thought of him. Besides, Ron was the brother of her best friend; dating him would make things much too complicated.

Ethel slowly got up off the swing. She took a deep breath and let out a deep sigh. She decided to walk up the hill to the white clapboard house and to see if her friend Nancy was home.

Maybe they could go for a walk down the road and across the little stream to where Tim O'Brian lived. He had taken quite an interest in Ethel. Ethel couldn't help but feel flattered. She quickly ran into the house to tell her mom that she was going up to visit Nancy. She thought it best not to tell Winnie of her intentions to walk to Tim's house.

Ethel then hurried out the door. She hoped to avoid any questions that her mom might ask. Winnie heard the screen door slam behind her as she stood and washed the dinner dishes.

Winnie worried about her daughters. She wanted more for them. Sally, her oldest, was struggling terribly since her marriage. Winnie was at her wit's end wondering how she could help her. Penny was struggling with her schoolwork, and Mary and Ethel were much too interested in boys. She knew Ethel had other plans than to just go and visit Nancy. She knew very well of Ethel's interest in Tim O'Brian. She also knew that the O'Brian brothers had a reputation with the girls, a reputation that she did not want Ethel to become a part.

Winnie could not help wonder if she had failed her girls. She had tried so hard to raise them the best that she knew how. She thought of her own life. She had hardly known her mom or dad. At a young age, she had been boarded out to live with others to work. She had worked as long as she could remember. Her divorce had been hard on her and the children. It wasn't just that there was no financial support. Winnie knew that her ex-husband had remarried and had six more children, but if he only could have just visited the girls once in a while or sent them a birthday or Christmas card so they could have known their dad.

Winnie thought of her beloved Margie. Margie had been her second-born. She had died at the age of twelve from a terrible accident while walking home from school. Somehow, she thought that Sally had never quite gotten over this. The other girls weren't much more than babies when the accident had happened and didn't remember Margie. But Winnie could remember every detail, from the small dimple on Margie's right cheek to her broad smile and piercing blue eyes that danced with delight. Ethel was a lot like her in a lot of ways. They both were full of life, energy, and adventure. Winnie brushed aside a tear as she reached for the towel to dry the dishes.

Ethel walked slowly up the hill to Nancy's house. Nancy had become a good friend. Nancy's mom worked in a large factory over in Grantville while her dad had a workshop in the basement of his house. Nancy said that her dad was good at woodwork and that he also took pictures and developed them. Ethel wasn't quite sure of James though. He was a short man, quiet in nature. When he spoke, he spoke with a stutter that seemed to embarrass him. Ethel couldn't explain it, but she felt uneasy around him. It was nothing that he said, just the strange way that he looked at her at times. Ethel thought Emma, on the other hand, was a kind and gentle spirit, except when James would upset her. Ethel had heard them argue quite loudly at times.

Ethel couldn't help wondering what a normal family would be like. She had seen it portrayed on the movies at the Saturday Matinees. Ethel wanted that kind of family, one where the husband worked and she could cook and clean and make the home a special place. Her husband would love and adore her, and they would have lots of children, and they would be one happy family. Her family would be different. Her children would have a dad, not like her dad who had run off and left them. How she had longed for years to see her dad. She would sit on the porch on her birthday and dream that he would come walking up and say, "Happy birthday, honey," maybe take her to get a soda, or just swoop her up in his arms and give her a big hug and kiss. She had long since given up looking for him or even hoping that he would be a part of her life.

Her thoughts were interrupted as Nancy called out to her. Nancy stood on the big upstairs porch shaking the throw rugs violently. Dust was flying everywhere. Even in her old clothes,

Ethel marveled at how pretty Nancy was. Her dark hair was pulled back and tied with a cloth sash. Her slim figure leaned over the banister.

"Can you come for a walk?" Ethel called up.

"Yeah, let me put the rugs back and give me a minute to freshen up," Nancy called back.

Ethel climbed the stairs to the porch and sat down on a chair to wait. Emma came out and, upon seeing Ethel, gave her a broad smile. Emma pulled a chair away from the banister and sat down to relax. She began to talk to Ethel and asked her about Winnie and the family. Ethel talked happily to Emma as she waited for Nancy. Suddenly, Shelby came barging out of the screened door and gave it a wild fling.

"Whoa! whoa! whoa! Slow down," Emma called out to her youngest daughter. Emma could see that Shelby was visibly disturbed. She reached out her hand toward Shelby to come to her. Emma patted at her dress and motioned Shelby to come sit on her lap. Shelby eyed Ethel up and then walked past her. She stomped toward her mother, emphasizing her anger with each step.

"So what is bothering you?" Emma asked as she took the young girl up on her lap.

"I'm mad," Shelby stated with a huff and rolled her eyes at Ethel as if she wished Ethel would leave.

"And why are you mad?" Emma continued. Shelby laid her head on Emma's chest as Emma gently patted the little girl she held in her arms and tried to calm her.

"I'm just mad," Shelby said a little more subdued.

Nancy came out of the house and announced that she was ready. "We won't be long, Mom," she said as she hurried toward the steps. Ethel followed close behind her.

Emma watched the two girls walk down the dirt road as Shelby cuddled in her arms. Emma was so tired. The factory was so hot where she worked, and the days were so long. She longed to spend more time with Shelby. She knew that she compensated her feelings by spoiling the child, but she didn't know what else to do about Shelby's angry outbursts except to pacify her.

Emma wished things could be different. She wished she knew how to be a better mom. Her mom had died when she was just a child much younger than Shelby. Her dad had remarried, but Emma had never quite got along with her stepmother. Emma had married James in an effort to get out of the house and to make a fresh start. But life had not always gone the way that she had dreamed. James was a small, frail man and was constantly sick and unable to hold a job. His stutter was perceived as a sign of ignorance, more than a handicap, and limited even more his choice of employment. This made it necessary for her to work.

She had lost two children as infants due to illness. Tom was her oldest. Ron was next, then Nancy and, last of all, her little Shelby. She had almost lost Tom and Nancy to rheumatic fever. The doctors had given up, but Emma had been determined that she would not lose any more of her children and nursed them back to health.

Between the doctor bills and James not working, she wondered how they would ever make ends meet. She went back to work as soon as possible and left the children in James' care.

The hard times divided her and James even more. Tension mounted, and their relationship became one of convenience and familiarity. Divorce was never considered. This was her life, and she accepted it. There were the children to think about.

Shelby fell asleep in Emma's arms. Emma looked down at her youngest daughter and stroked the hair from her eyes. She rose quietly and carried her into the house.

When Emma came back out, she was surprised to see that Nancy and Ethel had returned. She joined them and sat down in her favorite chair. Ethel saw Ron coming up the hill in the distance on his bike. She knew that he was returning from his job at the Western Union. Ethel turned to Nancy and jumped up quickly to leave, wanting to avoid having to talk to Ron.

"I better go home before Mom gets worried."

"Hey, I'll see you tomorrow at school," Nancy answered as she got up to go inside the house.

Ethel hurried down the steps and veered to the left as Ron approached from the right. Ron quickly jumped off the bike and walked briskly after her. Catching up with Ethel, he placed his arm on her shoulder. "Hey, slow down. I'll walk you home."

Ethel turned and gave him a weak smile and continued walking.

Emma watched the two of them walk slowly down the hill. Emma couldn't help but worry about her family. She was sure that Tom would be okay. But she worried about the girls. She had noticed changes in her family that she could not understand. Nancy would seem so withdrawn and quiet at times. Shelby was always full of anger and was far from being a delightful child. But Ron seemed to concern her the most at times. As a small child, he was always the more forward of the children, and as the years passed, he had grown sullen and downright bitter. His anger toward her was without reasoning, and she could not understand how to resolve it. She had thought it was due to her long work hours or to the continual tension and arguments between her and James. She felt that she had failed Ron somehow.

She remembered coming home one day from work when Ron was just six or seven years old. She found him crying outside the basement door. She bent down to ask him why he was crying. He lifted his head and, with a flash of his hand, angrily brushed the tears away. He glared up at his mom. "Dad loves me you know," he said.

"Of course he does," Emma said and stooped down to take him into her arms.

But Ron snapped back at her and withdrew from her touch, saying, "I know he will always love me, no matter what." Before Emma could speak, he pushed her aside and ran past her.

Emma ran into the basement to find James. "What in the world is wrong with Ron?" she implored. But James seemed uncomfortable and avoided her question by walking to the sink and washing his hands.

"James," she continued with her voice rising, "why is Ron so upset?" But with a wave of his hand, he brushed her off defensively and stated that supper was ready.

Emma had hoped it was only a stage that Ron was going through. But as she had watched the boy become a young man, she only saw his anger deepen. Somewhere long ago, she had lost the little boy, and it saddened her. "I hope he gets a good wife," she whispered aloud to herself as she watched Ron and Ethel walk down the winding road.

The little white house with red shutters.

CHAPTER

3

Ethel walked home from school with Nancy by her side. The smell of lilacs filled the air. The afternoon sun shined brightly and engulfed them in its warmth.

"Don't look now," Nancy whispered with a slight giggle, "but we're being followed."

Within minutes, Tim had joined them. He slid his arm around Ethel's waist and gave her a tight squeeze. Nancy gave Ethel a quick wink and said, "I've got to hurry home. I'll catch up with you later." Ethel gave her a grin and nodded and then turned to Tim.

They had become quite a couple. Ethel reveled at the feeling of being in love. Her heart would race in Tim's presence, and his attention to her was more than she had ever dreamed. She lived for his love and would do anything to please him. Her greatest fear was to lose Tim's love. She would count the hours until school let out so that she could be alone with him. They would walk the long way home. Ethel knew the times Winnie would work late, and she knew that John would be sleeping for his night shift. Surely, there was no harm in what she was doing.

As time went on, though, Mary began to question the time she was spending with Tim. "Mom's been asking me about you and Tim," Mary told Ethel one evening.

"What did you say?" Ethel asked nervously.

"I just said that you liked to stop off at the store and get a soda with him," Mary replied.

"Thanks," Ethel replied. "I love him so much, Mary."

"Don't thank me, Ethel," Mary continued as she gave her sister a stern glance. "It's you that I care for. I could care less about what happens to Tim O'Brian. I don't trust him. You need to be careful." Mary wished that she knew more that she could tell her sister, but she reasoned that Ethel probably knew more than she did at this point about the facts of love.

Ethel lay in her bed and let her mind drift. She couldn't help question the activities that Tim and her were partaking in when they were alone. She longed to ask her mom but dared not to, lest Winnie would forbid her to see Tim. Tim loved her, and that was all that mattered. She dreamed about the day that Tim would ask her to marry him. She would quit school, and they would start their family. Life would be perfect.

As summer approached and school was out, she missed Tim terribly. At first, they met secretly, taking long walks. Several times Tim had even taken her for a ride in his car. Ethel had not had many rides in cars. She felt like a queen sitting by his side.

But all of a sudden, Tim had begun to grow distant. Ethel had asked him to visit her house and had introduced him to Winnie. But little by little, his visits became shorter and shorter. Days went by and then weeks. Soon Tim didn't visit at all. Ethel wondered what she had done to make him stop loving her. She knew that she had gained a few pounds and that she hadn't been feeling well lately, but she couldn't understand Tim's actions and why he was avoiding her.

Ethel sat on the porch and waited for Tim to come by. Often Ron would stop by on his way to work and press her to date him. He had even asked Nancy to intervene on his behalf. Ethel thought Ron was nice enough, and in her loneliness, she began to enjoy their talks, but her heart still ached for Tim.

Ethel tried to lose weight but continued to gain. She had also missed her cycles and couldn't understand why. *Maybe that was just what happens,* she thought one day while sitting on the porch. She thought that maybe she should ask her mom if it was also normal for it to stop at times.

Ethel sat on the porch wondering, looking down at Tim's house that sat across the way on the opposite hill. It seemed far away.

"Care if I join you?" a voice spoke softly, interrupting her thoughts.

Ethel scooted over on the swing and made room for her mom.

"Mary says you haven't been feeling good," Winnie inquired, "and that you've missed your cycle a few times."

"Just a few times," Ethel answered, "and I've been feeling better again lately."

Winnie shifted in the swing uneasily as she continued, "Where has Tim been? He doesn't seem to come around much anymore?"

Ethel shrugged her shoulders. "I guess we kind of broke up," she mumbled.

"Ethel," Winnie said softly and peered into Ethel's face.

Ethel slowly raised her head to meet her mom's gaze.

"I think you're pregnant," Winnie said matter-of-factly.

"Pregnant!" Ethel said shocked. "How could I be pregnant?"

Winnie put her hand on Ethel's knee and patted it gently. She explained vaguely how it happens and asked Ethel if it were possible that she could be pregnant. Shocked, Ethel began to cry.

School started again. It took a few days of asking Tim to meet her after school so they could talk before he would agree.

He seemed to always have an excuse to avoid her. Ethel finally cornered him one day, and he agreed to walk her home.

Ethel had thought it all out. She hoped and envisioned in her heart that surely once Tim heard that she was going to have his baby that he would be excited and that he would take her in his arms and love her. He would tell her that everything would be all right. He would propose to her, and they would get married and make a home for their child.

Slowly, they walked home. Tim was quiet, walking with his hands in his pockets, his head hung down. Ethel waited until they had rounded the last bend before her house and then stopped where there were no houses nearby. "Tim," she began. She took a deep breath and then paused, "I'm pregnant."

Tim was looking down at the ground with a fixed stare. He kept his hands in his pockets and continued to look down, avoiding Ethel's pleading eyes.

"I'm going to have a baby," Ethel continued as if Tim hadn't heard. Tim still stood motionless, kicking a pebble with the tip of his shoes.

"Did you hear me?" Ethel nearly screamed, "I'm going to have a—"

Tim glanced up at Ethel and, interrupting her, replied in an angry voice, "And do you expect me to believe it is mine?"

Ethel's face turned ashen white. She felt as if all the blood was being drained from her body. She felt weak and faint and swayed as Tim's words cut through her heart.

Tim kicked the pebble as hard as he could and turned and walked away. Ethel stood and watched him walk away. Not once did he look back. Ethel turned slowly and walked up the hill to her home. She walked past the swing, around to the back, and sat down on the step in front of the back door. She lowered her head into her folded arms that rested on her lap and sobbed.

❀

It was pouring down rain a few weeks later when Ethel answered the door reluctantly. She was surprised to see Ron standing there.

Ethel invited him into the house and offered him a chair. She felt awkward. She knew that by now that all of Cutters Ford was aware of her condition. She knew that she would have to drop out of school. She had been staying home wanting to avoid people and their stares. She had even stopped going up to visit with Nancy.

"I just wanted to tell you that I'm dropping out of school," Ron said as he searched Ethel's face. He could not help letting his eyes wander over her body. "I quit my job," Ron continued. "I'm going to join the Marine Corps."

Ethel shifted uncomfortably, feeling Ron's gaze on her. "Are you sure this is what you want to do?" she asked.

Ron nodded his head and then paused, his eyes still locked on Ethel's face. "What will you do?" he asked cautiously.

Ethel looked up, feeling her face blush with embarrassment. "I'm not sure yet," she weakly replied.

"Maybe we could get to know each other, be a couple," Ron implored hesitantly.

"You do realize my situation?" Ethel asked somewhat puzzled and taken aback.

"Well, maybe I could marry you and we could raise the baby as our own," Ron continued and let the words tumble forth.

Ethel looked at him shocked. "But you know I don't love you," she replied gently.

"You could learn to love me," Ron pressed softly. He arose and went to sit beside Ethel on the couch.

Ethel could feel her head spinning. Ron took her hand in his. "I'll write you, and we'll talk more about it." Ron let go of her hand and stood up to leave. Ethel could feel his gaze upon her. She slowly lifted her head as Ron turned and walked toward the door.

"But why would you want to marry me?" Ethel asked.

Ron opened the door and glanced back at Ethel. Without answering, he turned and left shutting the door softly behind him.

Tim had never spoken to her again. Ethel had pushed the hurt aside, resolving that the most important thing to her was the baby that she now carried. Ethel guessed that she was almost six months pregnant when Ron came home for his first leave from boot camp. Ron looked much older in his uniform. This time when he asked her to marry him, she had agreed. They quickly got the marriage license after convincing both of their parents to agree to the marriage. Ethel was just fifteen years old and Ron was sixteen.

They moved into the little white house with the red shutters that sat at the very top of the hill above Emma's house. They would have to carry water from Emma and James' house, but Ethel didn't mind. She would be a good wife and mother. She would make the happy home that she had always dreamed of even if it had started out the wrong way.

Ron went back for more training in the corps. Their families all chipped in and gave the couple some used furniture and a crib.

January came, and Ethel went into labor giving birth to her son. She named him Ronnie. Ron came home from the service for a longer leave, and they slowly became a family. Ethel never heard from Tim again nor did she desire to. He never inquired about the son she had born, and he soon moved out of the valley.

Ethel tried to make Ron happy. She felt indebted to the man who had married her, but she hardly knew him. She made the little three-room house a home. She starched the curtains and waxed the floor. She carried the water and cooked Ron his favorite meals. But she couldn't help wonder why he had married her. He said that he cared for her. But to Ethel, he seemed unhappy. Often he was sullen and quiet and refused to open up or talk to Ethel. His drinking, which was mild at first, began to increase rapidly after he had joined the Marine Corps. Ron accepted the baby and his new life. His leave was soon up, and he had to go back. There was talk of Korea. *Maybe that was what was bothering him*, Ethel thought. A wife, a son, and a war—it was a lot for a young man who had just turned seventeen years old.

Ethel almost felt guilty when Ron had left. She enjoyed the peacefulness of the house. She wrote Ron often and budgeted the money carefully that he sent home, buying only the necessities. She would make her husband proud of her. Someday, he would love her, and she would love him too.

Ron did go to Korea. Ethel wrote to him and let him know that by the time that he would come home, he would be a dad again. The baby was born the following January, barely a year after Ronnie's birthday. Ron seemed to show more excitement at the birth of this son that was his. They named him Jerry. But Ron's drinking continued to escalate greatly after his return from Korea. Ethel tried to brush it aside and to make a home for their growing family.

It came as a surprise to everyone, that shortly after Jerry's birth, Ethel found that she was pregnant once more. By December of the same year, a third son was born. They named him Matt. Ron seemed to lose enthusiasm as his family grew and the responsibility with it. Upon being discharged from the corps, he immediately began to look for work along with his brother Tom. There were no jobs available in the small valley or the nearby town of Grantville. Finally, both Ron and Tom found employment about forty miles away. Ron had bought a car, and often Tom and he would drive the many miles, or they would stay the week and come home for weekends.

The young couple had little time to get acquainted as their new family continued to grow. By the following spring, Ethel gave birth to her fourth child. The doctor had encouraged them to make this their last, and they had conceded. Ethel was nineteen years old; Ron, twenty.

Ethel held the baby in her arms as they drove home from the hospital. Ron seemed quiet and subdued. He had received a speeding ticket the day before while hurrying to the hospital from the bar where he had been drinking. But nothing could dissuade the joy that Ethel felt as she held the small baby tightly in her arms. She pulled back the little pink blanket and peeked at the tiny face before her. They had named her Julie, for no other reason than that Ethel loved the name. Ethel reached inside the blanket and took the tiny hand in hers. Julie stirred in Ethel's arms. She opened her eyes and then squinted. She searched Ethel's face as her tiny hand grasped Ethel's finger and held onto it tightly.

The house was small, but Ethel had made it a home. They had managed to fit one bed for Ethel and Ron in the bedroom. Beside their bed, a few inches away, sat the crib they used for Julie, and a few inches from the crib stood the bunk beds where the small boys slept. Ronnie was three years old, Jerry was two, and Matt was one.

While Ron traveled back and forth to his job, Ethel worked hard to make the small house a home. She shopped for groceries for the family of six with the meager twenty dollars that Ron gave her weekly. This had to also include a case of beer for Ron and their cigarettes. Ethel washed the diapers and clothes at Emma's house. She would start the old wringer washer and then run up to the house to check on the children. She would carry buckets of water up to their house and then return and do the wash. She carried load after load of wet wash in an old peach basket to the clothesline and stood on her tippy-toes on the hillside to hang up the last few pieces of clothes on the clothesline.

Ethel felt awkward with James in the basement while she washed the clothes. She tried to converse with him but found it hard at first to understand his stutter. In time, she discovered that he liked country music. He played a guitar and loved Merle Haggard and Patsy Cline.

As time passed, both Ron and Tom had looked and found jobs closer to home. Ron had started to work at the factory where Emma worked. Ethel felt sure now that he was home that they could get closer as a family. The demands of life were hard on the young family. She knew that Ron drank too much. "I need to drink, Ethel," he told her. "You have just got to understand. I provide for the family. I work hard. What more do you want? There's no harm in me having a few beers." But the more he drank, the more argumentative he became. If Ethel protested, it only got worse. "How many men would do what I did?" he would continue on in a slurred voice from his drinking. He would bring up all that he had done for Ethel, including marrying her. Ethel had learned to just let him drink and vent off his frustration.

On Sundays, everyone gathered at Emma's for Sunday dinner. Tom was dating a nice woman and often brought her to Emma's dinners. Often after dinner, James would bring out his guitar and play country songs. Tom and Ethel would often join in and sing along. Emma sat back and listened to Ethel and Tom sing and looked at her growing family. She watched the grandchildren playing happily in the corner of the kitchen as Tom and Ethel sang. Often they would sing into the evening, finishing with Emma's favorite "Beyond the Sunset." In a few weeks, they were to all drive down to Clifton for a family reunion. Emma and James had not been back to their homes for many years. Finally, it seemed that Emma's family had settled down and found some happiness.

Life had fallen into a routine that Ethel hoped would grow into love. The children were growing, and slowly, the earlier demands of their family were lessening. They were a family now, and Ethel smiled as she sang and glanced over at her children. She turned and gave Ron a smile. Ron gave her a weak smile back and then rose to get another beer. *Surely things would get better,* Ethel thought.

Julie at seventeen months old.

CHAPTER

4

Nancy looked at the three small children playing on the couch. She often watched her niece and nephews. Julie was two years old and did everything she could to keep up with her three older brothers. Matt was three; Jerry, four; and Ronnie, five years old.

"No you don't," Nancy called out as she ran to get Julie who was running toward the stairs. She swooped the giggling little bundle up into her arms. Julie laid her head on her aunt's shoulder as Nancy carried her back into the room. Matt and Jerry sat quietly and played with their toy cars. Julie saw her brothers and wiggled and squirmed to get down from her aunt's embrace. "Let's go outside onto the porch," Nancy said to Julie and diverted her attention away from her brothers.

The lilac bush beneath the two-story porch was in full bloom. The fragrance filled the air. The sun shone brightly, making Julie squint and rub her eyes. "Wook," Julie said to her aunt and pointed to the squirrel that was running up the trunk of the large oak that sat in the front yard.

"Yes, I see," Nancy answered and lovingly touched Julie's button nose.

Nancy looked at the little valley that lay below her. The main road winded through the little town, houses lining either side.

She glanced at her watch. *Mom and Shelby should be home soon*, she thought as she bounced Julie gently on her hip. They had gone with Ethel, Ron, and Ronnie to do their weekly grocery shopping. Ron often helped out by taking Emma with them so that she could get her groceries. Nancy glanced at her watch again and remembered Ron had told her that they might be a little later than usual. He thought he might go out to Junction City and pick up a radio for his car.

Nancy was happy for her brother and Ethel. She hoped that they were finally working out their problems. She loved her brother and even admired him for marrying her friend. She could not help wonder why he had hastily married her. Even Nancy knew that it was unlike her brother to do such an unselfish act. She figured it was just his desire to break loose from home and to do whatever he wanted to do.

Nancy had tried to tell Ron more than once at the Sunday evening dinners that he was drinking way too much. He would brush her off by saying, "Name someone who doesn't drink too much." Nancy would start to reply but stopped short knowing that he would not listen to her. What bothered Nancy the most were not his sullen and withdrawn spells, but the way he continued to flirt with other women.

On Saturdays, they would often go bowling or to a dance. Tom and his new wife, Lisa Sue, along with Ethel and Ron would join Nancy and her new boyfriend Mark for an evening out. It was true that most everyone drank too much at these parties, but with Ron, it was always a given that he would come home drunk. He didn't hide his flirtations, and more than once, Ethel had caught him in the dark hallways with another woman. He would tell Nancy the same thing that he told Ethel. "I'm not doing anything wrong, looking but not touching," he'd say slyly and walk away. Ron and Ethel's house was close enough to hers that Nancy would often hear their heated arguments escalate throughout the night, long after they had arrived home.

Ethel had shared with Nancy that Ron constantly told her that she should be more understanding of his drinking and flirtatious ways. He continually reminded Ethel of all the things that he had done and was doing for her. Nancy knew that Ethel was not happy but saw her determination to make the marriage work, if not for herself and Ron, then at least for their four children.

Nancy glanced down at Julie now asleep in her arms. She pushed the tight ringlets of curls away from the tiny brow before turning to go back into the house. Suddenly, she turned. Far in the distance, she could hear the sound of sirens piercing the stillness. They seemed to be coming from all directions. She walked to the banister and peered through the trees to the valley below and focused on the main road. The ambulances from Grantville raced furiously around the tight bends and headed out to Route number 4, the road that led to Junction City.

Winnie stepped out onto her porch. She could hear the sirens grow louder as they approached. Winnie and John had moved from the little red insulbrick house and had just recently bought a small duplex that sat on the main highway that cut through the town of Cutters Ford. Winnie raised her hand to her brow and peered down the road as John joined her on the porch. "Must be a bad accident," John remarked as the ambulances sped past.

Winnie sat down on the porch swing beside little Ronnie who had quit playing and came running to the porch at the sound of the sirens. She put her arm around her young grandson. She was glad that Ethel and Ron had dropped him off to be with her. They sat, swinging slowly, and John went back into the house. It seemed only minutes later that the ambulances sped back past the small duplex once more hurrying to the nearest hospital in Grantville. Winnie could only wonder what had happened as she took little Ronnie back into the house.

The truck driver saw the car approaching him in his rearview mirror. He could see that the car was speeding rapidly and was erratically out of control. "Are they crazy?" he said out loud to himself. With another glance in his mirror, he saw the car speed up even faster in an attempt to pass him. "They'll never make it around me!" he said, alarmed. He quickly veered to the right to yield his lane to the woman he could now see driving the Pontiac that rushed past him. "No!" he screamed as he saw the blue green Chevy approaching, "She's going to hit that car!" He sat shocked as he came to a stop on the shoulder of the road, still clutching his steering wheel. He looked ahead and shook his head hopelessly. "She's going to hit them!"

The blue-green Chevy hardly had a chance. Ron was talking to Ethel as he heard Emma scream from the backseat of the car. Ron saw the Pontiac coming straight at him head-on. It was only a few hundred yards away, and she was in his lane. Ron grabbed his steering wheel tightly and yanked it to the right while breaking. The car came to a quick stop on the shoulder of the road. Ron took a deep breath. Ethel, Shelby, and Emma watched in horror. The woman driving the Pontiac now had the whole road to herself. It appeared that they had avoided a fatal collision. But within seconds, the woman began driving faster and more erratically. She began to lose control, drove off the road, and was once again heading straight toward them.

The impact made a death-curdling sound that echoed throughout the countryside. Metal crushed, glass splattered, and then there was complete silence. The truck driver rushed from his vehicle with others that had now stopped. The woman in the green Pontiac lay slumped across the steering wheel. The steering wheel had broken and pierced her chest. She was breathing slightly and unconscious.

The Chevy sat crushed like a tin can. Its windshield had splattered where Ethel's head had hit it before she was thrown from the car. Fourteen-year-old Shelby began to cry as rescuers came to help her from the wreckage just as the ambulances arrived. Emma could see them working feverishly on Ethel's still body that lay by the side of the road on a stretcher. Emma's leg felt broken, and she could not move it. She could see that Ron had been hurt also but that he was conscious. She had thrown herself in front of Shelby seconds before the impact. She knew that they were all hurt badly and bleeding, but they were all conscious except Ethel. Only Ethel wasn't responding.

The rescuers began to carefully lift Emma from the car as the others loaded Ron into an ambulance. Shelby stood in shock, crying. Emma continued to ask the attendants about Ethel as they attempted to put Emma into the ambulance. The sounds of sirens seared loudly as the woman from the Pontiac was whisked away. "Please," Emma cried out to the attendants. "Is she alive?" The rescuers did not answer but began to pull the sheet up over Ethel's lifeless body as the others tried to turn Emma away. "No!" Emma screamed. "No!" she shook loose and turned around to look at Ethel. "Please," she pleaded with the attendants. "Please don't cover her up. Please help her—her children," Emma said weakly. "Oh God, please…her children." The rescuers uncovered Ethel. Her head was bleeding badly; they quickly lifted her into the waiting ambulance and sped off. Shelby and Emma were placed in the last remaining ambulance.

Tom ran up the hill to talk to his sister Nancy. He had recently married Lisa Sue and had moved into the little, yellow house that sat below Emma's.

Nancy laid the sleeping Julie down on the couch. The boys continued to play contently. Nancy looked out the screen door. She saw Tom rush up the porch steps. Nancy hurried out to meet him. James had also heard the sirens and had come to join them.

"Must be a bad accident," Nancy said to Tom.

"Nancy, where did Ron and Mom go?"

"Well, they were all going grocery shopping over at Grantville, and then Ron said that they would probably go out to get a radio at Junction…" Nancy's voice trailed off as the realization hit her that they were heading to Junction City.

Tom seemed alarmed. "I don't have a good feeling about this," he said as he rushed down the steps. "I'm going to ride out there."

Lisa Sue joined Nancy as Tom rushed past her. "I wish we had a phone," Nancy said as she watched Tom drive down the road.

Hours passed before Tom returned. When he did, both Lisa Sue and Nancy suspected that there was bad news when they saw that only Shelby got out of Tom's car.

"It is only a miracle that they all are alive," Tom said, seeing Lisa Sue's and Nancy's alarm. Nancy took Shelby to her bedroom and then rejoined the others that were sitting in the living room. Tom told all of them the details of the accident as best as he could. "No," he said before they could even ask. "Ron was not drinking. Apparently, the woman from Johnstown had had a fierce argument with her husband and was on a death wish. They said that she was traveling over eighty miles an hour when she hit Ron's car."

"But Ronnie?" Nancy asked, sheer horror rising in her voice as she remembered that her nephew had been in the car.

"He's okay," Tom continued. "Ethel and Ron had dropped him off at Winnie's before going to Junction City. If they hadn't, he probably would've been sitting on Ethel's lap. Mom has a broken leg. Ron is pretty banged up and has a busted kneecap where it went into the dashboard. Ethel is…" Tom choked up a little. "Ethel is in pretty bad shape. She is unconscious and has serious head injuries. It took about fifty stitches to sew her up. They are surprised that she's alive," he said weakly hanging his head and wringing his hands together nervously.

"And the other woman?" Lisa Sue asked slowly.

"She's alive. The steering wheel just missed her heart. But they think that she will make it," Tom replied.

James got up without saying a word and went downstairs to the basement. Nancy looked around the room. Tears filled her eyes as she looked at little Matt and Jerry sitting on the couch staring at the adults. Their toy cars rested on their laps. They seemed to sense that something was wrong, hearing the mention of their mommy's and daddy's names. Julie lay beside them asleep. Matt searched Jerry's face as if wanting him to explain it all to him. But Jerry said nothing. Matt turned to Julie and leaned over her to see if she was okay. He bent down and gave her a kiss on her pudgy cheek.

"What will we do with the children?" Nancy asked Tom and Lisa Sue.

"We'll just have to take turns caring for them and take it one day at a time," Tom said slowly. "Well, I'm going to run up to Winnie's and John's and break the news to them. I'll take them over to the hospital. They should be with Ethel if…I mean when she comes to," Tom said wearily as he arose to leave.

"Drop Ronnie off here on your way back through," Lisa Sue called after Tom as she followed him to the porch. "We'll take care of him."

"I will," Tom called back over his shoulder as he hurried into the car and slammed the door shut. He gave Lisa Sue a quick wave before racing quickly down the hill.

Days sped by and then weeks. Emma and Ron had both been discharged and were still recuperating from their injuries. The family was exhausted from the ordeal. The children were distraught, not understanding the confusion that had entered their lives as they were shifted from Aunt Nancy's and Emma's and Aunt Lisa Sue's to Gramma Winnie's and others. Julie cried continually for her mommy.

Ethel's recovery was slow. It had taken weeks for her to even begin to recognize people and to regain her memory. But she was slowly recovering. She had asked Winnie one day, "Who was the nice man that always came to visit me?"

Winnie winced slightly before answering her softly, "That is Ron, your husband." Ethel had seemed puzzled as she rubbed her forehead as if to try to make her mind remember.

Nancy had her hands full trying to help everyone. Lisa Sue came up often and helped. James withdrew to his basement workshop and said very little to anyone.

One day, Nancy went out to sit and watch the four children play on the blanket that was sprawled out across the porch. "Ronnie, make sure you lock the gate so that Julie doesn't fall down the steps," she cautioned as Ronnie went to go down the porch steps to get a ball that had fallen.

"I will, Aunt Nancy," he said as he pushed the gate hard to hear it click shut.

Jerry walked over to his Aunt Nancy and crawled up on her lap. "When is Mommy coming home, Aunt Nancy?" he asked softly and looked up and searched her face for an answer.

"I don't know, honey," Nancy replied. But she is getting better," she said, smiling.

Matt watched his brother with his Aunt Nancy and listened carefully at Jerry's question and Nancy's answer. Nancy saw Matt's deep blue eyes searching hers with a longing to understand. She smiled at him as he reached over and took Julie's hand in his. Julie looked at her big brother and squeezed his hand before rolling over and pouncing on him. Matt squealed with delight as he wrestled with Julie. Jerry squirmed off his aunt's lap and ran over to join them. They rolled across the blanket, laughing and wrestling together. Ronnie came up with the ball and tossed it onto the porch before turning and locking the gate. He flopped down on the blanket with the other three and joined in wrestling with them.

Everything will be fine soon, Nancy thought as she watched the children play and marveled at the love and closeness that they shared. *It has to be*, she thought longingly.

Family Car Crash of 1956

CHAPTER

5

The wind snapped through the trees and billowed through the tree-lined hollow making a loud whistling sound. Winter was near. It had been six months since the accident.

Ethel put Julie's hat on her head and snapped it around her chin. "Button up your coats," she called to the boys as they rushed out of the door to go down to their Gramma Emma's. "Are you coming?" she called to Ron in the next room.

Ron lay on the couch watching the Thanksgiving Day football game. "Go ahead. I'll be down in a few minutes," he groaned.

"Your mom will have dinner ready soon," she called back as little Julie pulled her mom toward the door.

Ethel let Julie lead her rather than pick her up. Ethel was still regaining her strength but had miraculously fully recovered. Her hair was nearly grown back. The scar, though massive, had healed completely. Except for a few regular headaches, she was doing fine.

"Where's Ron?" Emma asked as Ethel and Julie entered the basement door.

"He's coming," Ethel answered as she took Julie's hat and coat off and laid them on the large pile of coats that lay on top of the old Victrola.

The boys had already sat down on the long wooden bench that they always shared. Lisa Sue pushed the bench tight against the table so that they could reach the table. Ronnie, Jerry, and Matt all sat quietly, their eyes fixed on the large turkey that sat in the middle of the table.

The kitchen consisted of the small sink with an electric stove that sat beside it. In the corner was a small refrigerator. In the middle of the room were two old, massive maple tables that had been pushed together to make one large table. Long cotton tablecloths covered them. Across the room was a cupboard that had been painted yellow and held most of the dishes and glasses. On the far wall was a yellowed picture in a plastic frame of Jesus knocking on a closed door. The cement block walls had been painted white. To the left of the old Victrola was a wooden door that was stained brown. It led to the furnace, coal bin, and James' workshop. Circling around past the workshop was the washroom where the old wringer washer sat. Another wall and a door separated it from the humble basement dining room. Small windows lined the basement walls and were covered with simple cotton curtains. Such were the meager surroundings that welcomed the family together for dinner every Sunday and during the holidays. Emma had worked hard to keep her family together and to make the house a home.

Ron entered the kitchen. He still slightly limped from his knee injury. Ethel placed Julie in the wooden highchair that James had made for the grandchildren to sit in. Tom carved the turkey, and everyone began passing the plates of food while talking all at the same time.

After dinner, the family went upstairs. The men talked about the football game that was playing on television, and the women were anxiously discussing Nancy's recent engagement and her upcoming wedding. Shelby fleeted around demanding everyone's attention while Julie, Matt, Jerry, and Ronnie ventured off into the next room to play hide and seek. The four children had become inseparable.

Shortly, Emma called out to the children that *Lassie* was on TV. Quickly, the foursome ran into the room and flopped down in front of the television set. Emma reached down and handed each of them their own box of Cracker Jacks. Ronnie reached over and helped Julie open hers. Matt squealed with delight as he pulled the little prize from the mixture of caramel popcorn and peanuts. Julie squealed too, following her brother's example, not sure why he had squealed. Jerry reached over toward Julie and helped her to find the prize that was in the box of popcorn, wherein she squealed again in delight. Once more, the family pressed on looking for happier days and easier times.

✳

The seasons had come and gone nearly as fast as the children were growing. A year and a half passed. Ethel and Ron had struggled to get the woman that had caused the accident to get her insurance to pay the doctor and hospital bills but to no avail. They had finally driven the twenty-five miles to the county seat and had hired a lawyer to help them. The woman's insurance finally conceded to pay all of the bills plus a small settlement.

Ronnie was now seven years old and going into the third grade. Jerry was six years old and was going into the second grade. And Matt was five years old and going into the first grade. Julie was four years old.

Ethel watched the small trio walk through the front yard, past the giant blue spruce, and onto the dirt shale road that affronted the small yard. She stood waving from the small porch as they walked side by side down the road. They were dressed in their new jeans and cotton shirts. Ethel had polished their old shoes into a fitful shine. Their hair was neatly combed. Ethel stood watching them march down the road like little men before seeing them disappear around the far bend. A tear slid down Ethel's cheek. She felt as if she was sending them off to war instead of school.

"I want to go too," Julie said as she tugged on her mom's dress.

"Next year, honey," Ethel said and ran her fingers through Julie's curly hair. "Come on, Julie," she called as she went back into the house.

"In a minute, Mommy," Julie answered. A rail surrounded the little front porch. Five small steps led down from the porch to a small dirt path that meandered downhill leading to Emma's house and to the dirt road. Julie grabbed the rail with her tiny hands and placed her feet on the bottom rung of the rail and pulled herself up. She balanced herself while leaning over the rail, stretching her neck to try to get one last glimpse of her brothers, but they were out of sight. Julie reluctantly and carefully climbed down.

Julie ran into the house and shut the door behind her. "Can I have a nana, Mommy?" Julie asked as she entered the kitchen. She pulled the kitchen chair away from the table and climbed up onto it.

Ethel gathered the breakfast dishes and carried them to the small sink. The tiny gas stove beside it was turned on to heat a pot of water. "No, honey, you can't have them. You know they are for your daddy's lunch."

"Just one," Julie pleaded. She struggled with her little fingers scrunching four of them into her palm and let one lone finger stand up. "I really like nanas, Mommy," Julie peered up at the bananas that were on top of the small cupboard that sat beside the sink.

"No, honey," Ethel told her sadly.

Ethel hated that she could not give the kids something as simple as a banana. There just wasn't enough money. She had been married to Ron for seven years now, and Ron was still only giving her $20 a week for groceries. She had switched from buying whole milk to the cheaper canned or powdered milk. She continually had to limit her children with what they ate to get by financially. Ethel could feel the anger rise within her. Ron insisted that his beer and the cigarettes were to come out of the grocery money. He wanted his special snacks that he could have with his beer: the pickled sausages, cheese and crackers, and his favorite pork rinds. She had tried to tell him that the children were growing and needed more to eat, but Ron would answer her, saying, "Well fine, Ethel. I'll just stop off at Lindy's for a beer and snack." Ethel knew that Ron was always looking for any excuse to be able to stop at the little tavern that sat at the foot of the hill on the main highway of Cutters Ford. More often than not, he stopped there after work anyways and drank a few beers before coming home. Ethel had found it was easier to just pacify Ron than to argue with him. If she argued with him, it only gave him an excuse to drink more when he got home.

Ethel took the tea kettle of boiling water and poured it into the small dishpan. She took the agate dipper from the metal bucket and scooped some cooler water to it and added the soap. She began to wash the dishes and let her mind wander. One highlight that Ethel looked forward to was that sometimes she would go to Bingo with her mom. If she would give the children their baths and tuck them in bed early, often Ron would agree to let her go. Winnie would usually buy her the Bingo cards, and they would split any money that either of them would win. Ethel rarely told Ron when she won. Often she would lie to him, denying that she had won. She felt terrible for this, but she knew he would either take the money or have her put it toward the grocery bill. Ethel would tuck the money away and buy the children clothes or shoes when they needed them. Sometimes, she had enough to get the children's pictures taken. Again, she would have to lie to Ron and tell him that Winnie had bought the clothes or had paid for the pictures. All she could do was to try to make it all work as peaceably as possible.

"Mommy," Julie said, interrupting Ethel's thoughts. "I'm hungry."

"How about some rice puffs or wheat puffs?" Ethel asked as she dried her hands and reached for the cupboard door.

"I don't like them their cereals, Mommy," Julie said slowly.

"I know, honey," Ethel said, looking inside the cupboard. "How about some oatmeal with raisins?"

"Okay," Julie answered gleefully.

Ethel took the steaming kettle off the stove and poured the hot water into her cup. She added a spoonful of instant coffee to the cup of water and stirred it vigorously.

Julie finished her oatmeal and scooted quickly off the chair. She reached up for her empty cereal bowl and carried it to the sink. "Here, Mommy," she said as she handed Ethel the bowl.

"Thank you, sweetie," Ethel said as she put the bowl into the dishpan.

"Drink, Mommy?" Julie asked.

Ethel scooped a little water into the agate dipper and brought it down, tilting it slowly to Julie's lips. Julie drank the water slowly. It ran down her chin and caused her to giggle. "Tank you," she said before wiping her chin with the back of her hand. She ran into the living room and climbed up onto the couch with her blanket.

Ethel dried her hands and came in to sit with Julie. "Do you want to watch *Betty Boop*?" she asked.

"Uh-huh," Julie said smiling.

"Do you mind if Mommy lies back down for a while?" Ethel asked.

"What about *Jack Lane*?" Julie asked.

"You get me up after *Betty Boop* goes off, okay?" Ethel asked as she bent down and kissed Julie on her cheek. You and I will watch Jack Lalanne together then."

"Okay, Mommy," Julie answered giving her mom a big smile. She snuggled down into her blanket and turned to watch the TV where *Betty Boop* was now singing.

A commercial came on, and Julie sat up and peeked at her mom sleeping in the bedroom. She got up and ran into the kitchen. She looked at the bananas sitting on top of the tall cupboard. She began to pull the chair from the kitchen table over to the sink's ledge. The steel chair made a loud rumbling noise as Julie tried to pull it. Julie stopped and ran back into the bedroom to peek on her mommy to see if she had awakened her. She was still asleep. Julie tiptoed away and then ran back into the kitchen. Quietly, she once again pulled and pushed the chair toward the sink. She then climbed up on the chair, and grabbing the sink's edge, she hoisted herself up onto the small counter. From there, she could stretch on her tippy-toes and reach the loose bananas on top of the cupboard. Julie took the banana in her hands and looked at the treasure before laying it down on the sink. She climbed carefully back down onto the chair. She grabbed the banana from the counter and gingerly climbed off the chair and pulled the chair quietly back to the table. Still holding the banana, she went into the living room and climbed back up onto the couch. She turned to the TV and smiled happily. *There could be nothing better than watching Betty Boop and having a banana to eat*, she thought.

Julie started to peel the banana with her tiny fingers but suddenly stopped and looked at the banana. *Mommy had said no*, she thought, fingering the banana slowly. *Just one*, she tried to convince herself, and then again, she thought, *No, Mommy had said that they were Daddy's*. She laid the banana down beside her. Another commercial came on, and she sat and stared at the banana. Maybe if she asked her mommy again. Julie ran into the bedroom and climbed up onto the bed. "Mommy," Julie whispered into her ear. Ethel did not stir. "Mommy," Julie said again, louder this time.

"What, honey?" Ethel mumbled sleepily.

"Can I have a nana, Mommy?" Julie asked. Ethel did not answer and had fallen back asleep.

"Mommy," Julie said loudly. She shook her mom gently to wake her. "Can I have a nana?"

Ethel opened her eyes and saw the deep brown and green eyes peering into her face. "No, honey. Mommy told you already that they are for daddy's lunch."

Julie slid off the bed and walked slowly back to the couch. All Julie could think about was the banana. She sat on the couch, swinging her legs over its edge and continued to look at the banana more than *Betty Boop*. Shortly, she heard her mom snoring. Julie bit her lip as a new idea sprung into her mind. She ran once again into the bedroom. "Mommy," she whispered. "Mommy," she said a little louder and gently shook her mom to wake her. Ethel now sound asleep did not answer her. Julie climbed up onto the bed and sat thinking. She climbed up over her mommy and gently pulled her mom's eyelids open with her tiny fingers. Ethel still did not wake but stirred a little. Julie leaned down and whispered into her mommy's ear, "Can I have a monkey bar?" Julie asked.

"What?" Ethel mumbled as she awoke.

"Can I have a monkey bar?" Julie asked in a slight whisper.

"Uh-huh," Ethel mumbled and rolled over in the bed.

Julie raced off the bed and ran to get the banana. Now she could eat it because her mommy had said that it was okay. She peeled it as quickly as her small fingers enabled her to and gulped down the banana. Julie thought it tasted so good that maybe she could eat another one. She ran again to her mommy's bed and again asked her for a monkey bar. Ethel again said yes, and Julie went to climb up to retrieve another banana.

Soon it was time for Jack Lalanne, and Julie ran and threw all of the banana peels away. She had eaten three of the four bananas. She then went to wake up her mommy. This time, she shook her and called out loudly to her mom. Julie climbed up on top of Ethel and straddled herself across Ethel's stomach. "Giddyap,

Mommy," she yelled. Ethel woke up and rubbed her eyes as Julie said, "*Jack Lane* time, Mommy."

Ethel stretched and reached for Julie and pulled her down to her and hugged her. "You mommy's girl?" she asked.

"Uh-huh," Julie answered giggling. She hopped off the bed and ran into the living room as Ethel sleepily followed. It was only 9:00 a.m. "Come on, Mommy," Julie called. Ethel stretched out onto the floor to do exercises with Jack Lalanne. Julie lay beside her trying to do the exercises. They laughed together as Ethel took Julie and balanced her on her legs while holding Julie's hands tightly.

It was later in the day before Ethel noticed that the bananas were nearly all gone. She saw the empty peels in the garbage. "Julie Anna," she called as she went out to the little front porch to find Julie. "What are these?" Ethel asked holding up the banana peels.

"But, Mommy, I did ask you, and you said yes," Julie answered sheepishly not sure if she was in trouble.

"When?" Ethel asked a little confused.

"This morning when you were in bed," Julie answered.

"Are you sure?" Ethel asked still puzzled. "I thought I told you no."

"The first time you did, Mommy," Julie answered honestly. Julie took a deep breath and let out a long sigh before continuing. "But the next time when I asked you for a monkey bar, you said uh-huh." Julie let her eyes search her mom's face.

"Monkey bar?" Ethel repeated questioningly.

"People have candy bars and monkey's have monkey bars," Julie explained.

Ethel stood there holding the banana peels and looked at Julie. She burst into laughter before saying, "Well, I guess that is true."

Julie gave her an impish grin, relieved that she was not in trouble. Ethel turned to go back into the house to start dinner. She knew that Ron would have a fit but couldn't help laughing.

Julie sat down on the edge of the porch and dangled her legs over the edge. She rested her chin on the bottom rail and looked down the hill wondering when her brothers would finally come home.

"Hi, Daddy," Julie called down to her dad as he got out of the car. Julie watched him carefully.

"Hi, Julie," he said as he walked up the path. Julie stood up on the porch and watched her daddy come up the steps. She liked this daddy. He didn't walk funny, and his words weren't slurred.

Ron reached down and swooped Julie up into his arms and carried her through the front door. Julie wrapped her tiny arms around his neck and kissed him on the cheek. She wished she had this daddy all the time. He kissed her on the cheek. "You daddy's girl?" he asked.

"Uh-huh," she answered as he set her down. Julie ran back out the door. *Surely her brothers would be home soon*, she thought.

Ron turned on the television to get the news and sat down on the couch. He picked up the newspaper from the little coffee table and began to read.

"Ethel, bring me a beer," he called out toward the kitchen.

"Dinner will be ready soon," she answered.

"I don't give a damn," he said. He tossed the paper aside and got up to go into the kitchen and continued speaking. "Forget it. I'll get it myself."

He opened the small refrigerator door and grabbed the beer. He opened the cabinet drawer and grabbed the bottle opener and slammed the drawer shut. He turned to Ethel and asked, "What's for dinner?"

"Chili macaroni," she answered.

"Damn it!" he said as he snapped the lid off the bottle. "Is that all we ever eat?"

"Well, if you'd give me more grocery money and cut back on the beer, I could get something else," Ethel said matter-of-factly.

"Jesus Christ! Don't start, Ethel…" he fumed.

"Please, Ron," Ethel interrupted. "Curse if you want, but don't use the Lord's name in vain."

"And when did you get so religious and holier than thou?" Ron continued. The front screen door slammed shut loudly. Julie stood watching her parents argue. "And where in the hell did all the bananas go?" Ron yelled. Julie turned and ran back out the door as her parents continued to argue.

Julie ran down the steps as she saw her brothers coming up the road. Her little sleeveless dress blew around her as she ran down the dusty path barefoot calling out her brothers' names.

Their shoes were dusty, and their shirts were hanging untucked half out of their pants. The young warriors looked tired. Ronnie led the way. He had jet-black hair and dark eyes. Jerry had dark-brown hair and dark-brown eyes and was very thin favoring his dad's stature. Matt favored Ethel's family with his rich blue eyes and blond hair but still had his dad's distinct features. Julie was a mixture. She had brownish-green eyes and curly light-brown hair. She had an impish smile that could melt the heart of all three of her big brothers. She adored them, and they loved her dearly.

Julie finally caught up with them. "I get to go with you to school next week," she said excitedly out of breath.

"You mean next year," Ronnie said to Julie and smiled.

Julie stopped and put her hands on her hips. "That's what I said," she insisted, "next week."

"No," Jerry said, taking her by the hand. "Next week and next year aren't the same."

"How come?" she asked puzzled.

"You'll see," Matt assured her.

"What's for dinner, Julie?" Ronnie asked

"Noodles," Julie answered, still thinking about *next year*.

"Oh boy, chili mac," Matt said.

Ronnie and Jerry echoed the same, "Oh boy."

"I don't like it if Mommy puts beans in it," Julie said.

"Oh, they're okay, Julie," Jerry teased. "They'll put hair on your chest."

"But I don't want no hair on my chest!" Julie exclaimed.

Matt leaned toward Julie and whispered in her ear, "Jerry's just teasing you."

Julie grinned up at Jerry. "Daddy's in a bad mood," Julie continued, updating her brothers.

"When isn't he in a bad mood?" Ronnie mumbled.

"He's always in a bad mood," Matt agreed.

"Uh-uh," Jerry said, trying to defend his dad. "Sometimes he's not. Why is he upset?"

The three boys knew they could get a lot of information out of Julie even if she did get a little mixed up at times.

"'Cause," Julie said, taking a deep breath and letting out a worried sigh. "'Cause Daddy doesn't like noodles, and 'cause I ate his bananas. I got Mommy in trouble," she continued on sadly.

"No you didn't," Ronnie said and put his arm around her as they neared the house.

"It's not your fault, Julie," both Matt and Jerry echoed.

Everyone was quiet at the supper table that night. Ethel asked the boys how school went and for them to show her their papers after dinner. Ron went in and lay down on the couch as soon as he finished eating. Ethel got up to clean up the table and to do the dishes. She wiped the little wooden table clean and told the boys to come and do their homework. She put a pot of water on the stove to heat for their baths.

"I don't have no homework," Matt said proudly to his mom. "I like my teacher too," he continued on.

"I don't like mine," Jerry said. "She's mean."

"Mine's okay," Ronnie stated.

Julie was still sitting in her chair as she ate her dinner. "Mommy," she whispered, "I ate it all 'cept those beans. I no like them."

"You did fine, honey," Ethel said and took her bowl. "How about you getting the first bath since your brothers are doing their homework?" she asked Julie, grabbing her arm gently before she could run away.

"I don't have no homework," Matt said again proudly.

"How about you doing Mommy a favor and go down to Gramma Emma's and get us a bucket of water?"

Matt went and grabbed the bucket off the sink. He took the agate dipper out of the bucket and laid it down on the counter. "I'll be right back, Mommy. Watch how fast I am."

"Okay," Ethel answered as she wiped Julie's face and arms with the warm water and soap. Finishing, she patted Julie dry and put fresh pajamas on her. The boys were getting old enough to bath themselves.

Ethel wasn't religious, but she wanted her children to know about God. She didn't know that much about God. She remembered the nuns used to bring them some food and presents at Christmas when she was a little girl. Shelby had started to take the children to the little church that sat at the top of the next hill. They had gone several times, and Ethel could tell that the boys had enjoyed it. Julie had loved it also. She seemed to think it must be like real school and felt grown up to be allowed to go. Ethel got up from the couch and followed the children into the bedroom. She tucked them in and said a prayer with them.

A few hours later, Julie awoke in her bed. She could hear her mom and dad talking in the living room. Julie peeked through the pink and blue balls of the baby bed that she still slept in and watched them as they talked. She was glad that they were not arguing. She heard them talking about buying a bigger house and moving. She heard her daddy tell her mommy that he would start to give her more grocery money. Julie smiled when she saw them kiss. She lay back down and grabbed her blanket and fell asleep.

Julie at two and one half years old with Santa.

CHAPTER

6

Christmas was fast approaching. Julie stirred as she heard her brothers getting ready for school. She stood in the bed and looked out the window. It was snowing. Julie pounced out of the bed with a leap. She grabbed her blanket through the rails of the bed and ran into the living room. She could smell the fried eggs that she knew her mom had made earlier for her dad. Julie climbed up onto the couch and sat watching everyone hurry about. Matt was looking for his shoes. Jerry was looking for his homework, and Ronnie was looking under the cushion of the couch for his hat. Minutes later, the trio yelled good-bye as Ethel hurried them out the door. Julie ran to the front window. She pressed her nose against the frosted windowpane and watched her brothers walk down the path.

Once they were out of sight, she reluctantly turned and walked toward her mom. Ethel sat on the couch and sipped her cup of coffee. Julie climbed up and sat down beside Ethel. She took her little blanket and reached over her mom and draped it partially onto Ethel's lap before plopping down beside her mom again. She carefully put the remaining part of the blanket onto her lap and then snuggled down into the cover and cuddled close to Ethel's side. Ethel put her arm around Julie and patted her softly.

Shortly, Julie sat upright. "Mommy, I want to go outside and play in the snow," she said excitedly.

"Maybe later, honey, when it warms up a little, okay?"

"Okay," Julie said and then added, "Can I go down to visit Aunt Lisa Sue too?"

"Well, not today, Julie. Aunt Lisa's busy with the baby."

"Oh," Julie said.

Later, Ethel bundled Julie up in her snow pants and jacket. "Don't go too far or stay out too long," Ethel said as she put Julie's gloves on each hand.

"I won't, Mommy," Julie said excitedly. She felt so grown up to be able to go outside by herself. She took a deep breath and tried to sound grown up like Ronnie and said, "I will come in as soon as I just start to feel cold."

"Okay," Ethel said and patted Julie's head tenderly as she opened the door for her to go outside.

Julie walked down the little path that led to Gramma Emma's. She stopped between the two houses and looked all around her. "Here would be a good place to make a snowman," she said out loud to herself. Matt, Jerry, and Ronnie will be surprised when they come home and see Mr. Snowman waiting for them," Julie squealed with delight at the idea of surprising them.

Julie eagerly started to pack the snow with her gloves as she had seen her brothers do many times. But the snow would not come together and pack right for Julie. "I can't do it by myself," she said in a huff aggravated at the snow that stuck to her gloves. "I wish Matt and Jerry and Ronnie were here," she said disappointed and flopped down in the snow to sit. *I know,* she thought to herself. She jumped up as fast as the bulky snow pants would let her. *I'll just make a real little person like me.* Julie shoveled the snow with her gloved hands into a pile the best she could. She packed it gently and then added some more snow. Shortly, she had a very little person. She stood back to look at her creation. She put her hands on her hips and tilted her head at the configuration. *Maybe it would be better if it had eyes, nose, and a mouth,* Julie thought. Quickly, she knelt on the ground and brushed the snow away and found a little stick. She stuck the stick into the little pile of snow for a nose like she had seen Jerry do it. Now all that she needed were the eyes and mouth.

Julie brushed her snow-covered gloves against her coat and hurried down the path to Gramma Emma's house. She straddled her legs to climb up onto the porch that led to the basement kitchen where they ate Sunday dinners. She knew that Gramma Emma was at work and that Aunt Shelby was in school, but Pap Pap James was home. She opened the screen door and knocked on the big wooden door, but no one answered. Julie balanced herself on the doorstep and reached for the doorknob and turned it. Slowly, the door opened, and Julie went in. No one was there, and the kitchen looked large and empty.

Julie knew where Matt and Jerry and Ronnie had gotten the coal before. She had gone with them the last time. She walked past the Victrola and toward the wooden door that led to the coal bin. She hoped that she would not get into trouble, but she knew that Gramma Emma did not mind if she got a few pieces of coal. She had let them the last time. Julie opened the door and went in. A dim light hung from the ceiling not far from the basement window. Julie went to the coal bin. She straddled the boards that ran across the opening to the coal bin and then hopped inside. She fingered the bigger pieces of coal and looked for just the right ones that would make good eyes for her snowman. She then found some smaller pieces that would be perfect for the mouth. She put them all into her pocket. *That should do it*, she thought gleefully and turned to leave. Startled, she jumped back. There stood Pap Pap James at the furnace watching her. "Hi, Pap Pap," she said as she climbed back over the boards to leave.

"Wait a minute, Julie," he called to her. "I want to show you something," he said to Julie. He took her hand and led her back to his workshop.

❋

It was later that evening when Matt asked Ethel if he should wake Julie up from her nap for supper. "Yes, Matt, get her up, or she won't want to sleep tonight," Ethel replied as she set the table for dinner.

Matt went in to wake Julie up, but she was already awake. "Come on get up. Supper's ready," Matt told her.

"I don't want any supper," Julie said. She rolled over in her bed away from Matt.

Matt ran to the other side of her bed to face her. "Hey, you sick?" he asked. But Julie didn't answer him.

Matt went back to the kitchen. "She won't get up," Matt told Jerry.

"Come on we'll get her up," Jerry said to Ronnie with a grin.

Ethel heard Julie crying and told the boys to leave her alone and to quit teasing her. She called them to come back out to the kitchen. "Go ahead and eat," she told them as they sat down.

Ethel went into the bedroom to check on Julie. She put her hand on Julie's head; there was no fever. "Mommy shouldn't have let you go out in the snow to play," Ethel said out loud to Julie. Julie reached for her mommy. Ethel picked her up and carried her to the couch.

After dinner, Ethel got the boys ready for bed but let Julie stay up. Ron had not come home, and it was late. She knew that he was at Lindy's and knew that the later it got, the worse he would be when he got home. "Honey, let mommy give you a warm bath and comb your hair," Ethel said softly to Julie.

Julie got up and went into the kitchen. Ethel set her on the little wooden table and combed her tight curls that were knotted. She washed Julie's face and hands with the warm water. But when Ethel went to take Julie's clothes off to put on the pajamas, Julie screamed, "No!" She crossed her arms and locked them around herself.

"Julie," Ethel said alarmed and surprised at Julie's reaction. "But Mommy has to put your pajamas on."

"No!" Julie said again as she tightened her arms around herself. Ethel reached to move Julie's arms, but Julie started screaming and crying.

"Julie, what is the matter with you? Tell Mommy."

But Julie said nothing.

"Julie, Mommy won't hurt you," Ethel said lovingly to Julie.

Julie raised her head. She looked deep into her mom's eyes. Julie let her eyes search her mom's face carefully.

Ethel could see the desperation in Julie's eyes that were etched in fear. "Julie, you know that Mommy won't hurt you." Ethel stood looking at Julie. Julie's head hung downward, and she avoided looking at her mom. Ethel was totally confused and troubled at Julie's unusual and erratic behavior.

Julie slowly lifted her head and once again looked at her mom cautiously. Julie bit her bottom lip tightly, and then slowly, she began to speak. "Pap Pap hurt Julie," she said in a low whisper.

"When?" Ethel said, trying to calm her voice so not to upset Julie more.

"When I got coal for my snowman's eyes," Julie said through sobs.

Ethel knelt down and took Julie into her arms. "It's okay, honey. It's okay," Ethel said as she held Julie tightly in her arms.

"I shouldn't have went into the coal bin," Julie said in a low voice as she began to cry uncontrollably. Ethel drew Julie close to her, trying to comfort Julie and to get more information.

"No, honey, it's not your fault," Ethel said. She stroked Julie's hair softly and then carried Julie in her arms to the couch. Ethel sat down and rocked Julie slowly as she held her little girl in her arms tightly as if to never let her go. Ethel asked Julie how Pap Pap James had hurt her, but she only pointed to her panties and cried harder. Ethel had wanted to question Julie more for details, but every time she inquired further, Julie would start to scream and cry, saying, "No, Mommy. No, Mommy." Ethel's mind raced and was distraught as she tried to sort it all out. She bit her lip tightly holding back the tears and anger that was raging within her.

Shortly, Julie fell asleep, and Ethel laid her down on the couch. Ethel took the little pajamas and began to change Julie's clothes gently so not to wake her. Ethel suddenly stopped aghast and shocked at what she saw. Anger rose inside of her as the tears flowed down her cheeks. Ethel quickly put the fresh pajamas on Julie. She took a warm blanket that was beside the space heater and draped it over Julie. Ethel sat down on the couch and took the sleeping Julie into her arms and tucked the warm blanket around the little girl tightly. Ethel's mind continued to race, thoughts tumbling endlessly as her anger soared within her.

The door opened suddenly. The cold air rushed in with the staggering Ron. Ethel gazed at him sternly. Her eyes were filled with emotion.

"What?" Ron said loudly as he stood still in the open doorway.

"Shut the door, Ron," Ethel said in an angry whisper. She got up carefully and took Julie into the bedroom and laid her in her bed. She covered her up with a heavy quilt before turning to go back to the living room.

Ron sat on the couch with a beer in his hand. His head drooped forward and swayed, incapacitated from his night of drinking.

Ethel shook her head back and forth hopelessly. *It would be futile to try to attempt to talk to him*, she thought. But she was too livid with anger to let it go.

"What in the hell is your problem tonight?" Ron asked Ethel defensively as if his drinking wasn't enough of a problem.

"What is my problem?" Ethel replied letting her full anger rise within her.

"Don't start!" Ron yelled back.

"Ron, keep your voice down!" Ethel answered back in a hushed whisper while enunciating her words in anger. "Do you have any idea what happened to Julie today?" Ethel continued as angry tears streamed down her face.

Ron sat on the couch silently avoiding Ethel's glare. "Do you know what happened to your little girl today?" she repeated again.

Ron turned his head slowly and looked at Ethel. He saw her tears and turned away from her. He waved his hand in the air weakly and said, "Not tonight, Ethel."

Ethel grabbed Ron by the shoulders and shook him. His head wobbled like a ball on the string. "You listen to me, Ron," Ethel demanded angrily and, then having his attention, proceeded to tell him the details.

Ron sat quietly, looking somewhat shocked but not alarmed. Ethel thought the booze had numbed him and maybe that he didn't quite understand the magnitude of what she was telling him.

"Ethel," he started in a calm but slurred voice, "she's a four-year-old girl. She gets mixed up at times."

"Mixed up! Mixed up!" Ethel screamed letting her voice rise. "She was terrified, Ron! Don't you even care?"

"Ethel, you know that she's a tomboy. She's always getting hurt. You can't be sure of what really happened," Ron said groggily.

"How can you say that?" Ethel asked. She couldn't believe what her ears were hearing. "I thought I was going to have to keep you from going down there and killing him for what he did to Julie." Ethel waited to get some reaction out of Ron. She searched his face with her eyes looking for any sign of emotion but to no avail. Pleading, she continued, "How could James hurt her, Ron? She's just a baby."

But before she could say anything else, Ron raised his hand in protest.

"Leave it alone, Ethel."

"Leave it alone?" Ethel asked, feeling totally perplexed. She could not understand his reaction. It made no sense to her.

"I'm telling you to leave it alone, Ethel. I mean it," he said sternly and then got up slowly. He tried to steady his legs and then staggered into the bedroom to go to bed.

Ethel sat motionless on the couch in a daze. Her mind spun as her thoughts raced, summing up the evening's events. "What can I do? What can I do?" she murmured softly out loud to herself. "What should I do?" she said out loud to herself as she began to sob. She put her head in her hands that rested on her knees and sobbed loudly. She tried to understand Ron's reaction. She tried to reason with the situation, at what she had seen, and what Julie had told her. She recalled the look of horror and fear on her little girl's face and cried all the more. There was no reasoning or explanation that could explain away a situation that could never be fathomed or understood.

Ron lay quietly in the bed, but he could not fall asleep. The moonlight streamed through the window and fell like a soft blanket illuminating the tiny form that lay in the bed beside his. He longed for another beer but dared not get up and face Ethel's wrath again. A tear streamed down his face as he looked at the little girl beside him. *What could I do?* he thought to himself. He turned restlessly in the bed toward the wall unable to look at Julie. *Why stir up a big mess and cause trouble? No one would believe her*, he thought. *No one ever believes a child.* Ron's thoughts continued as he tried to rid himself of the insidious plague on his mind. *She's young. Maybe she will be able to forget about it all in time.* He continued to toss and turn, longing for some resolve, some peace, but finding none. His soul lay tortured as the memories of his own childhood came racing upon him. Tears flowed down his cheeks forbiddingly. "My God," he cried quietly, "now the grandchildren."

The house was too quiet, even for the boys. A cloud seemed to hang over the family. Even Ronnie couldn't explain it to Jerry or

Matt. Julie was quiet and withdrawn and wouldn't let their mom out of her sight. She cried at the least little thing.

Ethel and Ron hardly spoke to each other. "I'd rather they argued," Jerry said to Ronnie one day.

"Not me," Matt piped in.

And so it went all week until Sunday. The boys went to Sunday school, but Julie stayed home. Ronnie had asked Ethel what was wrong. It wasn't like Julie to want to stay home and miss Sunday school. Even Matt's coaching her to come with them could not change Julie's mind. But Ethel said nothing, leaving young Ronnie's question unanswered. She kissed the three of them good-bye and hurried them out of the door.

Ethel watched Julie carefully and held her in her lap continually. She didn't ask Julie anymore about the incident or press her for details. Ethel prayed to God that Julie could forget it. Ron refused to talk about it. If she even approached the subject he would give her a fixed look and then turn away. Ron had not said a word to Emma or James, and Ron had forbid Ethel to say a word to anyone.

Later that day, Ethel pulled the pots and pans out of the cupboard to cook supper. The boys sat in front of the TV watching Abbott and Costello. Julie was napping. Ethel could not help but think that Julie napped a lot since the incident. Ron had the day off and lay on the couch sleeping. He awoke upon hearing Ethel in the kitchen and got up.

"What are you doing?" he called out to Ethel.

"I'm getting ready to fix dinner," she replied.

Ron got up from the couch and went into the kitchen. "You do know that it is Sunday?" Ron asked sarcastically.

"Yes," Ethel answered firmly. She turned from the stove and glared at him.

"Well?" Ron stated.

"Well, what?" Ethel quizzed back.

"Well, you know that we have to go to Mom's for dinner."

Ethel sat the pot down loudly on the stove and stared unbe-
lievably at him. "You think that I'm going down there and taking
the kids to dinner after what happened this week?" she yelled.

Ron turned and saw all six eyes looking back at him from
the living room. "Quiet down, Ethel, the kids are listening,"
he whispered.

"Quiet down! Are you nuts?" she yelled even louder.

"Well, we have to go to dinner, or Mom will be upset, and the
family will wonder!" he declared.

"She'll get upset, and the family will wonder, why?" Ethel
repeated the words incredulously back to Ron and let her pent
up rage release. "Then tell them why, Ron!" Ethel shouted at him.

"I'm taking the boys and going down to Mom's. You and Julie
can stay here if you want," he said loudly back and then turned
and walked away.

"So you are just going to push all of this under the rug and
pretend that it never happened?" she yelled after him. But Ron
did not answer her. He rounded up the boys with their coats and
hurried them to the front door. Ronnie, Jerry, and Matt looked to
their mom in the kitchen. She stood at the stove, staring blankly,
tears streaming down her face.

"Go on!" Ron ordered the boys as he followed behind them
and slammed the door as he left.

Ethel took the pot from the stove and put it into the cupboard.
She paused and leaned on the stove to collect her disheveled
thoughts. She wished she knew what she could do. She had
gone down to Emma's the day after the incident against Ron's
wishes and admonishment to leave it alone. She had stormed into
Emma's house, her anger rising afresh. Emma had never seen
Ethel so distraught and tried to get her to sit down and calm
her. Ethel let her words out in a torrent of emotion and then
exclaimed that if James ever got near Julie again that she would
kill him. Emma's mouth had dropped open, her eyes full of alarm
as she gently shook her head in unbelief at Ethel's words. "But,

Ethel, think of what you are saying," Emma had said as she put her arm around Ethel. "I know James has his problems, but surely, you can't think that he would do something that horrible? Julie is just a little child. She must be mistaken. Talk to her about it."

Ethel had stepped back from Emma. She had wiped the tears off her cheeks. Emma had begun to speak softly again, but Ethel had raised her hand in a halting motion and had walked away.

Ethel put the last pot back into the cupboard and walked to the kitchen table and sat down. She began to sob uncontrollably at the helplessness and desperation of the situation. It was no use. If no one would believe her, then no one would surely believe a four-year-old little girl. There was no way Ethel was going to question and upset Julie all over again.

Weeks passed, and the quiet tension continued to penetrate the home nestled high on the hilltop. Julie began to be more like her old self as the excitement of Christmas approached. Her brothers had become very protective of Julie after gleaning bits and pieces of an adult world that they could not truly understand. Ethel and Ron were back on speaking terms on an as needed basis. Ron had told the family that Julie hadn't been feeling well and that Ethel had stayed home with her.

After the third week, everyone wondered what the problem really was all about. But the family asked very few questions. The family seemed to live by the adage of "Ask me no questions, and I will tell you no lies." Life would continue on; things were better left unsaid, and if you ignored something long enough, it would surely go away. This was not a way of thinking but a true way of life that everyone adhered to. The only problem was that it was not true, and it didn't work.

Ron had tried to be nicer to Ethel after the incident with Julie. He had grown to love and appreciate Ethel. The thought of losing her or the children was something that he could not bear to deal with. He could never show weakness and tell Ethel this, but he did begin to try harder. He came home after work instead of stopping off at Lindy's. He quit complaining about the money. He even sat and played some games with the children. He taught them to make houses out of a deck of cards. Ethel liked the change that she saw in Ron. She tried harder too. At times like these, she felt a deep love for the man who had fathered all of her children.

The week of Christmas came, and Ron and Tom went out to Lisa Sue's family home in the country to look for a Christmas tree to cut down. They found one for each of their families and then a smaller one for Emma.

Nancy and Mark had married. Afterward, Tom and Lisa Sue had one son and another child on the way. Shelby was in high school.

Ron was quiet as they drove back from the country. The trees were stuffed in the trunk of the big car. Ron hoped that somehow Christmas would change things. If he could just get Ethel to come to Emma's for Christmas dinner, maybe their life could get back to normal.

It was Christmas Eve. Ron and Ethel decorated the tree as the children slept. It had taken them awhile to settle the four of them down in their excitement for Christmas.

"The kids are pretty excited," Ron said to Ethel as he strung the lights around the Christmas tree that sat in the corner of the small living room.

"Yea, they are," Ethel said smiling.

"Even Julie seems excited," Ron ventured. "She seems to be doing a lot better these days," Ron continued on, cautiously not wanting to approach the subject and argue with Ethel.

Ethel nodded but said nothing. It still troubled her that Ron had not spoken up or defended his daughter. Ethel bit her lip to hold her peace. She wanted the children to have a happy Christmas.

"Ethel," Ron continued on, "I know that we plan on going to your mom's tomorrow afternoon for Christmas day, but…"

Ethel cringed inwardly trying to hold her tongue; she knew where Ron was going with the conversation.

"Do you think that we all could go to my mom's in the evening for dinner?" Ron asked. He paused and looked at Ethel as he held a Christmas bulb in his hand. He saw her distraught look and continued on before she could speak, "It's just we've been going to dinner at your mom's house on Tuesday, and then you don't go to my mom's for dinner on Sunday. The family is wondering what is going on. They know that Julie can't be sick this long, and they've quit asking me why you both aren't coming to Sunday dinners. It's awkward, you know."

Ethel hung an ornament and said nothing. She turned away from Ron and faced the tree trying to hide the anger that was rising within her. She bent down to the box of ornaments and aimlessly stared into the box before picking up an ornament randomly. She couldn't help thinking, with all that had happened, all that Ron was worried about was that it was awkward and to care what people thought…what his family thought. Well, she would like to tell them what she thought.

"Please, Ethel," Ron asked softly and put his hand on her shoulder. "I've really been trying."

Ethel knew that he truly was trying, and she wanted desperately for her family to be happy. She wanted Ron to be happy. He really had changed, and everyone had been so happy lately. Things were finally coming together. Her family was finally coming together. The least she could do was to try also. She reluctantly pushed her anger aside.

Ethel fingered the tiny angel ornament in her hands nervously, giving thought to Ron's pleas. She touched the angels feathered wings tenderly before turning slowly to face Ron. "We'll work something out," she said before changing the subject to the children and Christmas.

Julie at age three and a half. Julie and Matt at Hanson's Park.

CHAPTER

7

Matt and Julie sat inside the tiny bedroom and looked out the window. The forsythia was in full bloom, and the tulips were bright with color. Winter was past, and the beauty of spring seemed to beckon in a new season.

"You shouldn't scratch them," Matt said to Julie as she sat scratching her arm furiously. "Mommy said they'd leave scars if you scratch them."

"But they itch so much," Julie said as she continued to scratch her arm.

"You two gonna be okay?" Ethel said, poking her head past the bedroom door.

"Yea, Mom," Matt said sadly.

"Julie, quit digging those chicken pox, honey, or you'll have scars," Ethel scolded gently.

"Told you," Matt echoed.

"But we wanted to look for Easter eggs with Jerry and Ronnie," Julie said. "It's not fair."

"I know, but there will be next year," Ethel told them both as she went to kiss them good-bye. "I'll be down at Gramma Emma's if you need me, okay? I'll be up to check on you and to bring you your dinner."

Ethel turned to go and glanced back once more at the two little faces that were pressed against the window watching the Easter egg hunt. She shut the door behind her and headed toward the path that led to Emma's house. It was still hard for Ethel to go down to Emma's house and harder yet for her to talk to James. On Monday's, she would go down to do the wash, and often, he would try to start up a conversation with her. She often looked at him and tried to figure out how he could talk to her as if nothing had happened. *Did he think maybe that Julie had not said anything or was he just trying to pretend it never happened?*

Ethel knew that everyone in the valley liked the quiet man who did odd jobs of cutting grass and were amazed at his woodwork. He was a likeable person overall. So how could Ethel only see the hidden side to this man, she wondered.

She would never doubt what Julie had told her. Ethel was just glad that Julie seemed to be back to her old self. She worried about Shelby still living at home with Emma at work all day. Ethel had noticed things that made her uncomfortable with Shelby and James. She did not trust James at all regardless if everyone else did. Ethel had approached the subject with Emma one day when James wasn't around. Ethel hinted to Emma about the concerns that she had for Shelby. She even mentioned a little about Julie's fear of her grandfather. But Emma had replied, "Ethel, surely you're mistaken." Ethel assured her that she didn't feel that she was mistaken and voiced her concerns about Shelby being left alone with James. But Emma had kindly told Ethel that she was sure everything was okay and that though James had his faults that he'd never hurt anyone. Ethel knew that there was no use pursuing the subject and let it drop.

Ethel could not help but notice how much Ron was like his father. You never really knew what to expect out of either one of them. Everyone saw only one side of their personalities. Sometimes, Ethel wondered if she really could get to truly know either of them. It seemed the more she tried to please Ron, the more withdrawn he would become. He had slowed down on his drinking before Christmas, but once she had given into going back to Emma's, he gradually started to drink again. It wasn't long before he was stopping off at Lindy's most evenings after work and coming home drunk. The more he drank, the more they argued.

When it seemed more than she could bear, Ron would be nice for a while, and things would settle down for a time. She thought that he might be having affairs. She had asked him several times, but he would wave her off and tell her that it was all in her imagination. Ethel loved her children, and she was sure that Ron did too. She wanted the marriage to work. She wanted her children to have a mom and a dad. She couldn't stand the thought of putting them through the agony of a divorce.

By summer, things were becoming unbearable. It was late, and Ron had not come home from work. It was nearly 2:00 a.m. when Ethel heard his car pull up. He saw her as he entered the front door and knew that she was angry. He walked past her into the kitchen and got himself a beer. He popped the cap off with the opener and let the cap hit the floor and roll under the table. He walked in and sat down beside Ethel and put his arm around her.

"Now, Ethel, before you start," he said, his voice breaking up as he struggled with forming his words. "Now, let me explain."

Ethel pushed his arm aside, saying nothing as he reached for a cigarette and offered her one.

"It's not what you think," he continued, enunciating every word.

"And what do I think, Ron?" Ethel asked angrily.

"You know," he said as he waved his hand in the air. "The same old, same old," he continued, appearing to struggle with his thoughts as well as his words.

Ethel got up to go to bed. There was no use getting into an argument with him and waking the children. He grabbed her arm and pulled her down to him. "Come on, honey," Ron pleaded.

Ethel could smell his breath. It reeked of alcohol and smoke. As she went to pull away, her eyes saw the red stain on the collar of his shirt and another one smudged on his neck. She could feel the anger and rage rise within her as she jerked her arm from his grasp. "I guess that lipstick on your collar and neck is just my imagination too?" she asked, letting her voice rise. Ron retaliated in fierce defense. His words made no sense in his drunken state, but he raised his voice all the same.

Julie awoke hearing the shouting from the next room. She stood up and peeked over the crib and looked through the bedroom doorway. She could hear their heated words. She lay back down and grabbed her blanket and looked across at her brothers in their bunk beds. She was surprised to see that all three of them were in the bottom bunk and wide awake.

"*Sh!*" Ronnie whispered and put his finger to his mouth and motioned Julie to be quiet before she could speak.

"Why are they mad?" Julie whispered as low as she could.

"We don't know." Matt whispered back.

"I'm scared," Julie said.

"Come on over with us, Julie," Jerry said. "Just be real quiet."

Julie hated the old baby bed that she slept in. She felt that she was too old for a baby bed, but her mom had said that they had neither the money nor the room to get her a real bed. She knew that the baby bed would creak when she would climb over the rail no matter how hard that she would try to be quiet.

"Help me, Ronnie," she whispered as she grabbed her blanket and straddled the rail.

"I got you, Jul," Ronnie said quietly as he reached up and helped pull her down into the bed with them.

Julie sat listening and looked at Matt, then Jerry, and then at Ronnie before asking, "But why are they so upset?"

"It's about a woman," Ronnie answered in a low voice.

"About Mommy?" Julie asked trying to understand.

"No," Jerry said, "another woman."

"Another mommy?" Julie asked again, puzzled and confused.

"No!" Ronnie answered, trying to be patient with his little sister while trying to hear the adults talk in the next room.

"Another woman kissed Daddy," Matt whispered into Julie's ear as Jerry pulled her back to lie down.

"Go to sleep, Jul. We'll explain it to you in the morning," Jerry said as he covered her up with her blanket.

But as the voices rose, Julie sat back up in the bed with her brothers.

"Fine!" Ron yelled as he headed for the front door. "And you wonder why I don't come home."

He slammed the door hard behind him as he left. Ethel could hear him stumble down the steps. She sat down on the couch and began to cry. But upon seeing the half-empty beer bottle sitting on the coffee table, she wiped her eyes and jumped to her feet. She grabbed the bottle and headed for the front door. She stormed onto the front porch. Ron had just made it to the car and was opening the car door to get in.

"You forgot something!" Ethel screamed at Ron while waving the beer bottle in the air.

Ron turned and glared at her and then ignored her as he turned to get into the car.

Ethel stood on the porch with the beer bottle still in her hand. The very smell of it reached her nose, infuriating her into a rage. She took the bottle and, as hard as she could, pitched it right at Ron. It barely missed him as he flopped down onto the car seat. He started the engine and pulled out, spinning rocks as he drove away.

Ethel went back into the house that she had tried so desperately to make a home. She walked over to the bedroom door and shut the door softly. She knew that the children had to be awake from all of the noise. She sat down on the couch and began to cry.

"What can I do?" she sobbed. She cried for herself, her children, and her family.

❋

Julie fleeted around excitedly. There was no calming her down. "What can I do, Mommy?" she asked.

"You can get the blanket that is on the couch and take it to the car if you want," Ethel answered. "Matt, you and Jerry grab the ice cooler, and, Ronnie, if you want to play ball grab your ball and bat," Ethel continued to give the children instructions.

Julie had taken the blanket to the car and had hurried back. "Now what, Mommy?" she asked.

"Just help your brothers, honey. Ask them what you can do to help," Ethel said.

Julie ran and followed her brothers up and down the hill to the car and back to the house.

"Do you have our swimsuits?" Julie asked her mom, tugging on her dress to get her attention.

"Yes, Julie," Ethel answered. She then turned to Matt, "Matt, why don't you get Julie and play outside until we're ready to go."

Matt grabbed Julie's hand and hurried outside.

Julie loved going on the family picnics. Next to Christmas, it was her favorite time. Everyone was coming: Uncle Tom and Lisa Sue and her little cousins and Gramma Emma. Julie loved Gramma Emma. Sometimes even Gramma Winnie and Pap Pap John would join them too. Julie thought that her mom and dad always seemed so happy at these picnics.

Soon everything was packed, and they were ready to go. All four of the children hurried into the backseat. Julie knew they were going out to Hanson's Park. It wasn't a real park, just a few picnic tables, a river, and no sand, but Julie didn't care. The picnic tables would be full of food for the family. Ronnie, Jerry, Matt, and she would swim until the skin on their fingers and toes would wrinkle.

Julie squeezed into the backseat between her brothers. Jerry and Ronnie had called out shotgun, which meant they got to sit by the window. Julie could never seem to remember to say it first. But Julie didn't care about sitting in the middle today. Julie nestled down in the backseat. They drove down the dirt road onto the main highway. Julie leaned over Matt and toward Ronnie to look out the window and then sat back in the seat. "Sit still," Matt said and gave her a gentle poke with his elbow. But Julie couldn't help it; she was just so excited.

Ethel turned around and looked at her four children. She could see the excitement on all of their faces. "Come on, kids. We'll sing some songs," she said.

Julie smiled from ear to ear. She listened to Ronnie's deeper voice blend in with Matt's and Jerry's higher pitch. Julie tried to learn the words and joined in on the chorus.

All the way to Hanson's Park, they sang songs and talked.

"Look how big the onion's are," Jerry exclaimed as he pointed to the corn. Ron and Ethel burst out laughing.

Ron had not apologized. It was not his way. He would just back off from drinking and be a little nicer to Ethel until she would give in to keep the peace for the family. He once again had reminded her that she should surely forgive him for his indiscretion as he had forgiven her for her mistake and even married her in spite of it. Ethel knew it would have done no good to explain to him that they were not married or even a couple when she had made her mistake. Ron reminded her that he worked hard, brought home a check every week, and that he was a good dad. So Ethel forgave him once again and hoped that there would be happier days for all of them.

But except for her love for her children, she was not happy. Ronnie was now eight years old. Jerry was seven; Matt, six; and Julie, five years old. Fall was rapidly approaching. Ethel had thought that with Julie going to school soon that maybe she could get a job at a sewing factory over in Grantville. She had heard that they were hiring. She knew she could catch the city bus that always stopped at the bottom of the hill. Ethel thought that maybe if they could get on their feet more financially, things would get better between Ron and herself. She approached Ron about it one evening. She thought that he would be thrilled at the idea. But he had flatly refused to discuss it and had forbidden Ethel to apply. "Don't I bring home a check every week?" he had continued on defensively. "No wife of mine is going to work." Ethel dropped the conversation. She couldn't help but think that there might be more to it than Ron was saying.

She had learned a long time ago to read between Ron's words. His actions spoke much louder than the words that he spoke. Ethel knew that he was insidiously jealous of her though she didn't know why. They often had arguments after bowling on Saturday nights. Ron would accuse her of flirting with one man after another. Ethel thought at first that he was just being defensive of his own flirtations and joked it off. But in time, she realized that he was serious with his jealous outbursts. She couldn't help but think that he objected to her going to work more because he wouldn't have control over her than the mere fact of a bruised ego pertaining to his providing. As it turned out, Ethel could not go to work anyway. Julie's birthday fell past the deadline, and she would have to wait another year to go to first grade.

Julie was so upset when her mom told her that she wouldn't be able to go to school that year. Unlike the year before when she was four, Julie now knew what was meant by next year.

Julie gradually pushed the subject of school aside and concentrated on enjoying the remnant of summertime with her brothers. She dreaded when they'd go back to school, and she'd have no one to play with.

Julie sat on the little concrete porch eating her peanut butter and jelly sandwich and watched her brothers tear off the crusts from their bread and play with them before dangling them in their mouths. Julie laughed out loud at them. She took a drink of her Kool-Aid and set it back down as she enjoyed her sandwich.

Matt finished first. He grabbed the two cookies from his napkin that his mom had given him and stuck them in his pocket. "Hurry up, you guys," he said as he stood up. "Let's go for a hike."

"Okay," Jerry said as he crammed the last of his sandwich into his mouth and put his cookies into his pockets also. Ronnie did the same and jumped up to join the others.

"Hey, you gotta wait for me," Julie said, trying to eat now as fast as she could.

"Well, hurry up, slowpoke," Jerry kidded.

"Run and tell Mom where we are going," Ronnie said to Matt as he stood and laughed at Julie. Her cheeks looked like a chipmunk's as she pushed the rest of her sandwich into her mouth and tried to chew without choking.

"Here, Jul," Jerry said. "Wash it down with some Kool-Aid." Julie took the little plastic cup and sipped it slowly.

"Mom said we could go but just be back in time for supper," Matt said as he rejoined them.

Julie stood up quickly. She quickly swallowed the remaining food in her mouth and washed it down with the last of her Kool-Aid. She grabbed her two cookies to put them in her pocket like she had seen her brothers do. "Hey, I don't have any pockets," she said to Matt as they headed up the hill toward the woods. "Put them in your pocket for me, Matt, please?" Julie asked.

"Okay," Matt said. He took the cookies and put them in his pocket.

"Don't you eat them, Matt," Julie said with a twinkle in her eye.

"I won't, Jul," he answered her back as he ruffled her curly hair with his hand.

"Ronnie, Jerry, Matt," Ethel called out after them. "You watch Julie doesn't go near the cliff and keep her with you."

"We will," Ronnie, Jerry, and Matt all answered back at the same time.

"I will too, Mommy," Julie repeated her brothers words, trying to sound grown up.

"Wait up," Julie called after her brothers as they got ahead of her.

"Well, come on. Hurry up," Jerry called back to her as he stopped to wait for her to catch up.

"Jerry, will you wait for me? I have to use the bathroom," Julie asked as she looked at him and pleaded with her eyes.

"Can't you wait?" Jerry asked perplexed.

"Uh-uh," Julie answered.

"Go ahead," Jerry said as they stopped at the old outhouse. He called out to Matt and Ronnie to wait up.

Julie knew that her brothers would wait for her. She knew that they kind of fussed at her, but she knew that they enjoyed her being with them. Julie pulled the door shut with the metal lock and locked the door so that it wouldn't fly open. She climbed carefully up onto the wooden seat to sit. The hole that was cut in the seat was so big that she was always afraid that she might fall down inside of it, and no one would find her for hours. She was much more afraid of falling down the hole in the outhouse than of falling over the cliff. *At least in the summer it isn't cold*, Julie thought. *In the winter, the wind blows straight up the hole and—*

"Hurry up, Jul," Jerry called out to her and interrupted her thoughts. "What'd you do, fall in?" he said jokingly.

Julie looked at the closed door and hung on a little tighter to the edge of the seat. "That's not funny, Jerry," she yelled back.

That evening when they came back home, there was not a clean spot on any of them. Fortunately, Ethel had put the old aluminum washtub at the rain spout and had caught the water from the thunderstorm the night before. She already had some water heating on the stove to warm it up a little. Ethel knew that when they had left for the hike that they would all need a tub bath when they returned home. Ethel would be glad someday when they would have running water and indoor plumbing. It was getting harder and harder as the children got older.

"Shotgun," Julie called out as they came running down the little path that led to the back door.

"Me first," Ronnie said.

"I mean, me first," Julie said correcting herself. She could never get it straight what to call out to be first or to sit by the windows in the car.

"Uh-uh," Matt, Jerry, and Ronnie called out together.

"Yes," Ethel said to them. "She called out first. So she gets to get the first bath."

Julie gleamed with joy. Finally, she had remembered first before her brothers. She hated to be the last one who bathed in the tub. It got all yucky after about the third bath even if her mom did keep adding fresh, warm water.

"Oh, Mom, don't let her go first," Ronnie pleaded. "She always pees in the water."

"No, I don't!" Julie said firmly and stomped her foot as she gave Ronnie a stern look.

Matt and Jerry broke out laughing. Ronnie joined in and laughed too.

The summer began to fade, but the evenings were still humid and warm. One night when it was extremely hot, Ethel spread a blanket out on the freshly mowed grass. Ron stretched out on the blanket with Ethel beside him. He turned on the transistor radio and tuned it to the baseball game. His favorite team, the Pittsburgh Pirates, was playing. Ronnie, Jerry, and Matt sat down beside their dad and listened to the game with him. Ron explained the game to them as the announcer called the plays. Julie sat between Ethel's legs and watched her dad and brothers. Ethel brushed Julie's hair carefully, getting the tangles out from the day's play. The stars shone bright in the clear night sky. The crickets sang loudly, and a warm, gentle breeze blew over them.

Below, the lights of the valley shined in the darkness and faded in the distance.

Happier days—Matt, Ronnie, Jerry and Julie

CHAPTER

8

The cool breeze blew the tight curls from Julie's young face as she stood on the small porch and leaned as far as she could over the banister. She peered down the dirt road hoping to get one more glimpse of her brothers as they hurried down the dirt road to go to school. Summer had been quickly ushered out by the autumn winds.

"Julie, come on back into the house," Ethel called out to Julie. Julie reluctantly obeyed. She shut the door behind her and flopped on the couch. Ethel watched her from the kitchen. *She is absolutely lost without her brothers*, Ethel thought to herself as she cleaned up the small kitchen. Julie was restless throughout the day. Ethel hardly knew what to do to settle her down.

"Hey, you want to help Mommy clean up the house, and then we'll walk down to the store and get a soda?"

Julie smiled at Ethel and ran to the kitchen to get the broom. Ethel began to sing the familiar songs, and Julie hummed along trying to learn the words. "My daddy is only a picture, in a frame that hangs on the wall, each day I talk to my daddy, but he never talks at all," Ethel continued the sad refrain.

"Oh, Mommy, let's not sing that song," Julie implored. "It's just too sad. It makes me cry." Julie couldn't imagine not having a daddy. The song relayed the story of a little boy who only had a picture of his daddy to talk to because his daddy had died. Julie didn't want her daddy to die. She wished that he would not drink so much beer. She hated that daddy, the way he treated her mommy and made her cry. Sometimes Julie would get so mad that she just wanted him to go away or something and come back as the nice daddy that she had glimpses of sometimes. "But no... no," she said to herself, struggling with the troubled thoughts that tormented her mind. *I don't want my daddy to die and only be a picture on the wall.*

Ethel saw the troubled look on Julie's face and started to sing another song. "Abba, dabba, dabba, dabba, dabba, dabba, dabba, said the monkey to the chimp." Ethel sang out, "'Abba, dabba, dabba, dabba, dabba, dabba, dabba,' said the chimpy to the monk." Julie repeated back giggling as she sang the silly song. Julie laughed through the whole song, half humming while trying to learn the words and half singing as she tried to mimic her mom.

Later, they walked down to the store. They sat on the store's little porch and enjoyed their sodas. Julie carried the bottles back into the store when they were finished. She took the pennies for the bottle deposit and put them gleefully in the little pocket of her dress.

Julie walked out the door of the little store and was surprised to see her brothers talking to their mom. Julie squealed with delight that her brothers were home from school. They all walked home together. Julie talked endlessly to her brothers going from Matt, to Jerry, and then Ronnie. She asked them about school and the swings and the merry-go-round. Ronnie looked on at his chippering little sister and nodded with a smile to Jerry and Matt to pacify her.

Julie was glad that the next day was Saturday. She had learned the days of the week and knew that on Saturdays and Sundays her brothers had no school.

Later the next day, Ethel asked Matt and Jerry if they would go down to the store to get a can of milk for dinner. Ronnie had gone off the hill earlier to play with some school friends. She wished that she had thought to ask him. Ethel dug in her purse for a quarter.

"Can I go too?" Julie asked, jumping up and down in front of her mom.

"Oh, Mom," both Matt and Jerry yelled out, rolling their eyes at each other, "Does she have to come too?" Julie looked crushed.

"Take her with you," Ethel urged the boys.

"But she always comes with us," Jerry said.

"Yeah," Matt chimed in, "we always have to take her with us everywhere we go."

"Take her with you," Ethel repeated firmly, giving both boys a parental stare as if to say don't argue with me on this.

"Can we have some money for candy?" both boys asked at the same time.

"Not today," Ethel said sadly to the boys. She knew the quarter was the last of the change that she had found in her purse.

Matt and Jerry ran out the front door. Julie ran behind them, trying to catch up. "Hey, you guys, wait for me," Julie called out to them and ran as fast as she could.

"Well, come on if you're coming," Jerry called back to her as he motioned for Matt to slow down. Jerry stood kicking the loose stones with his shoe as he waited for Julie to join them.

Julie quickly ran up to Jerry. She gasped to catch her breath. "You mad at me, Jerry?" she asked sadly.

"Nah," Jerry said as he tousled her curly hair with his hand. Jerry knew that what he was really angry about was that Matt and he had not been allowed to go with Ronnie earlier. The trio walked down the dirt road and crossed the tiny bridge that crossed over the small stream. Now on the main highway, both Matt and Jerry walked protectively beside Julie, careful to keep her off the road as they walked to the little store.

"Hi, Goldie," they all three called out as they entered the store and saw the older lady standing behind the counter.

"Mom wants a can of milk," Jerry said as he fumbled in his jean pockets to get the quarter.

"Here you are," Goldie said and placed a can of milk on the counter as Jerry handed her the quarter.

"Do you want a little bag?" Goldie asked Jerry.

"No, that's okay," Matt answered for Jerry as they turned to leave. Jerry stood holding the milk, staring in a daze at the candy counter, wishing they could have some.

"Let's take the shortcut home," Matt said to Jerry as they left the little store and headed down the steps.

"Sure," he answered as he walked slowly and tried to shake the bad mood that he was feeling.

"Wish we would've got some candy," Matt said gloomily.

"Me too," Julie said as she pouted, copying her brothers.

Jerry decided to take the shortcut home and turned to the right instead of the left. They walked past Lindy's. Matt searched the cars to see if their dad's car was there. "Dad's still at work," Jerry said to Matt as if reading Matt's mind.

The dirt road wound to the left. This would take them up the hill to the church where they went to Sunday school. Another small road veered to the right, which would then led to a small path, which they could take to go home. Julie wondered if it was really a short cut but hoped the little adventure would shake her brothers out of their bad mood.

As they neared the branch in the road, Matt and Jerry suddenly both stopped. "Hey, look," Jerry said. "There goes Tony Mesner."

"Let's go see what he's doing," Matt urged Jerry.

The boys took off running with Julie following behind them.

"Hey, Tony," Matt yelled. "What are you doing?"

Tony ignored Matt and turned away from Jerry's look too. Jerry ran ahead of Tony and asked, teasing, "Hey, whatcha doing pulling a wagon?"

Matt joined in with Jerry and started teasing Tony too, "Yeah, you a sissy or something?"

"Yeah," Julie chimed in, not sure why they were picking on Tony.

"Leave me alone," Tony said as he tried to go around Matt and Jerry.

"Make me," Jerry said.

"Me too," Matt said as he stood firmly beside Jerry.

Julie leaned down and picked up a handful of rocks and tossed them into the grocery bag that was in the small wagon that Tony was pulling. As Matt and Jerry continued to bully Tony, Julie continued to scoop up more handfuls of rocks tossing them into the wagon and groceries. Soon Tony began to cry and pushed past them and hurried up the hill toward his home.

The three stood looking at each other, not even sure why they had picked on the boy. He had never done anything to them. Julie dropped the handful of rocks that she still held in her hands. They watched Tony go up the hill pulling the wagon behind him. Tony turned briefly. Julie could see his tear-streaked face. She glanced at her brothers and saw the shame on their faces that she was feeling in her heart. Neither of them said a word as they turned and walked slowly home.

"What in the world took you so long?" Ethel asked them as they walked in the door.

"We...we just took our time," Julie answered slowly. She looked over at Matt and Jerry and, catching their glance, said no more.

"Well, come wash up for dinner," Ethel called out to them.

Shortly, Ronnie came barging through the door and went to the kitchen to the small basin to wash his hands. "Hey, Mom, Pap Pap James called out to me on the way home and said to tell you that someone wanted to talk to you on the phone."

Ethel quickly dried her hands and hurried down the path that led down the hillside. She hoped it wasn't Ron saying that he'd be coming home late. Emma had recently had a phone installed, and as nice as it was to have one so accessible, Ethel hated when Ron would call with an excuse to stay out late and drink.

It was only minutes later when Ethel returned. All four children jumped as the door flew open. All eight eyes were looking at their mom who now stood in the doorway staring down at them as they sat Indian style in front of the television watching Popeye the Sailor Man.

"What in the world did you do to that poor boy?" Ethel yelled. "Whatever were you thinking?" she continued on letting her voice crescendo. None of them answered. Ronnie moved up to the couch, glad that he knew nothing about what his mom was talking about. He could see by the look on their faces that somehow they were fully aware of what their mom was asking.

"Matt?" Ethel asked. "Jerry?"

But there was no answer. "And, Julie, you…throwing rocks into Tony's grocery bags?" Julie hung her head in shame, embarrassed at what she had done. She felt simply awful. "Well?" Ethel asked them again as she continued to look at them, her hands placed firmly on her hips. But the trio had no answer. "Well, you'll talk when your father comes home," she said as she turned off the television and went into the kitchen to finish dinner.

Julie knew that later after supper when her dad found out what they had done that they were going to be in big trouble. "We're going to get the marine belt this time," Julie said to Matt as she whimpered softly.

"Yeah, we probably will," Jerry said and then added solemnly, and I think we kind of deserve it."

"I don't know why we did it," Matt said.

"Me neither," Jerry replied back.

"We're in big trouble," Julie repeated to them. "Maybe we should run away?"

Both Jerry and Matt gave her a look to get real. Julie could only shrug her shoulders and bite her lower lip. As much as she anticipated the punishment, nothing could make her feel worse than the shame that she felt in her heart for what she had done.

It was as they had expected. Their dad was very upset at them once he had learned what they had done. Unlike their mom, he didn't ask why they had done it but went promptly to the bedroom and retrieved the old marine belt.

Later that night, Ronnie asked them why they had picked on poor Tony Mesner. There was a stillness in the room and Julie waited to see if either of her brothers had an answer, for within herself, she had none. Jerry spoke up and broke the quietness of the moment. "I was just in a bad mood."

"I just felt angry at him because he had said that he had candy and we didn't," Matt said solemnly. Julie vowed she would never do anything like that again.

Julie had tossed restlessly all night. In the morning, Ethel woke them up. Julie could see that her mom was still upset with them. "Get dressed," Ethel said firmly. "We're going for a walk."

"Me…too?" Ronnie asked a little confused, not used to seeing his mom be this upset at them for so long.

"No, you can stay here, Ronnie," Ethel said.

Julie glanced at Matt and Jerry to read their faces, but they appeared as blank and bewildered as she felt.

Ethel opened the door and waved her hand for them to go on. She marched them down the dirt road, onto the main highway, past Goldie's store, and up the other dirt road. They walked up the hill past the little church and further up the hill than Julie had ever gone. She glanced at Jerry and Matt and started to open her mouth to ask them a question. But before she could speak, they both shook their heads slightly to tell her to be quiet.

It wasn't long before Julie realized what her brothers had already figured out. "Now," Ethel said firmly to her children as they stopped in front of the small dilapidated house, "all three of you go up to the door and knock on it. You tell Mrs. Mesner that you are sorry for what you did. And then you ask to speak to

Tony, and you tell him that you are sorry. Julie, you tell them too," Ethel admonished her.

The walk home seemed so long. No one said a word, not even their mom. Julie hoped she would never hurt anyone that way ever again.

✳

It was a cool fall day. The dampness hung heavy in the air, making it feel much colder than it really was. Most of the leaves had fallen except for the brown leaves that hung limply on the large oaks.

Ethel had just come in from hanging the last load of wash on the clothesline. Her hands were cold and red. She went directly to the stove to boil some water for coffee.

Soon, Julie heard the rumble of footsteps on the front porch and knew that her brothers were home from school. She ran to let them in. She opened the door quickly. "Hey, where's Ronnie?" Julie asked loudly.

"*Sh!*" Matt whispered to Julie as he pulled her outside and shut the door behind her. Julie looked past the rail of the porch and saw Ronnie standing below.

"Oh my goodness!" Julie squealed.

"*Sh!*" Jerry said as he clapped his hand over her mouth. Julie pushed his hand aside and ran softly down the steps over to where Ronnie was standing. Beside him stood a little red cocker spaniel wagging its tail. Julie knelt down to pet him as Jerry and Matt ran down the steps to join them.

"Do you think that Mom and Dad will let us keep him?" Julie asked.

"I don't know," Ronnie answered and then turned and smiled at Julie.

"That's why we want you to ask them, Julie," Matt said as he patted her gently on the head.

"Where's his home?" Julie asked as the dog licked her fully across her face.

"We don't know," Ronnie replied. Julie looked at Ronnie with an impish grin. "Honestly, we don't know," Ronnie continued. "He just followed us home."

"With a little help," Jerry added, laughing.

"Well, just a little," Matt added.

"So will you ask Mom and Dad for us, Julie?" Ronnie pleaded with his little sister. "They always say yes when you ask."

"Should we ask Mommy first?" Julie asked and turned to look at her three brothers with a twinkle in her eye.

"Yeah!" they all agreed as they took their new furry friend around to the back door while Julie ran up the steps and through the front door.

They were all surprised when Ron and Ethel agreed to let them keep the dog. "What can we name him?" Ronnie asked. Everyone started to call out names.

We could call him Ike after our president, Mr. Eisenhower,"Ron suggested, surprising the children with his input and enthusiasm.

"Yeah!" the four agreed as they jumped up and down with glee. They didn't care what they called him as long as they got to keep him.

A few days later though, Ron said to Ethel, "We better change the name Ike to Mamie."

"But why?" Ethel asked a little puzzled.

"He's a girl," Ron said smiling.

Ronnie played ball with Mamie every day after school. Jerry scratched her belly after she rolled down the hill with them playing in the grass. Matt fed and gave her water. Julie would sit on the porch with her every day as the two of them would wait for the boys to come home from school.

It seemed the family was turning a corner of life. The happier times seemed to bring the growing family closer together. Nearly every night at dinner, the topic of conversation was on buying a bigger house. With the growing excitement, the family seemed to knit together with anticipation. Ron came home from work instead of stopping at Lindy's. Julie sat listening to the conversation around her as she dipped her buttered bread into the gravy.

"Will we have running water?" Ronnie asked excitedly.

"I think so," Ethel said and gave Ron a smile as she continued to butter Ronnie's bread.

It was early spring after Julie's sixth birthday before Ethel and Ron had found the right house for their price range. They were waiting to get approved for the mortgage.

One evening, Winnie and John came to their little house for dinner. Julie could see as they came in the door that Gramma Winnie had brought one of her delicious cakes. Julie adored Gramma Winnie and Pap Pap John. Pap Pap John always brought them a treat. He would slip them each a shiny nickel or a piece of Wrigley's Juicy Fruit chewing gum. Julie loved to crawl up on Gramma Winnie's big lap and get lost in her large arms as she wrapped them around her and gently bounced her on her knee.

After dinner, the adults sat at the table to talk while the children went in and watched television. "Sally is in the hospital again," Winnie told them.

"Where will Tonya go to live this time?" Ethel asked sadly. She knew that every time that her sister had a nervous breakdown, she would be in the hospital for a while. Tonya, Sally's youngest daughter, was left at the mercy of the family to take her in.

"We don't know," Winnie replied as she scooted her chair away from the table to have more room and to get comfortable. Winnie crossed her hands in front of her and moved her fingers nervously while searching Ron's and Ethel's faces. "Your sisters…Mary and Penny say they can't take Tonya to live with them this time. They have their hands full with all of their young children. Mary has her four young children and one on the way. And Penny wouldn't even consider it with her own situation and her three little ones," Winnie continued on speaking briskly. "Ethel…Ron…we wondered if maybe you could have Tonya come live with you if you get the new house."

Ron stared at Winnie and John but said nothing. "I just don't know, Mom," Ethel stammered as she looked over at Ron to see his reaction. "We'll have to think about it."

Everyone dropped the subject as quickly as it had come up. Winnie pulled a pack of cards from her purse. Ron and Winnie didn't always get along, mostly because of the way that Ron treated Ethel; however, they loved playing cards together.

A few weeks later, Ron and Ethel received the news that their mortgage had been approved. The house was everything they could have imagined. It was an older home but well taken care of. It sat at the foot of the hill across from Goldie's little store and Lindy's Tavern. The children could still walk to school and to church or to Gramma Emma's and Gramma Winnie's. The house had a large fenced in yard with a large barn out back. There were pear, plum, and cherry trees for canning. Ron could park his car in the barn. A concrete sidewalk led from the barn to the house and encircled around the whole house leading to a small basement. Though modest, it had everything that they needed and more. There was a big front porch surrounded by lilacs and rose bushes. A living room adjoined the kitchen at one end and a small landing at the other. The kitchen had two large windows and a back door that led to a screened rear porch. Off the screened porch was another door that led to a laundry room. The landing off of the living room led to a downstairs bedroom to the left and to the right a stairway that led to the bedrooms upstairs. At the top of the stairs immediately to the left was a bedroom. Directly to the right of the stairway across a hallway was another bedroom. In between the two bedrooms was a large bathroom, and at the end of the hallway was a large closet that led to an attic. All that was needed was for Ethel and Ron to give the bank the deposit and to sign the papers. Ron and Ethel had agreed to use the money from the car accident as their deposit.

Julie and her brothers were so excited. They were finally able to see the house. Julie was beside herself once she saw the house.

Her thoughts raced with all of the excitement. As if starting school this year wasn't enough to be excited about, now they were going to move to a new house, a house with an indoor bathroom. Julie had stayed in the bathroom the longest and flushed the toilet over and over again and tried all of the faucets, turning them on and off over and over again.

Julie couldn't imagine what else her mom and dad could have to share with them when one night they had set them down to talk. She knew that they weren't in trouble because they had not done anything wrong. Yet Julie sensed a seriousness in her mom's demeanor.

Ethel and Ron had fully discussed the situation at hand and had come to a decision but wanted to know how the children would feel about it. Ethel began to talk with them as Ron sat back on the couch and listened. "You all know your cousin Tonya?" Ethel asked. "Well, your Aunt Sally is in the hospital, and Tonya needs a place to live until she comes home."

"Like when you were in the hospital?" Ronnie asked. He was old enough to remember his mom's car accident.

"Kind of." Ethel nodded and gave him a smile. "Well, your daddy and I thought since we were moving into the bigger house that Tonya could come to live with us. She would share a room with you, Julie, and could be like a big sister."

This was not the good news that Julie had expected. She hadn't known what really to expect, but she wasn't sure if she should be happy to have a big sister or not. She had big brothers, and that was great, but she hardly knew Tonya except to see her at Gramma Winnie's house at Christmas.

"How old is she?" Jerry asked curiously. He was not sure what to make of everything.

"She's fourteen," Ethel said, "and all I can tell you is that she needs a home, or she will have to go to live in an orphanage."

"Oh," said Matt, "that would be sad."

"Yeah," echoed the others.

"So if you think we can make it work…" Ethel asked and then paused and searched Ron's and the children's faces.

"Yeah, Mom," all four of them answered at once.

Tonya moved in with them the next week. She would sleep on the couch until they moved. Everything was changing so fast for Julie that she hardly knew how to react. Julie liked Tonya right away. She thought that Tonya was pretty with her reddish-brown hair and freckles. Julie thought that she looked almost grown up. Tonya was quiet at first. Julie would fleet around her trying to make her feel at home, asking her question after question. Ronnie had told Julie that Tonya was only ten years younger than their mom was. That sounded like a lot of years to Julie, but Ronnie didn't seem to think that it was. Julie had to agree that when her mom and Tonya were together, they seemed to be like sisters.

Julie climbed up on the couch one day beside Tonya to try to cheer her up. She showed Tonya her favorite doll. Mommy says we are going to share the same bedroom in the new house. "Do you think you will like it?"

"I think I will like it fine," Tonya said as she put her arm around Julie and reached for Julie's baby doll to button the little dress.

"You'll like our mommy," Julie told Tonya. "She'll take good care of you until your mommy is well."

Tonya smiled down at her little cousin. "Thank you, Julie," she said.

Moving day came just weeks before school started. Ethel was busy trying to move and get the kids ready for school. They put a new carpet in the living room and carpet on the steps. Julie couldn't believe the size of her bedroom and the big bed and dressers. Her bedroom was bigger than the old bedroom that they all had shared.

"Aren't you going to miss your old bed?" Ethel asked her, half teasing.

"No way!" Julie answered her mom emphatically and shook her head. "Mommy, that's a baby bed. Please don't tell anybody that I was still sleeping in a baby bed."

"I won't, honey," Ethel promised.

Julie felt like a princess in her new room. Julie ran to put her favorite doll down onto the bed that Tonya had just put fresh sheets and blankets on and then ran across the hall landing to her brothers' room. Their bunk beds were set up on one side of the room while another twin bed sat on the other side. Now each of the boys had their own bed. They were happy too. Matt was whistling; Jerry was joking. Ronnie was trying to get them to organize whose dresser drawer was whose. They all took turns running to the bathroom. They flushed the toilet over and over and washed their hands endlessly just to hear the water run. All of them could hardly wait to take a bath in the big tub. Julie thought the tub looked as big as a small swimming pool. They ran down the stairs barefoot just to feel the carpet between their toes and stopped to peek through the stair rails and watch their mom hang the curtains. Ron had gone across the street to Lindy's to get away from the hustle and bustle of the household. Ethel could only hope that Ron would not start making this a routine, especially since now they lived so close to the tavern. Ethel turned, hearing the children on the stairwell and glanced at the four young faces that were watching her. She smiled at them and treasured the joy that flowed from their faces.

"I have some bean soup cooking and some of Gramma Winnie's homemade bread," Ethel told them as she resumed hanging the curtains. "It will be ready soon."

"*Hmm*," they all said, then turned and ran back up the stairs. Ethel could hear their laughter resound through their new home. She could only hope that this was a new beginning for all of them.

Beloved Mamie—Julie with Mamie, Matt with
Mamie, Jerry with Mamie, Ronnie with Mamie

CHAPTER

9

Ethel took a deep breath and let out a sigh. She put the pork chops in the skillet and turned down the heat to let them cook slowly. She moved in a daze lost in her thoughts. The children had settled into the new house happily, and Tonya was adjusting to her new high school. Winter had arrived with its cold winter winds and made summer seem as if it had been a long time ago. Ethel glanced at Tonya who was sitting at the table peeling the potatoes. *She's had it hard*, Ethel thought to herself. *All her life she's been shuffled from family to family*, Ethel thought sadly. Tonya had just had her fifteenth birthday, and her interest in boys concerned Ethel. Tonya was more physically mature than most girls her age. She was receiving a lot of attention from the young men at school. Ethel knew all too well the dangers that awaited her young niece and was determined to make her aware of them. They talked often. But Ethel wondered if she was really getting through to Tonya. "But they like me, Aunt Ethel," Tonya would tell her. "No one has ever thought I was special until Bill." And then the next month, it would be Steve or David.

Ethel knew exactly how Tonya felt, and she also knew the dangers and consequences that could follow. Ethel had been surprised at Ron's interest in correcting Tonya. She had thought that he would have a more hands off relationship with her discipline. But he continued to set strict guidelines on her comings and goings. Ethel didn't know whether to be elated or concerned. Even after ten years of marriage, Ron confused Ethel. She wondered if she would ever truly get to know this man that she had married.

It was Monday night, and Ethel wasn't sure if she would go to Bingo with Winnie. Again, Ron continued to surprise her. In times past, Ron would complain and get upset if she went to Bingo. But of late, he would tell her to go ahead and go and would even give her some money. And if allowing Tonya to come to live with them hadn't surprised Ethel enough, Ron allowing Ethel to go to work surprised her even more. Ethel wanted so much to truly love him. She found herself at times so moved by his attempts to love her, the children, and now Tonya only to be totally confused by his unexplainable actions, whether it would be his drinking and flirting binges or his extreme mood fluctuations. She found herself always questioning his motives. His actions contradicted his words, and his words contradicted his actions. Try as she would, she could not understand Ron's erratic actions nor did she know how to make Ron happy. She found herself questioning her heart. Was Ron being nice to her because he loved her, or was he just setting up leverages so Ethel would overlook his outbursts and allow his drinking?

She felt so guilty for feeling this way toward Ron. But already Ron had begun to rant and rave about the extra financial hardship that Tonya had affected on their family. Usually, he would bring it up for no reason, most typically after Ethel had returned home from Bingo. He always drank heavy on the nights that she went to Bingo. So much, that by the time she would get home, he was usually more than ready to pick a fight. It would usually start with Ron complaining about Ethel working, then lead right into money problems, and then into the problems of Tonya living with them. Ethel would get so angry with Ron because he would always yell it out loud enough as if he wanted the poor girl to hear what an inconvenience she was to their family.

It was true that there were added expenses and problems, but Tonya was a big help to the family also. She helped with the upkeep of the house, the washing and ironing, and the meals and dirty dishes and watched the kids so that Ethel could work. Ethel's job was not only compensating for Tonya's keep but was also bringing in extra money for their budget. They were actually better now financially than they had ever been. It had been over six months since Tonya had come to live with them. Sally showed no signs of improvement or of being released any time soon. Ethel had grown fond of Tonya, and Ethel knew that Tonya liked her also. The children adored Tonya, and Ethel had watched Tonya open up her heart to their love. Tonya played games with the boys yet was able to make them listen to her when she had to discipline them. Ethel had watched Tonya brush Julie's curly hair and tie ribbons in it. Tonya would swing Julie around in circles, get her down on the bed, and tickle her and smother her with hugs and kisses. Everything was working out, and Ethel couldn't understand why Ron was so unhappy. But then again, she had never been able to understand his mood swings.

As Ron entered the kitchen, his presence interrupted Ethel's thoughts. She was not surprised when he went to the refrigerator and got a can of beer. He knew Ethel's eyes were focused on him, and he quickly opened the beer before Ethel could tell him that dinner would be ready soon. He pulled out a chair and sat down at the kitchen table and watched Tonya peel the potatoes. Ethel glanced over at Ron and tried to deduct his mood as she fried the pork chops. Ron continued to sit and watch Tonya. Ethel didn't know why, but this bothered her. She pushed the thoughts from her mind, feeling like a jealous schoolgirl. Tonya reminded Ethel so much of herself at that age. Tonya was high-spirited, and though still a child at heart, she had already blossomed into full womanhood. Still Tonya had never really had a childhood.

How could she even begin to learn the complexities of womanhood? Ethel could tell that she craved a father's love. Tonya's father had left their home at about the same age that Ethel's father had left her.

Tonya handed Ethel the potatoes and, without saying a word, got up and went upstairs. Ethel had noticed that if Ron was drinking, Tonya would back off and withdraw from him, but if he was sober, she would talk and kid with him.

Ethel put the potatoes on to fry and decided in her mind that she would not go to Bingo. She flipped the pork chops and turned the heat down on low before turning to go to the sink and wash her hands. As she turned, she saw Ron staring at her.

"Are you going to Bingo tonight?" Ron asked.

"I don't think so," Ethel replied as she returned to the stove.

"Why not?" Ron quizzed. "I thought you liked getting out with your mom for the evening."

"I do," Ethel said, not sure where the conversation was leading. Ethel could tell by Ron's tone and mood that she was headed for a rocky night.

"Then go ahead and go," Ron encouraged Ethel. He managed a weak smile.

"Why do you want me to go?" Ethel asked softly as she turned to face Ron.

"I don't give a damn if you go or not," Ron answered defensively. "I was just trying to be nice."

But the years had taught Ethel too many times that Ron's kindness usually cost her something. "Well, maybe I'll go," Ethel said reluctantly. She wiped her hands on the dish towel and called up to the children to come downstairs for dinner.

"Suit yourself," Ron said as he got up to throw the empty beer can away.

When Ethel returned home later that night from Bingo, she found the children and Tonya were already asleep. The house was quiet, and Ron was already in bed. Ethel quietly set the alarm clock and slipped into the bed beneath the covers beside Ron. She could still smell the alcohol that lingered on his breath. She was glad that he was sleeping it off. She sighed as she rolled over hoping that tomorrow would be better.

School turned out to be quite different than Julie had expected. To her surprise, it was nothing like Sunday school. At first, she cried every day, wanting her mom to come with her. But in time, she fell into a routine with her brothers. They all walked the winding mile to their grade school. Julie had heard her mom say that there was talk about getting a school bus to pick them up, but until that would happen, they would have to walk the long walk every day. Julie thought the winter winds would blow her away at times. The cold rains and the heavy snow made it hard for her to keep up with her brothers. "Wait for me, you guys," she continually would call out to them.

Winter passed and spring was ushered in by the gentle winds of March. The warm rays of the sun beat down on Julie's neck as she walked home from school carrying her books. "Hey, you guys, wait for me," Julie called out as she ran to catch up with Ronnie, Jerry, and Matt.

"Come on, Julie," Matt called out to her as she struggled up the hillside being careful not to wander into the road. Matt motioned to Ronnie and Jerry to go on.

Julie came running up to Matt. She stopped to catch her breath and gave Matt a sheepish smile. "Thanks for waiting, Matt," she said.

Matt tousled his little sister's hair with his hand and gave her a big smile. "Ronnie and Jerry went on ahead to see what Gramma Winnie was cooking for dinner."

"I love eating at Gramma's on Tuesday nights," Julie said. "It is Tuesday…right, Matt?" Julie questioned her older brother. She believed that he had all the answers.

"Yea, Jul, it's Tuesday today."

"I love Gramma Winnie's fried chicken," Julie exclaimed.

"Me too," Matt said, his lips watering at the thought.

"And her chocolate cake," Julie added.

"*Hmm*," Matt said.

"Do you think Aunt Penny or Aunt Mary will stop over tonight with our cousins," Julie asked as they neared Winnie's house.

"Don't know," Matt answered, still thinking of the fried chicken.

"It's warm enough that we could all play a nice game of tag or hide and seek if they do," Julie continued on.

"Whoops," Julie said as she stopped to pick up her book that had dropped. As she did, her report card slid from between the pages of the book. Suddenly, a gust of wind took it in the air like a kite without a string. Matt raced after it and caught it in midair.

"Hey, Jul, how'd you do on your report card," Matt asked as he opened the envelope before Julie could answer. "Wow...sis, this is great," he exclaimed. "You got all As." Julie beamed with pride at her brother's admiration. "Wait 'til mom sees it," Matt said as he handed it back to Julie. "Come on, Jul," Matt said as he took off running. "Let's see if Gramma made chicken."

Later that night, Julie sat soaking in the big bathtub. She pretended it was summer and that she was swimming in the river. She had gotten very dirty after dinner while playing marbles with Ronnie, Jerry, and Matt. They played teams. Ronnie and Julie played against Jerry and Matt. It wasn't for keeps, just pretend, and in the end, they all gave the marbles back to each other. Julie sat in the tub, making waves with her feet. She beamed with a joy of accomplishment. Ronnie had said that she was the best marble partner he ever had and that she was really good especially being a girl and all. And her mom had been so happy with her report card that she had shown it to Gramma Winnie and had made a big deal out of it. Gramma Winnie bent down and smothered her with one of her big hugs.

"Julie, hurry up," Ronnie called out to her through the bath-room door. "I have to use the bathroom." Julie quickly pulled the plug from the drain and hopped out of the tub. She grabbed the towel and, with one quick swipe, dropped it and threw her paja-mas on. She swung open the door and nearly ran square face into Ronnie who was waiting patiently leaning on the door frame.

"Can I sleep in your bedroom tonight?" Julie asked.

Ronnie laughed at the still dripping Julie and moved a wet curl from her forehead. "It's okay with us if mom says it's okay," Ronnie answered for himself, Jerry, and Matt.

Julie ran into her brothers' bedroom laughing. She ran and climbed up into Jerry's top bunk bed and dove under the cov-ers. Slowly, she crawled out, and leaning over the top edge, she peeked down at Jerry and Matt who were sitting in the bottom bunk playing a Chinese checkers game.

"We see you, Julie," both Matt and Jerry chimed in at the same time ignoring her stare.

"Get Ronnie to tell us the story of the purple people eater tonight," Julie squealed with delight.

"You sure?" Jerry asked. "You always get scared when he tells it."

"Uh-uh," Julie said as she hung further over the side of the top bunk to look at Jerry. "Not if I get to sleep with yous, I don't."

"Hey, you're going to fall," Jerry said as he looked up at the dangling Julie. "Come on down before you fall down."

Julie hung onto the edge with her hands and did a flip from the top bunk and landed onto the bottom bunk toppling upon her brothers.

"Hey, where in the world did you learn to do that?" Jerry asked, laughing.

"Yeah, where?" Matt chimed in laughing too.

"From you guys," Julie answered, laughing.

"Well, so much for the checker game," Jerry said.

"I won," Matt said. "I was ahead."

"Okay, you win," Jerry said as he winked at Matt letting him know to drop the subject. Then with a slight nod of his head, Jerry motioned to Matt ever so slightly and pointed a finger at the disheveled marbles. Matt slightly nodded his head, knowing from Jerry's hand signals that Jerry had an idea. Matt winked back as Jerry took the black marble from the checker game and put it in the palm of his hand and tightened his grip around it as he stuck his hand under the cover. Julie got up on her knees and bounced and pretended not to see them wink at each other. She knew they were up to something but had found it was sometimes more fun if she just played along with them.

"Hey…Jul," Jerry began, "while you were in the bathroom, Mom gave us some jellybeans for our snack."

Julie stopped bouncing and forgot about their trickery as Jerry mentioned the jellybeans. "Really?" she asked.

"Yep," Matt chimed in. "They were really good."

Julie started to squirm past them to run downstairs, but both Matt and Jerry blocked her. "No, there aren't anymore," Jerry explained.

"We weren't supposed to tell you," Matt added.

Julie dropped back on her heels and puckered her lip up at both of them as she crossed her arms indignantly. Quickly, Jerry moved and then said without hesitation, "Hey! Here, Jul. I found one that I dropped under the covers." Jerry took his hand from under the cover and opened it and showed Julie what she thought to be a black jellybean. Julie's eyes brightened, and she uncrossed her arms. Jerry and Matt both knew how much she loved black jellybeans. Jerry placed the little treasure carefully into Julie's hand and wrapped her small fingers tightly around it. "There, just for you."

There was something about the cold, hard texture of that black jellybean that reminded Julie of the wink in her brothers' eyes a few minutes before. Julie tightened her hand around the black marble pretending to be overjoyed with the proposed jellybean.

And then before either Jerry or Matt could stop her, she plopped it quickly into her mouth. She had only meant to startle them and turn the trick on them, but as Jerry and Matt grabbed at her hand to stop her, she accidentally swallowed it. Julie's eyes widened as she took a big gulp of air wherein both Matt's and Jerry's eyes widened in fear.

"I swallowed it," Julie called out as she coughed, hoping she could spit it back up.

"Why did you do that?" Matt asked, his voice rising.

"It wasn't really a jellybean, Julie," Jerry said, his voice alarmed.

"I knew that," Julie cried out, now scared by what had happened.

"Then why did you swallow it?" Jerry bellowed out trying to pat her on the back to get it back up.

"Because I wanted to trick you guys, and I accidentally swallowed it," Julie said, crying now, imagining they'd have to cut her open to take the marble out.

"Come on," Matt called out. "Mom will know what to do."

Jerry sprinted out of bed with Julie behind them as they ran down the steps to their mom. They nearly knocked Ronnie down as he entered the bedroom when they rushed past him. Ethel assured them that the marble would pass, and everything would be okay.

The days passed by, and spring ushered in summer. Julie rejoiced being out of school. Ethel and Ron worked, and Tonya watched over the children. Tonya taught Julie how to bake a cake and refereed the four of them on licking the icing bowl. Ronnie taught her how to play ball, and both Matt and Jerry gave up trying to duck out of the house without her and often asked her to go with them.

One day, they decided to go down to the old barn. They went in through the barn door and entered into the small room that was off to the side of the big doors where they often would play.

"Hey, this would make a swell clubhouse," Jerry said.

"Yeah," Matt agreed. "I never thought of that."

"Yeah," Julie joined in. "I'll run up to the house and get the broom," Julie volunteered. Julie hurried back and swept the floor and made a makeshift curtain for the window from an old towel. Matt and Jerry found an old couch that had been left in the barn and dragged it to the room. Afterward, Julie ran up and asked Tonya for some Kool-Aid and crackers. The three of them sat having their snack as they enjoyed their new clubhouse. Julie felt happy to be included in her brothers' adventure. She wished Ronnie was with them, but he had gone to play ball with some of the older boys in the neighborhood.

The next day, Ronnie joined them in their new clubhouse. He was impressed at his younger brothers' and sister's ingenuity. It became a special place for the foursome to hang out.

A few weeks later, they all went down to the clubhouse with the lunch that Tonya had made for them.

"School starts soon," Ronnie reminded them.

"Don't remind me," Jerry answered

"Me either," Matt retorted.

"Why not?" Julie asked. "I can't wait for school to start again!"

Julie felt excited at the thought of school starting soon. She could hardly believe that she would soon be entering the second grade. Matt was going to the fourth grade; Jerry, the fifth; and Ronnie, the sixth. Julie could not even imagine being in the sixth grade.

"I hope you don't get Mrs. Tomdrin," Ronnie said to Julie.

"Maybe you'll get Mrs. Hawkins instead of Mrs. Tomdrin," Jerry interjected as he gave Ronnie a queer glance.

"Ah, come on, guys, don't scare her," Matt whispered to Ronnie.

Julie loved her brothers. She felt for sure that there wasn't anything that they did not know. She may have gotten the good report cards, but Julie thought they were the smart ones. They may not have gotten all As on their report cards, but Julie felt that they were the reason that she did so well. They taught her how to do everything, from tying her shoes to helping her with her homework. What Julie loved the most though was the way that they would protect her, especially at school and everywhere they went. Oh, they could get pretty upset with her when she would tease them, and it wasn't beyond any of them to give her a good punch nor was it unusual for Julie to give them a good punch right back and then run to their mom or Tonya for protection. But never would her brothers let anyone else touch Julie when they were around.

Julie noticed that her brothers had dropped the subject about Mrs. Tomdrin and all too keenly had decided not to bring it up again. "Is Mrs. Tomdrin mean?" Julie asked Ronnie as she tried to get more information from him.

"Nah," Ronnie said as he tried to shrug it off, "she just makes you work a little harder than some teachers."

"Hey," Jerry interrupted, determined to change the subject. "Do you think Mom will let us wear our new school clothes to church tomorrow?"

"Let's ask," Matt said as they all four ran to find their mom.

The next morning, they all dressed in their new clothes to go to Sunday school. Tonya went with them and led the way up the winding dirt road. They had just rounded the last bend in the road when a car appeared. "Come here, girl," Ronnie called out to Mamie as the car approached them traveling a little fast. Mamie ran obediently to Ronnie. Mamie followed them to church every Sunday just as she would follow the foursome everywhere that they would go. She would wait at the church door for them until Sunday school was dismissed and then once again would follow them home.

"Oh, my shoes got all dusty from that dumb, old car," Julie exclaimed as she bent down to wipe them clean with her hand. She clapped her hands together to try to brush the dust off her hands.

"And when did you ever care about getting dirty?" Matt asked her, smiling, as Ronnie and Jerry burst out laughing.

"Well, these are my new shoes," Julie told them. Julie could see the small church at the top of the hill as they neared the top. "Why don't Mom and Dad come to church with us?" Julie asked her brothers.

"They just don't," Jerry answered.

"Well, how come they don't?" Julie pressed, not satisfied with Jerry's answer.

"Because Dad works on Sunday," Matt replied.

"Not always," Julie reminded him. "I bet they wouldn't argue as much if they came to church with us," Julie declared as they neared the front door of the little church.

"Maybe, you're right," Ronnie agreed, surprised at how his little sister thought.

Julie glanced at Mamie as the dog settled down beside the front doors before she turned and followed her brothers into the small church. Tonya went to sit with the other teenagers. Julie quickly slid into the pew where her brothers had sat down and squeezed in between Ronnie and Jerry. Soon Mrs. Hines started to play the piano. Julie listened to the music as she looked around the church. There were stained glass windows on either side. Each window portrayed a beautiful picture. One of Julie's favorites was Jesus walking on the water. The bright sun streamed through the colored glass causing brilliant, little rainbows to dance upon the floor. Julie hummed the song that was so familiar to her. She wanted to sing but did not know all the words. Soon the congregation began to sing. Julie opened the songbook, but some of the words were still too big for her to read. She leaned closer to Ronnie so that she could hear him sing so that she could learn the words. "What a friend we have in Jesus," Ronnie sang out with his deeper voice. Julie liked the song and let the words enter into her heart. "What a privilege to carry, everything to God in prayer. Oh what peace we often forfeit. Oh what needless pain we bear. All because we do not carry, everything to God in prayer."

Church was soon over. Julie thought maybe she'd wait and walk home with Tonya, but Tonya was talking to her friends. Julie quickly ran to catch up with her brothers. "Hey, you guys…wait up," she called out as she ran after them. Mamie, who had stayed behind with Julie began to run now too. Julie watched Mamie run past her. Mamie's large reddish-brown ears flopped up and down as she ran. "What's your hurry?" Julie asked her brothers as she finally caught up with them and tried to catch her breath.

"We're hungry," answered Matt.

"Hey, Jul, you got your shoes dusty again!" Jerry teased.

"Oh, it's okay now. Church is over. Mom will wipe them clean for me," Julie explained unconcerned.

Once home, they all hurried and changed into their play clothes before running downstairs to feast on the pancakes their mom had waiting for them. Julie poured on as much syrup as her mom would allow her. "Can we go on up to Gramma Emma's and take a hike in the woods?" Ronnie asked for all of them.

Ethel nodded and smiled at them as she placed four more pancakes on the serving plate.

As soon as they finished, they gave their mom a hug and darted out the door. Julie wondered if maybe her younger cousins could play with them. If not, they could go up to their old house and go into the old shed or take a walk in the woods. Later, Julie would go down and talk to Gramma Emma while she was peeling potatoes and sneak one or two. Gramma Emma couldn't quite cook as good as Gramma Winnie, but they always had fun at her house, whether they were playing hide and seek, hiking, or just exploring around the cliff.

It was early evening when everyone arrived at Gramma Emma's for Sunday dinner. Julie had just washed her hands and had squeezed onto the wooden bench beside her brothers. Julie was glad she was old enough to sit on the big bench and to let her little cousins have the baby seats. Uncle Tom and Aunt Lisa Sue had three children now. Aunt Lisa Sue was going to have another baby soon. Julie wondered where Gramma Emma would put them all. But Gramma Emma always seemed to have room for one more. Aunt Shelby had gotten married and lived in a little town not far away. Sometimes she would visit with her husband and little girl but not every Sunday. Julie missed seeing Aunt Nancy. Her husband was in the army, and they moved all the time. She only came home about once a year. She had two children and was expecting a third. Julie had hardly ever gotten to see these cousins but would often listen to Gramma Emma talk about them with the other adults.

After the dinner plates were cleared and the table cleaned up, Pap Pap James brought out his guitar. Julie climbed up to the fourth step of the stairs and sat down. She placed her elbows on her knees and rested her chin in her cupped hands. She swayed to the sound of the music that began to fill the little basement kitchen. Julie looked down at the others still sitting around the table. Some were talking and drinking coffee while they smoked a cigarette. Matt, Jerry, and Ronnie sat on a wooden bench watching Pap Pap James pluck the guitar as he stopped to tune it here and there.

Soon Uncle Tom and Ethel began to sing. Julie thought their voices blended together beautifully. She thought they could probably be on the Grand Ole Opry, if they tried. Julie knew they were practicing singing for Gramma Emma's family reunion next week. "I've got a mansion, just over the hilltop, in that bright land where we'll never grow old. And someday yonder we will never more wander but walk on streets that are purest gold." Julie listened to the words intently as the music filled the small room. Julie could not help but wonder how her family could sing the songs of heaven and Jesus and yet not ever want to go to church. She was sure that things would be a lot better if they would all go to church. Julie was learning a lot about the Jesus they sang about in Sunday school, and Julie could not help wondering if her family really knew him.

Julie hummed the melody as her eyes watched her family. She looked to the far left where the old yellow cupboard sat. Above the cupboard hung a picture of Jesus standing at a door knocking. Julie wondered if any of her family had ever noticed it hanging there.

School Days

CHAPTER

10

It was only a week later that Julie discovered what Ronnie meant about Mrs. Tomdrin. Julie started the second grade, and sure enough, Mrs. Tomdrin was her new teacher. She was nice to Julie. But Julie noticed that sometimes she could be very mean to the children that didn't do so well on their tests. Julie thought that this was unkind and unfair.

School was not the only thing that brought major changes to Julie's life. Things were changing at home, and Julie couldn't figure out why. It seemed that her mom and dad argued nearly every night about something. Julie would listen with her brothers from their bedroom upstairs. Usually, it was about Tonya. Tonya started to date boys, and she tended to bend the rules a lot. Boys liked Tonya, and Tonya liked the idea that they found her attractive.

"She can't be going out with every Tom, Dick, and Harry." Ron stormed one night after he had drunk a few beers.

"And why does it matter so much to you?" Ethel yelled back. "I told you I'd talk to her about it." Ethel just couldn't understand Ron's extreme interest. He seemed to get more concerned and involved in Tonya's activities than he did his own children. *It made no sense*, Ethel thought as she listened to Ron's outbursts.

"What do you mean, what's it to me?" Ron bellowed. "We're raising her, aren't we?"

"I told you. I'd talk to her," Ethel repeated again, not wanting to argue with Ron.

A few days later, Ethel sat on the front porch looking across the street to Lindy's where Ron's car was parked. *It was a mistake to live this close to the tavern*, Ethel thought. Ethel was so unhappy. She felt like she was drowning, and no matter how hard she tried, she could not find the shoreline to which she could swim. She could even endure this and live with her unhappiness, but she knew that it was affecting the children. Julie hardly slept in her room and clung to her brothers. Ethel would either find her sitting and watching for her dad to come home or she would try to avoid him altogether. The boys argued and began to fight all the time, releasing their tension on each other, which was so unlike them. It was all filtering down to the children, and Ethel did not know what to do. It wasn't just the arguing. It was just too many years of trying to make it work. *Was it wrong to want to be loved*, Ethel caught herself thinking. She thought of divorce. Ethel knew that her meager salary would never support her and the four children. She could barely get Ron to give her money now for the family. Ethel was sure he would never pay support, and she feared her children would have it the same as when she was a child. She would have to work several jobs, and the children would go unattended. There just didn't seem to be an answer. And where would Tonya live? Everyone said Sally would be well soon, but Ethel was sure she was not coming home for a long time. Besides, Tonya was in the eleventh grade. It would be a shame to uproot the girl another time when she was so close to graduating. Tonya loved the kids, and they had grown to love her dearly. Ethel began to rationalize. At least the kids had a dad unlike Tonya or herself. And when Ron was sober, he was a pretty good dad, and even as a husband, he could sometimes be nice. But even Ethel's rationalization couldn't relieve her of her weariness and sadness. The problem still remained, that lately, Ron was hardly ever sober or nice. And when he was nice, it was usually because he wanted something. After eleven years of marriage with Ron, Ethel was aware of how manipulating and intimidating he could be, and no rationalization could get her past that truth.

"Tonya, we need to talk," Ethel called out to her as she entered the front gate.

"Can we talk later, Aunt Ethel?" Tonya asked, trying to avoid her.

"No," Ethel answered and motioned Tonya to come over and sit beside her. Ethel had noticed that Tonya was avoiding her a lot lately and was withdrawn. "Listen," Ethel started slowly as Tonya came and sat down beside her. "You know how we love you, honey," she continued.

Tonya started to cry, burying her face in her hands. Ethel was startled and shocked at her outburst, not sure what triggered it. "Here it comes," Tonya said as she lifted her head up and brushed the tears hastily away. Her black mascara ran down her face.

"What?" Ethel asked puzzled, totally losing her train of thought.

"You love me, but I'll have to go live with someone else, right?" Tonya answered.

"No," Ethel said as she put her arm around her for comfort. "Why would you think that?"

"You think I don't know what Uncle Ron says to you all the time," Tonya continued. "I hear you arguing about me all the time. I'm nothing but trouble, and that's all I've ever been to everyone," she said before bursting into tears again.

"That's not what I was going to say, Tonya," Ethel said, stroking Tonya's back and pausing for a moment. "You know you always will have a home with us."

"That's not what Uncle Ron says while you're at Bingo," Tonya said, her voice trembling.

"What does he say?" Ethel asked, more puzzled than ever.

"Never mind, Aunt Ethel, please don't ask me," Tonya pleaded, sobbing.

"We'll talk later," Ethel said and dropped the subject as she patted Tonya's back gently. Ethel watched Tonya get up and walk away and go into the house. She looked once again across the street. She wondered and dreaded when Ron would come home. Ethel pressed her face into her hands and sobbed.

Ethel felt a tug on her arm and looked up to see Julie standing beside her. "You're home from school already?" Ethel asked as she quickly wiped her eyes.

"What's wrong, Mommy?" Julie asked and put her arm around Ethel's shoulder.

"Oh, nothing, honey," Ethel told her as she reached up and stroked Julie's tiny cheeks. "How was school today?"

But before Julie could answer, Ethel heard a chorus of voices call to her, "Hi, Mom." Matt, Jerry, and Ronnie came running through the front gate. Matt slammed the gate shut behind them and let it close with a loud clank. Ethel got up to give them a hug. She took Julie's hand as she opened the front door and ushered the children through the front door. Ethel paused before following them. She turned once more and looked across the street. Sorrow flooded her heart as she thought, *What can I do?*

Julie couldn't sleep. She had asked her mom if she could keep the bedroom light on for a while. She had wanted to go over to sleep with Ronnie, but her daddy had yelled at her and said that she had to sleep in her own bed.

Ethel quietly watched her daughter from the doorway. Her light-brown curls encircled her young face. Her eyes were fixed on the ceiling, and Ethel could see that Julie was in deep thought and totally unaware of her presence. *She looks so troubled*, Ethel thought. She entered the room slowly so as not to startle Julie. "I thought I'd tuck you in and turn out your light," Ethel said softly as she sat down on the edge of the bed beside Julie.

"Leave it on, Mommy, please?" Julie asked.

Ethel stroked her little girl's forehead and gently ran her fingers through Julie's hair, brushing aside the curls from her face. "What's wrong, Julie?" she asked.

"I just get scared," Julie answered as she turned on her side to face her mom.

"What are you afraid of?" Ethel asked.

"I don't know," Julie replied shrugging her shoulders.

"What are you thinking?" Ethel continued, pressing Julie gently for answers. Julie laid silently in deep thought. Ethel stroked Julie's back softly.

"I get bad thoughts, Mommy," Julie said in a whisper.

"What kind of thoughts?" Ethel asked softly.

Julie squirmed beneath her blanket. She felt so uneasy. She hesitated and then took a deep breath. "I get bad thoughts about daddy. Sometimes I wish he would never come home again." As Julie spoke the words out loud, they caused her to tremble.

"Is that why you watch for him at the window?" Ethel asked.

"I'm afraid he won't come home because I wished it," Julie whispered, unable to look up into her mom's eyes. I'm afraid he might get in a car accident and die. And then I feel so bad inside. Like I did when I threw rocks into Tony Mesner's groceries," she said as her lip quivered and she began to cry.

Ethel began to cry too as she reached down and pulled Julie up onto her lap. "Honey, your just upset because you hear Daddy and I arguing and that's why you think that."

"I don't like it when Daddy yells at you all the time," Julie confided to her mom.

"And it's that anger that makes you have the bad thoughts, honey," Ethel continued as she held Julie lovingly in her arms. "Try to understand, honey, they are not really your thoughts."

"But I think them," Julie muttered.

"It's just your mind trying to sort it all out, Julie." Ethel rocked Julie quietly in her arms.

"You really think so, Mommy?"

"I know so, honey. You talk to me when your heart is troubled, okay?" Julie nodded as she looked deep into her mom's deep blue eyes. *How could her mommy love her so much?* she wondered.

"Hey, I'm not very good at this, but how about if we say a prayer together and ask Jesus to help us?" Ethel said as she pulled back the covers for Julie to crawl under. Julie flopped onto the bed and dove under the covers pulling them up to her chin. She smiled up at her mom. Ethel tucked her in after they had prayed and said, "I'll leave the light on for you until you fall asleep, honey." She bent over and kissed Julie on the cheek. "You feel better?"

"Uh-huh," Julie answered.

Julie watched her mom go across the hallway and across the landing before going into her brothers' room to check on them.

Julie awoke in the morning with Tonya beside her. She snuggled up against her. Tonya still half asleep wrapped her arm around Julie securely.

Ethel called up the stairs for them to all get up and get ready for school and that she was leaving for work. Ron had left for work earlier. "Are you up?" Ethel called once again, waiting to hear their feet hit the floor before leaving.

Julie sat on the vanity stool so Tonya could comb her hair. Tonya then hurried all four of them downstairs where they quickly ate some cereal. Shortly, they all gathered their books and rushed out the door. Tonya closed the door behind her and locked it before running to catch up with the others.

They parted at Tonya's bus stop where she would ride the bus to the high school. "Julie, button up your coat, or you'll catch a cold," Tonya called to Julie as she hurried off.

Julie turned and smiled at Tonya. "I will," she answered as she fumbled with her coat buttons with one hand and waved goodbye to Tonya with the other.

"Come on, Jul, hurry up!" Ronnie called back to her. "We're going to be late!"

"Hey, you guys, wait for me!" she called out as she ran as fast as she could to catch up with them.

Later that evening, Julie sat at the kitchen table doing her homework. "Hi, Dad." Julie watched her dad open the refrigerator door. "Can Mamie come inside for the night? It's getting so cold outside."

"Yea, Julie," Ron answered. "I'll let her in."

Dad likes Mamie, Julie thought. As Ron reached for the doorknob, Julie put down her pencil and quickly ran to meet Mamie at the door. Julie nestled her head in Mamie's fur. "You're cold," Julie said as she petted her briskly, trying to warm her up. Mamie wagged her tail and shook herself all over before reaching forward and giving Julie a wet kiss with her nose and licking her cheeks.

"Come on, girl," Matt called from the living room. Mamie trotted into the room and flopped down between the three brothers that were sitting on the floor watching television.

It was only four weeks before Christmas, and Ethel really wanted it to be a happy Christmas for everyone, even Ron. She longed to feel close to him, but he had been so distant lately. No matter how much she tried, she couldn't seem to reach him or to get close to him. Maybe Christmas would help. They had always had nice Christmases. The children were in the Christmas play at church. Emma had said that she would go with Ethel to see them do their parts.

The weeks past quickly. Julie was so excited and nervous, along with Ronnie, Jerry, and Matt as they got ready to go to church for the play. Ethel quickly bundled them up and hurried them out the door, telling them that she would join them later at church with their Gramma Emma.

Julie stood proudly with the other children lined in a long row across the front of the church. She stretched her neck to look down the row looking for her brothers. She hated being separated from them. She always felt more confident when they were near. One by one, they recited their lines. Julie looked out at the audience and saw her mom and Gramma Emma sitting in the crowd. She wished they'd come to church with them all the time. Julie smiled a big smile as she finished her memorized lines and saw her mom smiling at her. Someday, when she was older, Julie hoped that she could play the part of Mary in the play. She couldn't help think how wonderful it would be to play the part of the mother of Jesus.

The days went quickly after the play. Ethel had stopped going to Bingo the last few weeks and was busy preparing for Christmas. It was Christmas Eve. Tonya and Ethel were making cookies and fudge for Christmas. Julie climbed up on the chair and helped to cut the cookies with the cookie cutter. Ronnie, Jerry, and Matt came into the kitchen to sample the cookies, and all four of them argued who was going to lick the mixing bowls. Ethel smiled as they worked it out. It was turning into a nice holiday.

Ron was in a better mood and had even been more affectionate lately to Ethel. *If things could just stay this way*, Ethel thought to herself later as she sat and wrapped the last of the presents before putting them under the tree. Slowly, she got up and went to bed. She knew the children would be up soon.

Julie heard her name being called in a hushed whisper and ran to meet her brothers on the landing of the steps. They tiptoed down the steps and paused halfway and sat down to look through the stair rails at the presents and the lit Christmas tree. "You go first, Jul," Ronnie instructed. See if Mom and Dad are awake first."

"Okay," Julie answered. She got up and tiptoed down the steps and peaked into her parents' room.

"We're awake," Ethel said sleepily before sitting up slowly. "You can go get your brothers." But with that said, three heads popped around the corner. Ethel only smiled at them as Julie let out a squeal and ran to the living room followed by her brothers.

Mamie laid by the gas space heater curled in a ball sound asleep as the children opened their gifts. Tonya sat in the big chair by the heater opening her gifts excitedly. There was a beautiful sweater and some makeup. Julie let out another squeal as she held the baby doll that had floppy arms, head, and legs like a real baby. She ran and gave her mom and dad a hug and kiss. Jerry got an erector set; Matt, some building blocks. Both were already excitedly opening the boxes to take out the pieces. Ronnie sat nearest the Christmas tree, mesmerized as he stared at his first hunting rifle. Now he could go hunting with his dad and Uncle Tom. Ethel and Ron let the children enjoy their gifts as they gave each other their presents. Ethel leaned over and gave Ron a kiss. He leaned toward her and kissed her back.

"I have one more gift," Tonya said after everyone had thought they had opened all the presents. Julie noticed that her brothers seemed aware of what was going on. Tonya handed Julie the present. "It's from me, honey," she said as she choked up a little.

"Thank you, Tonya," Julie said as she took the gift and sat down to open it. Everyone watched as Julie quickly opened the gift. Julie's eyes got as wide as saucers as she held the little Thumbelina doll in her hands. Julie wound the little knob on the back of the doll gently. The lullaby played, and the baby doll moved its head with the music. Julie squeezed the soft doll to her chest and jumped up and ran to Tonya. "Thank you so much, Tonya," Julie said as tears ran down her cheek, and she hugged Tonya.

"You're welcome sweetie," Tonya told her as she held Julie tight in her arms.

That night as Julie lay down with her two new dolls beside her, she couldn't remember a happier Christmas. They went to Gramma Winnie's house and then to Gramma Emma's. Julie played with her cousins and brothers and ate as many cookies as she wanted.

"You want me to tuck you in?" Ethel asked the smiling Julie as she entered the room.

"Mommy, I wish this day could last forever."

"Me too, honey," Ethel answered with smile.

Growing up—Julie, Ronnie, Matt, and Jerry

CHAPTER

11

Ethel raised the cup slowly to her lips and paused before sipping the hot coffee. She fidgeted in her chair as she waited for her friend to join her for lunch. She was no longer comfortable with the secret she had kept to herself. Bob was to join her for lunch. Ethel had convinced herself that surely there was no harm in simply having lunch with a friend. But it bothered her that if there was no harm, then why didn't she talk about it to others. She had not even mentioned it to Winnie. She was sure that if Ron knew about it, he would be very upset.

Bob saw the distressed look on Ethel's face as he slid across the seat of the booth where Ethel sat. Bob brushed his hand through his sparse hair. He studied Ethel's face as he motioned to the waitress for a cup of coffee. "Rough night?" he asked as he reached for the coffee that the waitress had brought him.

"Bob, I can't eat lunch with you anymore," Ethel spoke in a low voice as she stared at her coffee cup.

"And?" Bob asked, as she grew silent.

"I can't see you anymore."

Ethel and Ron both knew Bob from their Saturday night bowling leagues. Ethel wasn't sure how they had happened to meet for lunch the first time. It seemed innocent enough. Bob was a nice man, and Ethel had found herself enjoying their conversations even looking forward to them. She had learned that Bob himself had recently divorced. His wife had left him and took their two girls with her to Florida. She had left their oldest, a son, with Bob. Bob had been notified from his mother-in-law that the girls were not being properly cared for by their mother. Bob was trying to legally get custody of them and to bring them back home. Ethel could hardly believe what her ears were hearing but she knew that the information was true. Ethel had been appalled at the thought that a mother could leave a child. She could never understand how a mother could not take care of her children. Ethel could not imagine not having her children in her life. They were her joy, her reason for getting up in the morning, her reason for living. She thought that surely she would never leave them. There was always a lot of talk at the bowling alley. Ethel could only imagine what Bob had heard about Ron. She knew it was a mistake, but she had shared with Bob the despair and hopelessness that she felt with her marriage. Bob had listened quietly. She had also told him of her earnestness to make her marriage work. It was so comforting just to talk with someone. She was so lonely and so tired of trying to make things work. Bob was kind. He just listened, never pulling her one way or the other. Ethel found herself truly troubled as she began to like Bob.

Bob reached out and cupped Ethel's hands in his. "What brought this on?" He tilted his head slightly to one side as he continued to study her face.

Ethel avoided Bob's eyes and pulled her hands away from his grasp. "I want to make my marriage work, Bob. Ron has been trying again, and if he is willing to try, so am I."

"*Again* is the keyword," Bob said reluctantly. He did not want to interfere or influence Ethel. He knew all too well in his heart, he had come to have special feelings for Ethel. He studied her sad eyes before he continued, "For how long this time?"

Ethel shrugged her shoulders and stood up to leave. She patted him gently on the shoulders before telling him good-bye and walked slowly away.

Weeks passed by. Life to Ethel seemed a virtual roller coaster. One week Ron would be full of affection and would stay at home. But by the next week, he would stay out late drinking and come home wanting to argue. When she went to Bingo, he'd get mad, and when she'd stay home, he'd push her to go out. There was no rhyme or reasoning to his behavior. Ethel could not figure it out. Neither could she seem to ever please him. Nearly three months had gone by and she had only seen Bob in passing. Ethel was determined that surely after all of these years, her marriage just had to get better. They had been through so much together.

Ethel hurried through the house. She picked up the children's coats and placed them on the small red chair. She called up the stairway once again for the children to get up for school. She was going to be late for work if they didn't get up soon. Ethel knew that Tonya didn't like school. But Tonya had not been herself lately. She would either be withdrawn and moody or full of anger. Ethel had even found her crying a few times.

"Tonya, come on. You kids have to get up for school!" But there was no answer. Ethel ran up the stairs and into Tonya's room. She was surprised to see that she was awake. "Tonya, why didn't you answer me? Come on. You've got to get up. We're all running late."

"I'm not going, Aunt Ethel."

"Tonya, please…we don't have time for this today."

But Tonya just lay still, her eyes fixed in a daze. Ethel waved Julie out of the room and told her to get her brothers up and to get ready for school. Ethel sat down on the bed beside Tonya and gently put her hand on her shoulder and caressed it lightly. "What's wrong, honey?"

Suddenly, Tonya began to cry uncontrollably, deep, heavy sobs taking her breath away. Ethel leaned down and kissed her forehead. She began to stroke Tonya's auburn hair letting it fall between her fingers. "Talk to me, honey, please." But Tonya said nothing.

Ethel got the children ready for school and gave them their lunch money. She hurried them out the door and then ran across the street to the little store and asked Goldie if she could use her phone. She called into work and got the day off. Ethel made a pot of coffee and hoped that Tonya would come downstairs to join her so they could talk. Ethel paused as she stirred her coffee and tried to decide what to do. When Tonya didn't join her, she once again climbed the stairs and went into Tonya's room. Tonya looked at Ethel and then turned over to face the wall. Ethel tried once again to get Tonya to talk. "Aunt Ethel, please just leave me alone, please."

Ethel was at a loss as to what to do. She pulled back the covers and said in a firm voice, "Get up, and get dressed. We're going up to Mom's house!" Ethel waved her hand in the air before Tonya could stop her. "Now. We're going to get to the bottom of this!"

Winnie put a pot of coffee on and cut them both a piece of cake. John had just finished his breakfast after working the night shift and went up to go to bed. Ethel and Tonya sat down at the small kitchen table. Ethel briefed Winnie with her concern that she was at a loss as to how to help Tonya. They sat quietly. The silence hung over them like a cloud.

Winnie dried her hands on the old tea towel and sat down. "You need to talk to us."

"About what?" Tonya answered, letting anger replace her tears.

Ethel leaned forward on the table. "About what has been bothering you."

"Nothing is bothering me," Tonya squirmed uneasily in her chair. "I have one lousy day, and I don't feel well, and you go nuts."

Ethel felt the anger rising inside her. "You've been moody for the last month. It's not just today. You're not yourself, and I want to know what is bothering you."

"No! You're just concerned that you'll loose your babysitter!" Tonya shot back.

Ethel felt the words smack her. "Tonya, you know that's not true. You know how much you mean to the kids and me." Ethel brought her head to her hands and began to sob.

Tonya's anger melted at Ethel's words. She couldn't bear to see her cry. Tonya buried her head into her arms and burst into tears. Winnie jumped up and placed her arms around Tonya. She was totally caught off guard by Tonya's reaction. "What is it, child?" But Tonya only continued to cry. Ethel and Winnie looked at each other and then Tonya. Both were perplexed by the situation and waited for Tonya to lift her head before continuing on. Shortly, Tonya quieted down.

"I'm sorry, Aunt Ethel," she said slowly. "I haven't felt well lately."

Ethel reached out and took her hand and patted it gently. "It's okay, honey. But you need to talk to us." Ethel looked at the young girl, her face streaked with tears, a young girl who was far from being the woman that her body represented. Ethel knew that Tonya had been dating several guys. She knew that Tonya would almost always bend or break their curfew rules. But unlike Ethel's teenage years, she had talked to Tonya about boys, telling her what to expect. She had told her to not let them talk her into anything. Most of all, she had told Tonya the dangers of getting pregnant and how important it was to graduate from high school.

Tonya took a deep breath and peered deeply into Ethel's eyes. "I am sorry, Aunt Ethel." Once again the tears began to flow.

"Sorry for what?" Ethel pressed gently.

"I've always been a burden to everyone."

Ethel and Winnie sat quietly, listening, not wanting to interrupt her.

"Flip a coin. Find a home for Tonya," she said as she lifted her head. "I've never fit in anywhere."

"But I thought you liked staying with us and the kids?" Ethel asked softly.

"I do, Aunt Ethel, truly I did. But all I do is cause trouble. I…"

"Did?" Ethel asked puzzled, confused as to why Tonya talked as if she would no longer live with them. "You are not causing us trouble." Ethel's voice filled with compassion.

"I liked living with you, Aunt Ethel, truly I did. I didn't want to move again. I wanted to at least stay with you until I graduated."

"But you can," Ethel reached her arms across the table to grasp Tonya's shaking hands.

"No, I can't," Tonya said sharply as she pulled her hands away from Ethel's and clasped them tightly to her chest.

"But why?" Ethel cried out with her voiced raised. "Why can't you?"

Tonya let out her breath in despair and hung her head hopelessly. Tears began to stream down the sides of her face streaking her makeup. Slowly, she looked at Winnie and then at Ethel before letting her head drop. "I'm in trouble."

Winnie turned to Ethel who looked totally perplexed and then to Tonya. She took a deep breath and then with a firm but compassionate voice asked, "What kind of trouble?"

"I haven't gotten my period," Tonya blurted out the words before she could stop them.

The words hit Ethel like a ton of bricks, her eyes dazed; she sat speechless. It reminded her of the conversation she herself had had with Winnie over twelve years ago.

"For how long?" Winnie continued the conversation, her words gaining momentum and tone as she spoke.

"Since around Christmas," Tonya answered through her sobs.

"And who is the father?" Winnie pressed. "Is it the Collins boy?"

Tonya's face grew puzzled. Her words seemed to hang on her lips as if frozen in motion. She looked at Ethel and then at

Winnie as if surprised by the question. "Aunt Ethel, I love you so much, and I am so very sorry."

Ethel lifted her head and looked kindly into Tonya's swollen eyes. "Who is the father, dear?"

Tonya could not form the words. Her face was horror-struck as the realization of her pregnancy hit her. The words suddenly poured out with force, "I can't tell you!"

"But you must," Winnie insisted.

Tonya buried her head into her folded arms and sobbed, mumbling, "I can't. I can't. I can't."

Winnie arose and went to Tonya. She motioned for Ethel to leave and to give them some time alone. Ethel shoved the chair slowly away from the table. She walked over to the sobbing Tonya, bent down, and hugged her. She kissed the top of her head and stroked her hair. "I love you, honey," and then Ethel turned and left the room.

Ethel was cooking dinner when Ron walked in the door. Of all days, he had come right home from work today.

"Where's Tonya?" he asked as he went to the refrigerator to get a beer.

"She's up at Mom's." Ethel stared at the pot of chili and continued to stir it, avoiding Ron's stare.

"You want one?" Ron asked smiling as he popped the lid off the beer bottle.

"You know I don't drink," Ethel answered, not wanting to talk.

Ron hurried to the sink as the beer began to foam over the sides of the bottle. "For Christ's sake, Ethel, this beer is warm!" He shook his hand and grabbed the towel. He wiped his hand and then the bottle of beer and took a long drink. "So why is Tonya at Winnie's?"

"She just needed a break," Ethel answered.

Ron pulled out the kitchen chair and sat down and studied Ethel as he took another drink. "A break from what?"

Ethel felt her mind race; her words felt heavy in her mouth as if she could not form them to speak. The last thing she wanted to do was to tell Ron what was going on. *There would be no tomorrow*, Ethel thought. She hoped that she could avoid the subject until after supper.

"A break from what, Ethel?" Ron asked again. He watched Ethel as she avoided his stare.

"A break from what?" Ron repeated sternly. He tapped his fingers impatiently on the beer bottle and waited for Ethel to answer.

Ethel knew there was no avoiding the question. Ethel turned to face Ron and laid the spoon down on the stove. "A break from us, Ron."

"Good God, you mean she doesn't get enough breaks with all the dates she goes out on all the time?"

"Why in the world does it bother you that she goes on dates?" Ethel asked, trying to change the subject.

"Damn it, Ethel, it doesn't bother me!" Ron spewed the words out angrily. "I just asked a simple question."

"Hi, Mom! Hi, Mom!" came the ripple of hellos as the children came in the back door.

"Hi, Dad!" they all said. They were surprised to see their dad home so early and sitting at the table. They all glanced at their mom and then at their dad, as if in perfect unison they tried to sense the atmosphere that they had just walked in upon.

"Well…we'll just go upstairs," Ronnie said as he steered the other three of his siblings through the kitchen door. He sensed that there was trouble.

"Where's Tonya?" Julie called over the stair rail as Ronnie tried to push her up the stairs.

"Yeah, Ethel. I don't see you yelling at the kids for asking about Tonya." Ron pushed his chair away from the table as he stood up to get another beer.

Ethel spoke quietly. "I didn't yell at you." Ethel looked at the beer in his hand. "Supper is ready, you know," she said. Ron looked at Ethel and without saying a word, defiantly popped the lid off of the bottle, and slammed the bottle opener down on the sink. "So what aren't you telling me, Ethel?"

"We'll talk after dinner, Ron," Ethel said firmly. "First, I want the kids to eat." Ron started to speak, but Ethel raised her hand slowly for him to stop and brushed past him to call the children to come downstairs.

They ate in silence. Jerry hated the silence. He knew it meant trouble. Julie wasn't sure what was going on and started to ask again where Tonya was but stopped short when Ronnie gave her a kick under the table. She dropped it, taking Ronnie's tip, but decided to give him a kick back. Somehow, she missed her mark and nailed Jerry instead. Jerry went to kick her back but accidentally kicked Matt instead, wherein Matt yelled out, "Hey, what'd you do that for?" and then kicked Jerry back.

"You can all four stop it right now or go straight to bed," Ron said in a raised stern voice. They finished eating and asked their mom if they could go outside to play. "Why don't you just go upstairs for a while and do your homework while your dad and I talk," Ethel said as she got up and began to clear the table.

"Oh, Mom, do we have to?" Matt asked.

"Go on," she urged, shoveling them one by one toward the kitchen door.

"So?" Ron said. He crossed his legs and leaned back into the hard kitchen chair and lit a cigarette. Ethel turned her back to Ron and started to wash the dishes.

"What's the big secret, Ethel?"

"Well, you'll just get upset." Ethel knew there was no preparing Ron for what she had to tell him.

"I probably will," Ron answered, flicking the ashes from his cigarette into the ashtray.

Ethel put down the dish that she was washing and wiped her hands. She turned around and faced Ron and looked him square in the eye. "Tonya is pregnant," she said. She placed the dishtowel down and stood still waiting for the fallout of Ron's reaction. But to her surprise, Ron became quiet. He sat looking as shocked as Tonya had looked earlier.

"But how?" he asked, nearly dropping his cigarette.

"How?" Ethel answered back surprised and taken aback at his question.

"Shit! You know what I mean!" he stammered. "Who?"

"She won't say," Ethel replied. She waited for Ron to hit the ceiling and to start screaming, "I told you so." But as she stood there staring at his blank face, Ron said nothing. Ethel turned away slowly and continued to wash the dishes. Her mind raced in a blur concerning the unsettling events of the day. Ron sat quietly. He turned the brown bottle around aimlessly in his hands and flicked at the paper label. After awhile, he arose and went into the living room and turned on the television. Ethel finished the dishes and cleaned up the kitchen. Though she could not understand Ron's reaction to the news about Tonya, she could not help but be grateful for the quietness.

She didn't know whether his quietness was just the calm before the storm, as every beer that followed posed a pending eruption. They had no phone, so she had no news from Winnie concerning Tonya. Ethel thought of driving the car up to Winnie's house but that meant asking Ron for the keys and that could very well light his fuse. After awhile, Ethel tried another approach. "Ron, I think I'll take the kids to get an ice cream," she said half asking.

"Go ahead," Ron replied as he looked past her at the television. He reached into his pockets and handed the keys to her. Ethel took the keys quickly before Ron could change his mind and went to the steps. She called up to her children. The rumble of their feet hit the steps as they heard the words *ice cream* and ran out the front door. Ethel turned to go. She paused for a moment at the door and glanced at Ron before closing the door softly behind her. *Hopefully, he will be asleep when we get home tonight,* she thought.

Ethel sat quietly in the car and listened to her children talk about their school day as they enjoyed their ice cream.

"Mom, Ms. Cheshire is so mean," Ronnie said.

"Ronnie, now…you'll scare the others if they get her for a teacher," Ethel replied, her thoughts only half with the children.

"But she is mean, Mom. You should see her. She's got real thick glasses, and one of her eyes is cross-eyed, and she only has one breast."

"Why?" asked Jerry curiously. He knew for sure that he would have her for his teacher next year.

"Because the kids say she had it cut off from cancer."

"Boys," Ethel called out, "that is quite enough! You should never make fun of anyone, especially someone who is fighting cancer."

"I'm not, Mom," Ronnie continued hesitantly but wanting to explain further, "it's just…she's really mean." Julie kicked Ronnie lightly. She felt grown up as she put her finger to her lip and motioned him to be quiet. Matt who was sitting in the front seat peered over his shoulder and nodded to Ronnie to let it go.

"I want to ride up to Gramma Winnie's house for a few minutes, but I want you to wait in the car for me, okay?" Ethel asked the foursome. "Okay," they all replied in unison. They settled into quietness, knowing that it was better to not ask why. Julie pressed her nose to the window and stared at their home as they passed it by and rounded the bend to her Gramma's house. Ethel pulled in front of Winnie's house and parked the car. She grabbed her purse and ran toward the front porch without saying a word.

"What's up?" Matt asked and turned to Ronnie for an answer. Ronnie shrugged his shoulders.

"How come we can't talk about Tonya?" Julie asked.

"I bet I know," Jerry piped in.

"What?" Ronnie turned to him, wanting to know what Jerry had to say.

But Jerry just shrugged his shoulders and said, "Nah, I don't know either."

After awhile, Winnie's front door opened slowly, and Ethel and Tonya walked to the car. Julie could see her mom's troubled expression and that Tonya's eyes were swollen and red from crying.

Matt hopped out of the car and jumped into the backseat with the others so that Tonya could sit in the front seat. Julie glanced at Tonya's swollen eyes and gave her a loving smile. Tonya gave her a faint smile as she got into the car.

Ethel turned around and headed back home. Ethel's heart twisted in turmoil at the thought of going home. Tonya was still refusing to tell anyone who the father of her baby was. Ethel felt she couldn't endure any explosions or outbursts of attacks from Ron tonight. She only hoped that he was asleep. She parked the car at Lindy's, and before the engine could be turned off, the children jumped out of the car and ran across the street to the house. "Watch out for the cars!" Ethel yelled after them. "Ronnie, take Julie's hand."

Slowly, Tonya and Ethel got out of the car. Ethel looked up as she heard the iron gate clang. Ronnie was coming back over as the other three stood on the front porch. He stopped and looked both ways before crossing the street. "Mom, Dad has all the doors locked, and we can't get in," Ronnie said.

Ethel crossed the street as she felt in her purse for her house keys. She couldn't help notice how dark the house appeared. Ethel fumbled desperately in her purse for the keys as she hurried through the gate. She hoped that she had brought them with her. Tonya followed them across the street, her head hung down. Ethel found the keys at last and struggled in the darkness to get the key into the lock. The door squeaked on its hinges as Ethel slowly began to open it. She turned to the children and told them to be quiet and to go right up to bed. Ethel hesitated for a moment as she opened the door a little further. The house was quiet and pitch dark. Ron had not left a single light on. Ethel left out a sigh of relief, glad that Ron was in bed and that they could deal with everything tomorrow. The children pressed anxiously past her hurrying into the house. Suddenly, Ethel gasped as the smell hit her in the face. "Ronnie!" she yelled out as she grabbed at Julie's shirt to stop her from entering the house. Ethel pushed past Julie, Matt, and Jerry and grabbed Ronnie's arm before he could go upstairs. Ronnie turned quickly, hearing the fear in his mom's voice and now smelling the peculiar odor. "Ronnie! Take your brothers and sister outside!" she said in a tone that alarmed Ronnie and the others. Ronnie immediately grabbed Julie's hand. He pulled her along with himself as he pushed both Matt and Jerry past Tonya and back onto the porch.

Ethel glanced into the downstairs bedroom but could see nothing. All of the lights were out, and the house was completely dark. Somehow, Ethel just knew that Ron was not in the bedroom. The smell was coming from the upstairs. Ethel sprinted up the steps into the darkness, past the landing and into the bathroom darkness. Tonya hurried behind Ethel and tried to find her way in the darkness. Ethel was struggling to find the cord that hung from the bathroom light in the middle of the bathroom. She felt herself stumble over a hard lump and somehow knew that it was Ron's body. The smell was causing her to cough as she felt fear and panic rise within her. She swung her arm wildly in the air trying to find the cord to the light. Suddenly, she heard the children running up the steps. "Tonya!" Ethel screamed, "go get the children out of the house!" Tonya turned and ran down the steps and herded the children back out onto the porch. Ethel felt the small metal end of the thin light cord and pulled it. The light came on in a bright flash, and Ethel blinked and then froze horrified as she saw Ron sprawled out on the floor. She stumbled over his body and ran to the small gas heater beside the toilet and reached down and turned the small knob to the left turning it off. She gagged profusely as she tried to get air. She ran to Ron's limp body. He did not move. She tried to slap his face gently, but he did not stir. She shook him roughly, but again, there was no movement. Ethel was desperate. She tried to get under Ron's shoulders and move him out of the bathroom, but she couldn't budge his dead weight.

"Tonya!" Ethel screamed. "Help me!"

Tonya came running up the steps. Ronnie, Jerry, Matt, and Julie followed behind her as they heard their mom's terrified cries.

Ethel continued to try to pull Ron toward the steps.

"Aunt Ethel!" Tonya screamed as she entered the bathroom.

Ethel looked up from Ron's lifeless body and saw the five children standing beside her looking down at her in shock. Julie started to cry and scream while Matt and Jerry stood frozen in shock.

"Help me!" Ethel called out.

Tonya and Ronnie ran and began to pull Ron toward the steps.

"He's not breathing!" Ethel screamed to Tonya. "We must get him outside into the fresh air." By now, the other three children ran to their dad. Ethel grabbed under Ron's shoulders to drag him as Tonya grabbed his socked feet. "Ronnie," Ethel called out to her eldest. "Grab his middle." Jerry tried to squeeze in to help Ronnie. Somehow, they managed to half carry and half slide Ron down the steps and drag him onto the front porch. Julie and Matt followed behind them not knowing what they could do to help. They watched their dad's head flop lifelessly as he was carried down the steps and out onto the porch.

They were all coughing and gagging as they stumbled out onto the porch. The fresh air hit them in the face and rushed into their lungs. Ethel bent down and began once again to try to revive Ron. "Ronnie, run up the hill and get your Uncle Tom," Ethel said, wishing that they had a phone. "Ron!" she screamed as she shook him violently. "Breathe, breathe!" But there was no movement. Ethel slapped at his face and shook him all the more.

The children were sobbing and crying out, "Daddy, wake up. Wake up!" A million things raced through Ethel's mind about how she could get help. But all she could do was to try to continue to revive him. Her mind raced as she earnestly worked on Ron not knowing medically what she should do. The tears ran down her face, and her mind filled with all the sad times, bad times, and even some of the good times and then back to the present.

"Why did you do this?" she screamed out hysterically. "What possessed you to ever do such a thing?" She sobbed out loud as she pounded him on his chest. She sobbed and put her head on his chest. Tonya was screaming and crying and ran to the end of the porch. Jerry, Matt, and Julie huddled together with their arms around one another, crying and staring in disbelief.

Suddenly, Ethel felt something. Her head rose slightly up and down as Ron's chest began to rise and fall. He was breathing! Ethel lifted her head and looked down at Ron. She jumped to her knees as she saw his head move to the side. She slapped his face back and forth gently but firmly and tried to arouse him. Julie stood with her hands to her face; watching and sobbing, she glanced from her dad to her mom to Matt and then to Jerry. Matt and Jerry just wrapped their arms tighter around Julie as the tears ran down their young faces.

Ron began to stir. He opened his eyes and looked up at Ethel. He reeked of alcohol. Ethel leaned back on her ankles as Ron tried to sit up. She took a deep breath. The whole episode seemed to last forever but was really over within minutes.

Ron said nothing as Ethel helped him to sit up. He looked around trying to focus through his confusion. He looked at Ethel and then at the children and then to Tonya who was still crying at the far end of the porch. He turned and looked at Ethel and then buried his throbbing head into his drawn knees and leaned back against the porch banister for support.

Ethel heard the gate clank open and looked up to see Tom, Emma, and Ronnie rush in.

"He's okay," Ethel said as she looked up at them, her face still wet with tears. She slowly went to get up. Tom reached down and took her arm and pulled her up and steadied her as she tried to stand. Emma had knelt down beside Ron and was talking to him.

Tom took Ethel into the house as the children followed slowly behind them. Tonya stayed at the far end of the porch and watched Emma and Ron.

Ethel sat down on the living room chair as the four children sat down on the edge of the couch all in a row. They sat quietly and stared at their mom across the room. Tom had gone to the kitchen and opened the back door and windows to let the house air out. The smell of gas still hung heavily in the air.

Tom came to Ethel and gave her a glass of cold water. Tom waited until Ethel had taken a few drinks of the water and then asked her what had happened.

The night continued in confusion as Tom and Emma tried to get Ron settled down and into bed. Tom double-checked all the gas stoves while Tonya took the children upstairs. The boys went into their room.

Julie stood on the landing with Tonya and held her hand. "Why don't you sleep with your brothers tonight," Tonya said in a low voice.

"You sure?" Julie asked. She turned and looked up into Tonya's face. Julie thought she had never seen so much sorrow on anyone's face. She held Tonya's hand tightly in hers.

"I'm sure," Tonya answered. She gave Julie's hand a tender squeeze and then released it, turning to go back down the stairs. Julie opened the door to her brothers' room and went in. She climbed onto Ronnie's bed where all three of her brothers had gathered. They sat quietly. They seemed to feel comfort simply from only one another's presence. They waited until the house was calm before feeling assured that everything was okay, and then one by one, they fell asleep.

Julie, age seven; Matt, age eight; Jerry, age nine; Ronnie, age ten

CHAPTER

12

The morning sun streaked through the living room window and danced across Ethel's face. Ethel stirred on the couch and then sat up quickly. Her mind raced immediately as if the night before had been a bad dream. Slowly, she placed her head into her cupped hands. She glanced up and saw Tonya asleep, curled in a blanket in the armchair across the room. She pulled back the blanket that apparently Grandma Emma had placed on her before going up to Julie's room. They had all agreed that Emma should stay the night.

Ethel rubbed her head gently as if to erase the previous night's memories. She looked around the room. This was her home. Memories flooded in as tears began to well up in her eyes. She sat staring at the floor in a daze and continued to rub her head.

"Are you okay, Aunt Ethel?"

Ethel looked over at Tonya who was still curled in the chair. She tried to give her a faint smile. "Yeah, I'm okay," she answered softly. "I'm just going to make some coffee before the kids get up."

The coffee pot perked slowly, rhythmically, interrupted only by intermittent spurts. The smell of coffee filtered through the house, filling it with the warmth of home. Ethel poured herself a steaming cup and walked out the back door of the kitchen, onto the small summer porch. She grabbed her old sweater that hung from a nail and went out the screen door of the porch. She sat down on the steps and took in a breath of fresh air. Ethel was glad that it was Saturday. A few minutes later, she heard the patter of steps on the sidewalk. She leaned forward to look around the corner of the house. "Come on, girl," she called to Mamie. Mamie came walking towards her. She wagged her tail slowly and seemed to search Ethel's face. "How did you sleep, ole girl?" Ethel asked as she reached down and patted the dog's head. Ethel had put some old towels under the crawl space of the house for Mamie to sleep on. It had become her favorite place to sleep except for when she would come into the house on cold nights. Ethel continued to stroke Mamie's head and her long, floppy ears.

Ethel turned as she heard the screen door open. She looked up to see Tonya step out of the house and join her with a cup of coffee. Tonya sat down and squeezed beside Ethel on the small step. Tonya stared straight ahead. Neither said a word at first. The sun shined brightly with its rays of warmth falling on them. Ethel stirred her coffee aimlessly. "The peonies will be up soon," she said and pointed to the small redheads that were beginning to poke through the ground in front of her. Tonya nodded. "Julie will be eight years old this month," Ethel continued to talk to break the silence. Ethel could not bring herself to talk about last night. Not now. Ethel sensed more than ever that there was more to Tonya's pregnancy than she was capable of dealing with right now. The two sat in silence as Mamie lay down on the sidewalk in front of them.

After awhile, Ethel reached over and put her hand on Tonya's knee and patted it gently. She stood back up to go in and make breakfast. In the kitchen, she pulled out the big aluminum pot and put it on the stove as quietly as possible. She opened the refrigerator door and grabbed the opened canned milk and jar of chipped beef. Before shutting the door, she paused and looked at the half case of beer that sat on the bottom shelf. She looked away and rested her chin on the open refrigerator door. Tears stung her eyes. She heard the sound of footsteps coming down the steps. She wiped her eyes quickly and shut the door with her shoulder as she carried everything to the table.

"Are you making chipped beef gravy?" Julie asked slowly. She peered into her mom's face and searched it earnestly.

"Yes, honey," Ethel answered.

Julie could see the weariness in her mom's face. She went over to Ethel and reached around her waist and hugged her tight. She buried her head into her mom's dress. Ethel stroked her matted curls softly and said nothing. "I love you, Mom." Julie looked up at her mom and released her embrace.

"I love you too," Ethel said tenderly. "You want to go get your brothers up?"

Julie smiled up at her mom and ran to go upstairs. Grandma Emma stayed and helped Ethel clean up. Ethel told the kids to get ready to go with her. Ron, though quiet, was in what appeared to be a foul mood. Both Ethel and Emma both thought it would be good to get Tonya and the kids out of the house. Emma told Ethel that she would stay with Ron until she came back.

Ethel drove to Winnie's and told the children to stay outside and play. Tonya and Ethel joined Winnie and sat down at the kitchen table. Winnie and John were now aware of the situation as Tom had called them on their phone. John pushed his chair away from the table and stood up. He reached down and picked up his newspaper in one hand and coffee in the other and went into the other room.

Ethel didn't know if she could handle more of the same turmoil as the day before, but she knew that it was necessary for them all to talk. The trio sat in silence for quite awhile before Tonya broke the silence. "Aunt Ethel, I want you to know how much I love you and appreciate all that you have done for me."

Ethel looked across the table at Tonya. Her reddish-brown hair hung limp, and her face was swollen from the hours of crying. She was only sixteen years old. *What little world that she had known had come tumbling down upon her,* Ethel thought sadly.

"I want you to know how very sorry I am for all the trouble that I've caused," Tonya continued.

Ethel felt so tired. She wished that she could run away from life itself. She had no energy left, not even to respond, as she sat still, listening to Tonya. Winnie poured a cup of coffee for both of them and handed them the cream and sugar. She then pulled out a chair and sat down between them.

After a few moments, Ethel looked over at Tonya. Tonya glanced sadly at Ethel and propped her head in the palm of her hand for support. She stared down at the table and aimlessly circled the worn red pattern on the table with her finger in nervousness.

"Yes, you're in a lot of trouble," Winnie spoke softly. But you surely can't believe that you are the reason Ron tried to kill himself?"

Tonya sat motionless as the tears streamed down her face. She was too tired to cry anymore. She sat and said nothing as she continued circling the pattern with her finger. Ronnie, Jerry, Matt, and Julie knocked on the back kitchen door after trying to turn the doorknob and found that it was locked. Winnie got up and opened the door. Her robust form blocked the doorway. "We're thirsty," Ronnie said as the others looked on.

"Go on out and play, and I'll make you a pitcher of Kool-Aid," Winnie said. She shooed them gently away with her hand as she closed the door once again and locked it.

Tonya continued to look down unable to look at Winnie or Ethel. "But it is my fault," she said.

Ethel slowly turned her head and glanced at Tonya. "How can it be your fault?" Winnie pressed. "You're pregnant, yes, but what does that have to do with Ron? I've already talked to your Aunt Mary, and she said that you could come to live with them for a while." Winnie continued on, "You'll have to drop out of school anyways, so it won't make a difference whether you live in Grantville or Cutters Ford."

Tonya sat and listened to her grandmother talk of her situation as if it was something that could easily be worked out. Tonya felt numb as if all of her emotions had dried up within her. The reality of it all began to hit her. Ethel sat and stared at Tonya from across the table. She was puzzled at Tonya's reaction to Winnie's questions. Ethel stirred slightly in her chair. "Why do you feel that it's your fault, Tonya?" But Tonya did not answer Ethel's question nor did she look up. Ethel grasped her coffee with both hands and took a small sip. "What does this have to do with Ron?" Ethel pressed slowly.

Tonya buried her head into her now folded arms and shook her head back and forth as if to shake the answer out of her head.

Ethel slumped in her chair and turned her head toward the wall to avoid Winnie's glare. *Not this*, Ethel thought, tears streamed down her face as Winnie looked on, first at Ethel and then at Tonya. Her eyes darted back and forth between the two of them as she tried to put together what she felt that Ethel and Tonya somehow now knew but somehow she had missed.

"What?" Winnie asked Tonya as she reached over and shook her arm. "You tell me what's going on right now," she ordered Tonya firmly as Ethel stood up and ran out of the room.

Tonya lifted her head and looked straight into Winnie's eyes. "The baby is Uncle Ron's," Tonya cried out through her broken sobs.

Winnie let go of Tonya's arm and sat back into her chair. Nothing had prepared her for this. She could hear the children knocking on the back door, calling, "Gramma, we want some Kool-Aid." But she was too stunned to speak or move.

Beloved Tonya and Julie.

CHAPTER

13

The peonies were in full bloom as the sun shined down brightly on the tiny frame that sat by itself on the back porch steps. Julie swished the stick in her hand back and forth on the sidewalk. She watched the birds make a nest in the hydrangea bush that was at the corner of the house. She could hear her mom and dad yelling again from inside their home.

Ronnie, Jerry, and Matt had gone up to Gramma Emma's house to go hiking in the woods. Julie was not allowed to go with her brothers because for some reason; even though it was a Saturday, Gramma Emma was not at home. Julie sat alone, thinking, lost in her thoughts. She was now eight years old. Her birthday had come and gone. Except for the cake that they had up at Gramma Emma's that Aunt Lisa had made, her birthday had passed unnoticed amid the turmoil and confusion. However, Julie's thoughts were not on her birthday. All she could think about was her mom and dad. Nothing made sense to her anymore.

Everything had seemed to change overnight. She felt that her whole world was falling apart. Tonya had moved out and went to live with Aunt Mary. Julie wasn't sure of all the reasons why. She tried to piece it together with the information she had gathered from listening to her brothers. They told her that Tonya was going to have a baby but that she didn't have a husband. In between all of the adults yelling, her understanding was that because Tonya was not married that she should not be having a baby. Even though Julie understood this, she could not understand how anyone could get that upset over a baby going to be born. *Babies are so special*, Julie thought as she tossed the stick aside. Julie could not stand to hear the yelling from her parents inside the house. She stood up and walked down the sidewalk to the corner of the house. She leaned down and looked under the house toward the crawlspace to see if Mamie was there napping. "Come here, Mamie," Julie called. Mamie was curled up in a ball and asleep. Julie called to her again. Mamie stretched her legs and slowly opened her eyes without lifting her head. She looked at the little face peering at her from a distance. "Come on, Mamie. Come to Julie," she said and patted her leg.

Mamie got up and crept slowly out from under the house. She shook herself briskly and then stood and looked up at Julie as if to say, "What do you need, my little friend?" Julie walked down to the cherry tree and sat down beneath it in the soft grass. Mamie followed her faithfully and plopped down beside Julie and put her drooling chin on Julie's folded legs. Julie stroked her friend lovingly and bent down and kissed the furry neck. Mamie didn't move a muscle but rolled her eyes upward to look at Julie.

Julie continued to sit there and leaned her back against the large trunk of the cherry tree. She looked up into the cherry tree that was full of blossoms. They had picked the cherries last year, and her mom and Tonya had made cherry pies. Julie had helped them seed the cherries and had red hands for days. Julie smiled as she remembered. But now everything had changed. Tonya was gone, and she wasn't sure what was going to happen with her mom and dad. Everything was so mixed up. When she was up at Gramma Winnie's, she'd hear one thing, and when she was up at Gramma Emma's, she'd hear another. She was learning that it wasn't such a bad idea to listen in on adult's conversations, especially since they would never answer her questions. Often, she would follow her brothers and would listen in on the adults. When they were caught, the adults would be furious and told them that this did not concern them. Julie thought that it was strange that everyone would say that it didn't concern them when it was their lives that were being torn apart without knowing why. Somehow, it seemed that the adults thought that if the children didn't hear about it that they were somehow being protected from it. Didn't they realize that they were living through it and that explaining to them in part would help them to somewhat understand?

Julie stretched out on the grass as Mamie snuggled by her side. She continued to try to piece together the sequence of events into some kind of order as if she was putting together one of her jigsaw puzzles. If she could just get the pieces to line up, maybe she could see the picture and understand. Julie let her thoughts go back to the horrible night that they dragged her daddy out of the house. She could not understand the full concept of what her daddy had done, and she could not understand why he had done it. All she knew was that after that night, Tonya never came back to live with them again. She only came back to pick up her things.

Julie reflected back on the day when at Gramma Winnie's they were knocking on the door to get their Kool-Aid. It was unlike Gramma Winnie to forget or ignore them. When Gramma Winnie had finally opened the door they had seen their mom in the distant room with Tonya at the kitchen table. Even Julie knew that something was terribly wrong. Gramma Winnie had told them to go sit on the front porch, and then she had brought them sandwiches and Kool-Aid. While all four had quietly sat eating their sandwiches Jerry and Matt brought up about how their dad had almost died the night before. Julie had begun to cry. She had not realized that it was that serious. Ronnie kicked Matt and gave Jerry a poke to get them to drop the subject as he put his arm around her. "He's okay now, Jul," Matt and Jerry chimed in together to reassure her. Julie was sure that her bad thoughts had caused it all to happen, and she cried all the more.

Later that evening, Tonya came home to get her things, and Aunt Mary came and picked her up. Julie had noticed that her mom and Tonya had not said a single word to each other. Julie had never seen her mom look so sad. She would stare blankly and hardly knew that Julie and her brothers were even talking to her at times. She would nod to them or just say okay, but Julie could tell that she wasn't really listening.

That evening, Julie followed Tonya upstairs to their bedroom. She couldn't understand why Tonya was leaving. She climbed up onto their bed and watched as Tonya took her makeup out of the vanity drawers and packed them. She barely looked at Julie. "Are you mad at me?" Julie asked slowly after awhile.

Tonya turned and looked at her sadly and said, "Why no, honey," and then resumed her packing.

"Then why are you leaving?" Julie asked quietly. "Don't you like it here anymore?"

"I just have to go," Tonya answered reluctantly.

"I'll move my babies out of our bed, and I promise not to kick you anymore when I'm sleeping," Julie said, and then she broke down and began to cry.

Tonya turned and, upon seeing Julie crying, ran to the bed. She knelt beside the bed and grabbed Julie and hugged her and began to cry. "It's not your fault, honey, honest," Tonya sobbed. "You be a good girl, okay?" Tonya reached for the little Thumbelina doll that lay beside Julie. She picked it up and turned the little knob carefully and handed it to Julie. "You take good care of Thumbelina, and every night, you keep her with you and know that I'm thinking of you…okay?" Tonya leaned down and gave Julie a kiss on her forehead and then stood up to go. Aunt Mary was beeping her horn for Tonya to come.

"I will, Tonya," Julie had said as she lifted her head and watched Tonya. Tonya looked back one more time and then turned and walked away. Julie sat still on the bed as she heard Tonya's footsteps hurry down the stairs.

Later that night, Julie had asked all of her brothers to sleep with her in her big bed. She just couldn't bear to sleep alone. They heard their dad come home later that night. It remained so quiet that they all tiptoed to the door to listen. But they didn't hear their dad say a word to their mom nor did their mom speak to their dad. Shortly, they heard their dad's creaking knee as he came up the steps to go to the bathroom. They dove into the bed and pretended to be asleep.

Later, when it was quiet, Ronnie, Jerry, and Matt talked Julie into going downstairs to see what was happening. Julie agreed and pretended to go down to get a drink of water. Her mom was sleeping on the couch, and her dad was in his bedroom asleep.

The next morning, her mom woke them early to get dressed. She looked so very sad. The boys dressed quickly and ran downstairs to eat breakfast. Julie was trying to comb her hair, but she wasn't doing a very good job of it as Tonya had always helped her. Suddenly, she was startled when her dad appeared in her room. She had not heard him come in but saw him standing inside her doorway in the reflection of the mirror as she sat on the vanity bench. Julie sat motionless. Her dad hadn't said a word to her or her brothers since the night that they had found him in the bathroom. She turned around quickly to face her dad and dropped the hair barrette that she was ready to snap into her hair.

Her dad came over to her. Julie searched his face and tried to figure out what to expect. But his face was emotionless, and Julie felt a fear come over her. He knelt down to face her at eye level and looked her in the eye and then said firmly, "You're not to go with your mom today if she asks you to go with her." Julie didn't answer because she did not truly understand what her dad was asking her to do. "Do you understand me?" he asked and firmly grabbed her shoulders between his hands.

"I don't know what you mean, Dad," she answered.

"If your mom wants you to leave with her today to go to your Gramma's, tell her that you're not going," Ron repeated his words sternly.

"But I have to go with Mom…if she tells me to, Dad," Julie answered puzzled.

"If you go with her…then you're no longer my little girl," he finished and turned and walked out of the room and left for work.

Immediately, after he had gone, her mom came up and told her that they were going to their Gramma Winnie's house to stay for a few days and that Julie was to grab some clothes to take with her. Julie's mind flashed back to what her daddy had just told her. "Come on, Julie," her mom said as she put some of Julie's clothes in a bag.

"I can't go," Julie said in a low voice.

"Julie, please don't give me a hard time."

"But I can't, Mommy," Julie said and began to cry. "Dad told me that I can't go with you."

Ethel stopped completely what she was doing and stared, stunned at what Julie had said. "When did your dad tell you this?"

"A few minutes ago," Julie answered as she rubbed her sleeve across her nose to wipe it.

"It's okay, Julie. I'll talk to your dad," Ethel reassured her.

"But I can't go, Mommy," Julie said and started to cry again. "He said I wouldn't be his little girl if I went with you."

Her mom knelt down and took Julie in her arms and hugged her. Julie laid her head on her mom's shoulder and cried. "I promise you…it will be okay," Ethel reassured her.

They all walked up to Gramma Winnie's house. Gramma Winnie prepared a nice dinner for them all, and later that night, when Pap Pap John had gone to work, all five of them crawled into the big bed upstairs in the back bedroom. They all talked for a long time.

"How long are we staying at Gramma's house?" Ronnie asked.

"I don't know," Ethel answered. "Gramma doesn't have room for all of us to stay here."

"Are we going back to our house and live with Dad when you aren't mad at him no more?" Jerry asked.

"I don't know what we are going to do," Ethel answered sadly.

"I can't go back home," Julie said. "Daddy is going to be so mad at me for leaving."

"No, he won't," Matt said.

"Uh-huh," Julie repeated. "He told me not to go, and I did."

A whole week had passed before their dad had stopped by to see them. The four of them continued to listen in on the adult conversations until Gramma Winnie had caught them and made them go outside. Julie's dad had told her mom that he could not live without her and that he would rather die than be without her. He had pleaded with her to come home and not break up the family. Her mom had reluctantly said that she would come home to try and talk things out and then decide what to do. And so, when they did come home, things only continued to escalate and get worse.

Julie's thoughts were interrupted as Mamie shifted and sat up. Julie sat and watched Mamie staring at the little squirrel that had climbed up the nearby plum tree. "Ah, leave it go, girl," Julie said to Mamie as Julie stroked her smooth coat. Julie sat for a few more minutes and then got up and brushed the grass off her clothes and began to walk slowly to the house. Mamie followed her to the steps and watched Julie go into the house and then turned and walked away. Julie walked onto the summer porch and quietly shut the screen door behind her. She paused at the closed kitchen door. She could hear that her mom and dad were still yelling. She knew that it would not be a good thing to walk into their argument, so she turned back around and went out to sit on the steps and wait for her brothers to come home. Julie clasped her hands around her knees and drew them to her chest. She rested her head in her arms and rocked herself back and forth gently. Periodically, she would stop and look down the road to see if she could see her brothers coming down the hill.

Julie could not help but hear her parents' conversation. She could not understand a lot of what they were saying, and it puzzled her. But somehow everything was different now, something terrible had happened, and Julie knew that things were never going to be the same. This was a problem that was not going to just go away. Julie continued to listen to their words.

"How could you do that to Tonya!" Ethel screamed.

"Me!" Ron answered defensively. "You were never home! Always running to Bingo after work!"

"You told me to go!" Ethel resounded.

"Yeah right, Ethel. I twisted your arm! You were always too tired to give me any of your time, but you could run to Bingo with your mother!" Ron yelled.

"Oh, so this is all my fault?" Ethel asked Ron, shocked at his justification and lack of remorse.

"No, Ethel. I'm not saying that," Ron said as he tried to smooth things over. "I'm just explaining the circumstances that I was in. You don't really believe her do you…that the baby is mine?"

There was a pause, and Julie thought that maybe the argument was over. Julie thought that maybe her mom had walked away from her dad as she didn't hear her mom talking, only her dad. Julie stood up and went up the steps toward the kitchen door but stopped as she heard her dad continue.

"Ethel, you know Tonya. She was always lying to us and did whatever she pleased. Remember…I told you this was going to happen. Now she went and got herself pregnant by this Winston boy and wants to make up some cockamamy story that it's mine."

Julie was surprised to hear her mom speak. Her words sounded as if her mom was speaking in desperation and anger. Julie could hear the strain in her voice. Julie walked closer to the closed kitchen door and peered through the window as she continued to listen.

"Ron! I talked to the kids!" Ethel shouted. "Matt told me that he saw you both kissing on the couch!"

"And you are going to believe a nine-year-old boy?" Ron yelled back.

"Yes! Yes…I am!" Ethel yelled. "I believe them both. Now, I understand." Julie saw her mom shaking her head back and forth.

"Understand what?" Ron asked.

"Why you would withdraw from me when I reached out to you. I figured that you were probably having another affair, but I never, in my wildest imagination, thought you were capable of this."

"Ethel, you know how Tonya is, always walking around here in her tight sweaters and skirts. Do you think any twenty-eight-year-old man would've done differently? She was always flirting with me when you weren't around."

"She needed fatherly attention, Ron. That's all she was looking for, and you know it!" Ethel snapped back.

"You really believe that, Ethel!" Ron shot back. He could see that Ethel was weakening. "You know how she was on her dates…always coming home late. Come on, you know what was going on. Don't pretend to be naïve."

Julie continued to look through the window. She saw the rage and anger on their faces.

Ethel turned slowly and walked away from Ron. She was too tired to argue with him anymore, and she was too tired to sort it all out. She wanted to believe Ron. It would be easier if she could blame Tonya for it all. Then she could try to put it all behind her, and maybe this time, Ron would really straighten himself out. Maybe they could be a real family. But she just couldn't believe that Tonya was like that. Yes, a lot of what Ron said was true about Tonya, but she could never believe Tonya would deliberately destroy their family. If only Tonya would tell her what really happened. But Tonya wasn't talking to anyone. Everyone was afraid that she might have a nervous breakdown like her mom.

Julie saw her dad follow her mom into the living room. She heard it grow quiet inside, and she put her ear on the window to see if they had stopped arguing. She took a deep breath and let out a sigh of relief. She was sure they had stopped arguing.

"Hey, Julie," Matt said quietly as he tapped her on the shoulder. Julie jumped, startled at hearing Matt's voice. Jerry and Ronnie swung the summer porch door open wide and saw Julie turn and punch Matt in the shoulder.

"Hey, why did you do that, Jul?" Ronnie asked.

"Because he scared me," Julie said. "And I'm mad at all of you guys."

"Why?" Jerry asked.

"Because you all took off today without me," she answered back. "I've been alone all day."

"We'll make sure you can go next time," Ronnie assured her.

"But wonder if they won't let me."

"We'll talk them into it, Jul," Jerry said.

"Yeah, or we won't go," Matt chimed in.

"It's awful quiet inside. What's going on, Julie?" Ronnie asked.

"I think they quit arguing now," Julie answered. "I think we can go in now."

Ronnie reached for the white glass doorknob and turned it quietly. He put his finger to his mouth and motioned them to be quiet as he led the way. As they opened the door, Ethel came into the kitchen and sat down at the table and began to drink her coffee.

"Hi, Mom!" they all said in unison.

"Where's Dad?" Matt asked.

"In the living room," Ethel answered as she stared blankly into her cup and then watched her children go into the living room.

"Hi, Dad," Matt said softly trying to be cheery.

"Can we watch TV?" Jerry asked their dad.

Ron shrugged his shoulders to them and motioned to them to go ahead. Ronnie and Jerry plopped down on the floor. Matt went over to the TV set and turned it on flipping the channels until he got to the cartoons. Julie went over to the chair and sat down curling up into it. She pretended to watch the cartoons but tried to side-glance over at her dad who was sitting on the couch. Her dad had not said anything to her since she had come back from Gramma Winnie's. She figured that he was really mad at her for disobeying him by going with her mom. She guessed that she wasn't his little girl anymore.

They sat and watched the cartoons for a while. They waited for their mom and dad to either start talking or yelling. Jerry hated the silence and fidgeted nervously as he sat on the floor. Julie slipped down beside him and touched his fingers gently with hers. He looked at her and smiled, and she smiled back.

Ethel came in and sat down in a metal armchair that sat in front of the window. She reached over and turned off the TV and then stared at Ron. He said nothing. "I think we better tell the children what we've decided," Ethel said.

Ronnie, Jerry, Matt, and Julie turned to look at their mom curiously. "Kids, your dad and I are going to get a divorce," Ethel said hesitantly. Her words broke up as she choked up when she spoke.

"What is a divorce?" Julie whispered to Matt. But he didn't answer her. Julie looked at her brothers. They all looked puzzled and shocked.

"Where will we live?" Ronnie asked. "With you or Dad?"

"We have to work out all the details yet," Ethel replied as the tears flowed out of her eyes. "I can't stay here anymore."

Julie started to cry softly. She did not understand what was really happening. Matt put his arm around her, not too sure himself of what was going on.

"But why are you leaving us?" Jerry asked.

"I'm not leaving you," Ethel answered and started to sob. "I'm leaving your dad," she tried to explain. "I can't stay here with your dad another day…and he refuses to leave."

"Oh, yeah, Ethel, make me the bad guy," Ron spoke up for the first time. "I thought we agreed to do this without turning the kids against each of us."

Ethel ignored Ron's remarks. "I'm going to stay at Gramma Winnie's for now. I'll see you every day before school and after school," Ethel continued. "It's too much for Gramma Winnie to take all of us to live with her. She doesn't have the money or the room. So you will have to stay here with your daddy until we get the rest worked out."

Julie thought she understood it now. "Do we spend some days with you and some days with Dad?" she asked her mom while looking at her dad. She didn't want him to still be mad at her.

"Kind of like that," Ethel replied.

Julie jumped up and ran to her mommy and hugged her.

"That way you can still have your mommy and your daddy, but we just won't be living together anymore," Ethel explained and sniffled back her tears.

"Why?" Jerry asked. There was anger in his voice. "Why can't we still all live together?"

"Because your daddy and I argue too much," Ethel said. She took Julie's hand and knelt down on the floor with her brothers.

"It's because of Tonya…isn't it?" Ronnie blurted out.

"No, Ronnie," Ethel said. She looked over at Ron for his support. "You know that we argued before Tonya ever came to live with us."

"It's because I told you that Dad and Tonya were kissing, isn't it?" Matt said as he started to cry. He looked at his dad's angry glare. Jerry and Ronnie looked at Matt. This was the first that they had heard anything about that.

"Why didn't you tell us?" Jerry asked shocked.

"I was afraid to tell anyone," Matt answered as he tried to quit crying.

Ethel squeezed between the boys and put her arms around them and glanced back at Ron. "These are your daddy and my problems, not you kids," Ethel told them. "It has nothing to do with you kids," she continued and tried to console them.

That night after they had all gone to bed, they heard their mom slip quietly out the front door. Julie couldn't help but think that contrary to what her mom had said, it had everything to do with them. She lay down beside Ronnie in his bed as he put his protecting arm around her. She lay awake and tried not to cry, but she couldn't stop the tears that warmed her cheeks as they streamed down her face. She could hear the muffled sobs of her brothers, and Ronnie sniffled quietly behind her. Somehow, Julie knew that nothing would ever be the same again.

Gramma Emma

CHAPTER

14

Julie woke up. She could hear her dad calling to them from the bathroom to get up. She rubbed her eyes and slowly sat up. She looked down at Ronnie who was still asleep and then up at Jerry asleep in the top bunk. Julie rubbed her eyes again and then saw Matt lying quietly in his bed awake watching her. Julie gave him a weak smile. "Dad says we have to get up."

"Ronnie, I said get up!" their dad yelled louder.

Julie shook Ronnie lightly to wake him and then leaned down to his ear and said, "Ronnie, wake up. We got to get up."

Ron poked his head into the bedroom. "You kids get up and get dressed and go on to church." Ronnie, now awake, raised his head to listen. "Come right home afterward and play in the yard until your mom picks you up."

Julie sat on the edge of Ronnie's bed. She heard her dad's footsteps hurry down the steps. Jerry rolled over in his bed and didn't say a word. Shortly, they all heard the front door close loudly. There was a stillness that settled on the four, a quietness that seemed to engulf them. Slowly, one by one, they all sat up. No words were spoken as they sat perplexed and confused at their world that had been turned upside down. Julie thought it seemed like a bad dream and hoped that soon she would wake up and that things would be different.

The rest of the morning was a hodgepodge of confusing activity as the four children tried to get it together. Julie went to her closet at the end of the hallway and took one of her school dresses from the wire hanger. She grabbed her socks and shoes. Julie tried to get ready, but doing her hair was the hardest. She tried to brush it, but it was so tangled. She took a barrette and tried to clip it into the clump of hair that she held in one hand, but the barrette kept popping open. She finally got it to stay shut, but to her frustration, her hair stuck out real funny and weird looking so she popped it open and tried again.

Julie finally looked at herself in the mirror. She tilted her head back and forth and tried to see if she looked okay. She shrugged her shoulders not knowing the answer and slowly turned and went downstairs. She joined her brothers in the kitchen where they were eating breakfast. Julie couldn't help thinking that as she looked at her brothers that they didn't look much better than her. Ronnie's shoestrings were broken, Jerry's hair had a rooster tail sticking right up in the middle, and Matt's shirt was hanging half in and half out of his trousers with spilled milk from his cereal on the front of his pants. Julie went to get a bowl from the cupboard and a spoon from the cabinet and sat down beside them. No one said a word as they ate their cereal. They all seemed lost in their own little worlds.

Ronnie finally broke the silence. "Dad gave me the key to the house last night and told me to find a place on the summer porch to hide it. The boys stood up, and then pushing their chairs in, all headed to the back door that led to the enclosed summer porch. Julie picked up her bowl and drank the remaining milk, careful not to spill it on her and then rushed out to join them.

"What about over the door edge?" Ronnie suggested.

"We can't reach it," Matt said.

"Not even on your tippy-toes?" Ronnie asked.

"Nope," said Jerry.

After a few more suggestions, they all agreed to hide it in the old metal cupboard that sat in the corner of the porch. Julie convinced them to put it on the third shelf instead of the fourth.

They reluctantly headed off to church as Mamie followed behind them. Julie wanted to be happy, but nothing seemed happy anymore. She had hoped that church would help her to feel happy. She had always felt so good inside when she was in church. Julie walked up the hill slowly behind her brothers. She kicked a stone as she continued on. Julie remembered how, one time at church, she had felt that Jesus had come into her heart. It seemed a long time ago when she was about six years old. They were downstairs in Sunday school when all of the classes were assembled in the middle classroom singing songs before they were to go to their own classes. The teacher was singing the song "Come into My Heart." Julie liked that song. The teacher had told them to close their eyes and to sing it again if they wanted to ask Jesus to come into their heart while they were singing. At first, Julie peeked with one eye closed and one eye open to try and look for her brothers who were sitting further down the row with their classes. But then, she closed both of her eyes, and as she sang the words "Come in today. Come in to stay. Come into my heart, Lord Jesus," she could feel a wonderful feeling inside of her heart that she could not explain.

"Hurry up, Julie," Ronnie, Jerry, and Matt, all three, yelled in unison.

"I am," Julie called back. She didn't seem to care that she was far behind them. Mamie tagged along beside her and looked first at her and then at the boys ahead of her.

Julie remembered one of the first times that God had surprised her. It was just last year. Julie had become very angry at her mom and at Tonya when they didn't call her to lick the icing bowl, and when she came downstairs, it was already in the sink. She was so mad that she threw a crying tantrum. Both Tonya and her mom ignored her fit, which made her even madder. She ran upstairs and pulled the vanity bench out and crawled behind the vanity that sat catty-cornered in her room. She then reached under the vanity and pulled the bench back to hide herself. She'd teach them. *They'll be sorry when they can't find me*, she thought. She heard them looking but refused to come out. *They could just worry awhile*, she thought, but she shortly grew weary of it all and went back downstairs. She could tell that her mom and Tonya weren't really happy with her behavior, but she thought she'd be stubborn a little longer. Julie didn't like feeling this way, but she didn't want to say that she was sorry, so she tried to just ignore it and hoped they would also. But the next day in Sunday school, as she sat and listened to her Sunday school teacher, she was shocked at what she had heard. The teacher was teaching about Jonah and the whale. Julie thought it was a pretty neat story. And then her teacher looked at Julie right in the eyes and said, "Don't ever think you can hide from God. You may hide from your mommy, but you can never hide from God."

And then to Julie's dismay, of all times, her teacher asked, "Have any of you ever tried to hide from God? If so, raise your hand." Julie felt horrible. She had to raise her hand otherwise she'd be lying, and lying in church would be the worst thing she could ever imagine. So she slowly raised her hand. All of the kids stared at her, and none of them would raise their hand. Julie felt completely ashamed at first, but after church, she was amazed at how good she felt inside. She ran right home and told Tonya and her mom how sorry she was for what she had done.

But how could God possibly fix this problem with her family? Julie's mind seemed to cloud in confusion at the very thought of it. Mamie gave a slight bark and interrupted Julie's deep thoughts. She looked up and saw her brothers far up the hill. They had stopped to wait on her. Ronnie had his hands on his hips, and Jerry and Matt were motioning her to hurry up. Julie took off running and tried to catch up with them. Maybe Ronnie could explain to her how God could help them fix their family. Julie finally caught up with them and slowed her gait. "Ronnie," Julie began as she tried to catch her breath. "How can we get God to get Mom and Dad back together again?" she asked, speaking in gasps as she regained her breath.

"God can't do that," Matt said before Ronnie could answer.

"Why not?" asked Jerry with hope filling his voice for the first time.

"I don't know," Matt answered back and then turned to Ronnie. "Can God do that, Ronnie?"

Julie's eyes darted from Matt to Jerry and then to Ronnie. Ronnie walked slowly on in deep thought not answering them at first. And then finally, he said, "I don't know. We could all pray real hard, and maybe God could do it."

Julie thought that she heard a tinge of excitement and hope in Ronnie's voice. Julie just knew that somehow God would help them. They entered the little front door of the church and left Mamie outside. Julie looked at her brothers, and they looked at her and smiled. Julie thought that they too were hoping the same as she was. She hoped that God would surprise her again. A good surprise.

✳

The next few weeks seemed to pass in chaos. Julie could not bear that her mom was not there with them. She missed Tonya too. She longed for God to answer her prayer and to put her family back together again. Julie had thought at first that they'd stay a few nights with their mom and then a few nights with their dad. She didn't think it would be so bad because they would get to take turns with them. She had thought that maybe things would get better and that they wouldn't argue so much and that surely they'd get back together. Julie thought that maybe her dad would quit his drinking and wouldn't be angry with them all the time. But nothing was working out.

Every day they would get up and try to get ready for school. Julie could never get her hair fixed right. If they forgot to hang their clothes up, they would be all wrinkly when they went to wear them. Sometimes, Matt would forget and put on a dirty shirt, or Jerry would grab the last clean one. On their way to school, they would stop at Gramma Winnie's to see their mom. She would comb Julie's hair and tidy the boys up.

After school, they would once again walk home. But often their mom would still be working and wouldn't be at Gramma Winnie's. Their dad had told them that they were to come straight home if she was not there. On Tuesdays, they still had their dinner at Gramma Winnie's, and their mom joined them right after work. Julie could hardly stand it when it was time for them to walk home.

"Come home with us, Mommy," Julie pleaded with tears in her eyes.

"I can't, honey," Ethel replied and then started to cry.

Slowly, all four of them walked home together. Hardly a word was spoken. As soon as Julie entered the house, she ran up to her room and shut the door. She threw herself onto the bed and buried herself in her pillows and cried until she felt that she might burst inside. She took her beloved Thumbelina doll and wound it up and then clutched it to her chest. Julie knew that her brothers had cried a lot too. They always tried to hide it, but Julie could hear their whimpers way into the dark night and noticed that their eyes were often red and swollen. Julie thought the loneliness could not get any worse until her dad forbade her to sleep in her brothers' room and told her to keep her light turned off. Julie felt as if she was dying inside. It was as if the house itself had dried up and was dying too. She felt like Dorothy in the *Wizard of Oz*, soaring through the tornado in confusion, except that her house never landed and that there wasn't any yellow brick road.

They were never sure what to expect when they came home. Sometimes their dad was home waiting for them. Sometimes, he came home later. Often, he would tell them to take some Campbell's soup and to go up to Gramma Emma's house and stay the night. At other times when he did stay home, he would drink his beer until he passed out. Nothing seemed to matter anymore. Things were never going to be the same again. It was not enough for Julie to see her mom for only brief periods. The emptiness in her heart seemed to grow each day. The more days that passed, the more she missed her mom. She missed the sound of her voice, the touch of her hand. Her presence had made their house a home, and now she was gone.

Julie could never tell what kind of mood their dad would be in. On a few nights, he surprised her by sitting and watching TV with them. He would drink only a few beers, and at times, Julie thought that she received a glimpse of the dad that she used to hold onto so dear. Julie would begin to hope again. *Maybe he was trying to change so Mom would come back. Maybe God was hearing their prayers.*

Then there were the other nights when after getting ready for bed, Julie would lie awake in her dark room. She would lift her blinds so the light from Lindy's tavern would shine in. She would listen for her dad to come in the front door. She could hear how clumsy his steps were when coming in the door and up the steps and how slurred his speech was as he mumbled beneath his breath. Julie would clutch her dolls tightly to her side and close her eyes until she could hear his footsteps go back down the stairs.

But Friday's were different. Julie was learning to live for the weekends. On Fridays, they all got to go and stay at Gramma Winnie's and spend the night with their mom. They would all pile into the big bed in the back bedroom upstairs and talk. Julie could smell the sweet, fresh fragrance of her mom's perfume as she lay close by her side. Julie felt that surely everything would be all right as she would feel her mom's arms wrapped around her.

⁂

Julie walked briskly beside Ronnie. "You guys walk too fast," she said as her words puffed out between taking deep breaths. Julie slowed her pace, hoping that Ronnie would walk slower. "Is it Friday yet?"

"Yes, today is Friday," Ronnie answered without slowing his pace. He ruffled her hair with his fingers. "Come on, sis, or we'll be late for school!"

"Today's Friday," Julie chirped to Matt and Jerry. "We get to stay at Gramma's tonight with Mom."

"Tell her," Jerry said as he looked at Ronnie.

"Tell me what?" Julie asked as she looked at all three of her brothers.

"Dad said that we are to come home first, and then he'll drive us up to Gramma's," Ronnie answered.

"But why?" Matt asked. "We have to walk all the way home right past Gramma's house just to have Dad drive us back up there again?"

"Oh…it's just because he wants a chance to get to see Mom," Ronnie answered.

"Great," Jerry spoke slowly. "The only chance we get to see Mom, and they'll fight the whole time."

Later that evening, Ron drove them up to Winnie's. Matt and Jerry darted out the right car door while Ronnie and Julie darted out the left. They ran to the front porch and stopped at the door that was now blocked by Gramma Winnie's large frame.

"Go on in," she said and motioned all four of them to go past her. She still stood in the doorway as Ron approached.

"Is Ethel here?" Ron asked. He cleared his throat nervously with a dry cough.

Winnie stood firm in the doorway, her eyes narrowed sharply before she replied curtly, "You know she's here, Ron."

"Listen, Winnie," Ron's words came forth angrily. "This is none of your business."

Winnie opened her mouth to speak but was interrupted as Ethel came up behind her. "It's okay, Mom. I'll talk to him." Winnie gave out a loud sigh and with a wave of her hand in the air, she turned and walked away.

Ron stood still with one foot on the concrete step and the other one on the ground. He leaned his elbow onto his bent knee as he put a cigarette in his mouth and then stroke the match to light it. Ethel went and sat down on the swing and tried to gather her thoughts. Ron inhaled the cigarette deeply, then released the smoke slowly. He flicked the cigarette and let the ashes fall to the ground. He stared at Ethel and said nothing.

Ethel hated this quiet before the storm. She had experienced it for twelve years and could almost predict his next movements. She sat and waited and stared down at the porch.

"The kids are very unhappy, Ethel." Ron slowly watched her face to see the impact of his words.

"I know how unhappy they are," Ethel responded without looking up at him. "I see it on all of their faces."

"Then why don't you come back home where you belong?" Ron answered smugly.

Ethel looked up from the porch into his face. "Why don't I come home? You're asking me?" she repeated. "You know exactly why I'm not coming home!"

Ron said nothing. He continued to lean on his bent knee and swayed it ever so slightly. His eyes searched Ethel's face.

Matt, Jerry, Ronnie, and Julie slipped past their Grandpap John who was asleep on the couch. The noise of the TV drowned out his snoring. They slowly tiptoed to the screen door and sat down to listen to their parents talk. All three of the boys put their finger to their mouths and motioned Julie to be quiet right as her mouth had dropped open to say something. She quickly closed her mouth and sat quietly between her brothers.

Ron changed the subject. "You can't live with your mother the rest of your life! Or are you planning to move in with Bob?" he asked tauntingly.

Julie looked puzzled at her brothers and scanned their faces for an answer to her unasked question. But all three of them quietly motioned her to be still.

"You know Bob is not the reason that our marriage is breaking up," Ethel answered defensively.

"You deny that you're seeing him?" Ron asked. He let out another puff of smoke into the air and glared at her.

"You've got a lot of room to talk!" Ethel fired back.

Ron smirked at her and threw his cigarette to the ground. He paused and stepped onto the cigarette. Slowly, he moved his foot back and forth nervously on the already extinguished butt. He carefully planned his next move and then stepped up onto the porch. He walked to the swing where Ethel sat. All four of the children ducked from his view.

"Ron, listen," Ethel spoke pleadingly. "It's not about us anymore. It's about the kids."

"Well…you're the one who left them." Ron spoke smugly.

Ethel looked him squarely in the eyes for the first time. "Did I have a choice?"

Ron shrugged his shoulders. "I didn't tell you to leave."

"How could you expect me to stay after what you did?" Ethel snapped back.

"Oh, don't start," Ron said with a wave of his hand. "I never thought you, of all people, would leave our kids."

"Would you give me support if I take them? Like you said, I can't live with Mom forever."

"You have a home, Ethel," Ron said firmly.

Ethel knew that it was no use to continue to talk. She turned away from Ron to wipe the tears away. She stared blankly at the passing cars on the highway. She could barely get the weekly twenty dollars of grocery money from Ron when she lived with him. She knew that he would never give her support money and enable her to leave him. He had her over a barrel, and she knew it. He knew it. He was using the kids to play on her emotions. *What could she do?*

Ron spoke quietly and changed his approach. He could see that Ethel was weakening. "Ethel, I'll change. I promise."

To Ron's surprise, Ethel ignored his remark. Ethel turned and looked firmly into Ron's face. "You've got to help take better care of the kids if this is the way that it's going to be."

"I am taking care of them!" Ron shot back. "They have a home and food."

"They go to school in wrinkled and dirty clothes and spend every night eating Campbell's soup up at your mom's every night." "And," Ethel continued as she stopped Ron from interrupting her, "how can you let them stay at Emma's with James there?" Ethel finished and stared firmly into Ron's eyes.

"Oh, so now you don't like my mom either?" Ron asked. "After all that she's done to help us. Christ, Ethel, she has always treated you like a daughter!"

"You know it's not Emma that I don't trust!" Ethel let her voice rise. "You know it's your dad that I'm concerned about! So help me Ron…if he so much as gets near my kids, I'll kill him!" Ethel's face was flushed in frustration and anger.

"I told you, Ethel. I'll change." Ron put his hand on her arm softly and tried to calm her down.

Ethel jerked her arm from under his touch and rose to go into the house. "How many times have I heard that!"

"Yeah, Ethel, that's right," Ron said as she got up to leave. "Go running to Bob. You're no different than his wife Nina leaving your kids."

Ethel froze in her tracks and turned to face Ron. The color drained from her face as Ron's words slapped her hard.

Ron jumped up to leave. "That's right!" Ron continued as he hammered the words into her heart and then turned, brushing past her and hurrying to his car.

Ethel stood and stared at him in disbelief as he walked to his car. Ron grabbed the door handle of the car and jerked it open and yelled back to her, "And what about Ronnie?" Ron jumped into the car and slammed the door and then peeled out onto the highway.

As Ethel turned to go into the house, she saw the four peering faces looking up at her. Tears streamed down her face as she rushed past them and up the stairs to the bedroom.

The four children turned and watched their mom leave the room. Hearing the commotion, Winnie appeared at the kitchen door. She glanced at Ethel as she hurried by and saw the children sitting at the front door. Slowly, Winnie dried her hands on her apron. She walked over to the children and saw the forlorn look on all of their faces. "Come on," she said kindly. "Gramma Winnie's got some fried potatoes and pork chops." Julie paused and looked up at her gramma. Winnie looked down at her lovingly. Julie wrapped her arms around her gramma and buried her face in her dress. Winnie patted Julie on the back and then said to all four of them, "I've got chocolate cake for dessert." Julie let go of Winnie and ran to the table. She climbed under the table, trying not to hit her head on the metal rod, and squeezed up onto the chairs that were pushed tightly against the window by the table.

Shortly after when they all sat down, Ethel joined them. Her eyes were dry but red and swollen. They were all eating when Ethel asked the kids about school. They all started to talk at once wanting to tell their mom all of the details. They finished eating supper, and Winnie brought out the chocolate cake. They all ate the dessert and talked some more. Julie drank the cup of milk that Gramma Winnie had poured for her and licked her white mustache as she finished her cake.

"Mommy, I can help you do the dishes if you want me to," Julie said. She wanted so much to help her mom.

"Well, how about we all do the dishes for Gramma, and then we'll all sit down and play a game of rummy?" Ethel asked.

The boys let out a loud "yea!"

"But…I don't know how to play rummy," Julie said. "Only fish."

"Well, you watch, and Gramma will teach you, okay?" Ethel said. She looked deep into Julie's eyes and smiled.

It was late when they went to bed. They waited until Grandpap John went to work over at the railroad station before they went upstairs. They had all taken turns going down into Gramma Winnie's basement to take a shower. Ethel came down and shampooed Julie's hair. She wrapped her in a towel and dried her. Julie looked up at her mom's deep blue eyes that were still red from crying earlier. "Mom, I wish we still lived up at the little house on the hill," Julie said softly. Ethel said nothing but smiled as she knelt down beside Julie. She helped her put her pajamas on. "I didn't mind the outhouse that much," Julie continued. "I wish we could all live together again, Mom."

"I know, honey," Ethel whispered into her ear and then took Julie into her arms and hugged her. "Come on…speaking of out-houses," Ethel said as she took Julie's hand. "Let's go down to the outhouse before we go to bed."

Julie took her mom's hand and climbed the basement stairs and then out the back kitchen door to the back porch. "You go on down, and I'll stay here and wait for you," Ethel told Julie. Julie went down the steps and smiled back up at her mom. Ethel could see Julie's face as the porch light shined down upon her. She saw the earnestness and sorrow that was etched across her young daughter's brow. Julie hurried to the outhouse and closed the door behind her and felt for the seat in the darkness. It didn't matter to Julie if Gramma Winnie had an outhouse. She loved being at her house with her mom and brothers.

Julie squeezed between her brothers and her mom in the big bed. It was a warm May night. The window was pushed open and the small wooden framed screen was put tightly in place. There was a light rain and Julie could hear the pitter-patter of it hitting the adjoining roof. A light breeze blew through the window and it moved the shade. Julie could hear it rhythmically tap softly against the window frame. A fresh smell of earthen dirt filled the air. It mixed with the lilacs that were in bloom beneath their window. Julie took a deep breath of air and let it fill her with the scents of spring.

Ronnie broke the silence. "Mom, are you ever coming back home?"

"I'm not sure what we're all going to do." Ethel let out a sigh and then continued, "I want to try and get an apartment over in Grantville."

"Can we come and live with you then?" Matt asked.

"What about Dad?" Jerry asked.

"What school will we go to?" asked Ronnie.

"Can I bring my toys?" Julie chirped in.

"Wait," Ethel said lovingly. She propped her elbow onto her pillow and rested her head on her hand. "Listen, let me try to explain, okay?" Ethel hesitated, not knowing how to explain the situation to her children. "I don't make much money at my job. I only make about half of what your daddy makes at his job. I can only get a small apartment at first, but hopefully, it will be big enough for us all to get together on the weekends. That way you can spend three days with me and four days with your daddy. And…I'll still see you during the week after school."

Julie hated the word *divorce*. She knew now only too well what it meant.

"This way you can stay in your same school," Ethel continued.

"But, Mom, why can't you come back home?" Matt asked earnestly.

Ron poked Matt to get him to drop the subject.

But Jerry turned to face his mom and asked, "Why, Mom?"

Ethel spoke slowly. "Honey, I can't come back home." The streetlight shined through the window and made shadows on the wall. The quietness was broken only by the sound of an occasional car that passed by. Ethel knew that the children needed an explanation but pondered on how to explain it to them. She didn't want to tell them what their dad had done. She felt that somewhere down deep inside that Ron loved his children, even Ronnie. At times, he could even be a good father. She wanted to give the children answers that she did not have herself.

There were no apartments in the small town of Cutters Ford. Ethel couldn't afford to take the children with her without Ron's support. Ron would never leave and give her the house. And yet how could she leave them?

Ethel heard the deep breathing of her children as they all began to fall asleep except for Jerry. She could still hear his muffled sniffles as he lay by her side. Ethel reached out and put her arm around him. Her head throbbed. Ethel painfully thought to herself that no matter what she did, it would be wrong and that the children would suffer.

Julie—age eight.

CHAPTER

15

Julie carefully got out of bed so as to not awaken Jerry and her mom who were still sleeping. Matt and Ron had already gotten up and gone downstairs. Julie took a deep breath. The smell of bacon, eggs, and coffee drifted up the old wooden stairway to greet her. Quickly, Julie darted down the steps and rounded the corner to go into the kitchen. Gramma Winnie stood at the stove frying eggs. Julie found an empty chair and sat down. Grandpap John still had his work clothes on as he glanced over at her and gave her a warm smile. Julie smiled back at him with a twinkle in her eyes.

Julie finished eating and decided to help clean up the dishes. Gramma Winnie took an apron from the cabinet and wrapped it around her. She pulled the tie around twice before tying it into a bow. Julie looked at the big apron and laughed. "It looks like a big ole dress, Gramma!" Julie pulled up a chair to the kitchen sink and began to scrub the hardened egg off the dirty plates. Ronnie, Matt, and even Jerry had now finished eating and had gone in to watch TV. Ethel had joined them at the table and sat quietly rubbing her head. Winnie took the pot of hot coffee and poured Ethel a steaming cupful.

Ethel sipped her coffee as John scooted back his chair and stood up to go to bed. As he passed by Ethel, John's kind eyes met hers. He paused for a moment and seemed to want to say something but could not find the words. He gave her a gentle smile and said, "It'll be all right, Ethel."

Julie finished the last of the dishes. She hoped Gramma Winnie wouldn't ask her to do the pots and pans. Quickly, she hopped off the chair and pulled off the apron. She gave her mom a quick kiss on the cheek and ran into the room to join her brothers.

"I'll have the kids go outside and play so that we can talk," Winnie said to Ethel.

"Oh, please don't, Mom," Ethel said. "Let them stay in. I don't want them to feel like they're being pushed outside."

Winnie dried her hands on the tea towel briskly and then pulled out a chair to sit down beside Ethel. Winnie took Ethel's limp hands into hers. "What are you going to do?"

"I just don't know, Mom," Ethel replied.

"Surely, you are not going to let the kids live with him," Winnie said matter-of-factly.

"I don't know what to do," Ethel said slowly. "Despite all that Ron has done, he has never been unfair to the kids, even with Ronnie. Maybe he will change if he has to bear more of the responsibility." Ethel paused and then looked over at Winnie.

Julie approached the kitchen door to get a drink of water and sit with her mom. She stopped short when she heard Ronnie's name mentioned. She tiptoed back into the living room and told her brothers. Ronnie knew that they would be seen if they all got up to go toward the kitchen. Slowly, he stood up and turned down the TV volume. Then they all scooted toward the open doorway where the space heater sat and tried to hear the conversation.

Winnie scooted her chair closer to the table and leaned closer toward Ethel. "But what about Ronnie? Are you really going to let Ronnie stay with Ron too?"

Ethel hung her head and rubbed her forehead fiercely as if by doing this she could somehow erase the turmoil and find an answer. But there were no answers.

Julie, along with Matt and Jerry, turned to look at Ronnie. "What is Gramma saying?" Julie whispered the question to her brothers in hope that one of them would answer. But none of them answered. Matt poked Julie with his elbow to be quiet. Julie wanted to let out a cry but instead squeezed tightly up against her brothers in an effort to hear more of the conversation.

"Ethel...at least let Ronnie stay with me until the divorce," Winnie continued.

"Gramma Winnie always likes Ronnie more," Jerry spoke out quietly.

"Yeah," Matt echoed.

"I think she loves all of us," Julie added defiantly as she tried to defend her gramma.

"Then why does she only want Ronnie to come live with her and not us?" Jerry asked Julie.

"I don't know," Julie said. The tears came down her cheeks against her will. *I can't lose Ronnie too*, Julie thought.

The kitchen was quiet now. Julie thought for sure the conversation was over, but her brothers didn't stir. They only sat still and continued to quietly listen.

"But, Ethel..." Winnie's low voice barely broke the silence.

The four children had very quietly inched their way into the next room in an attempt to hear the adults who spoke in not much more than a whisper.

"Ronnie isn't even Ron's real son. He can't stay with him," Winnie continued.

Ethel's voice broke the whispered hush as Winnie's words smacked her sharply. Her words came out louder than she had expected. "Mom, he's the only dad he has ever known. I don't want Ronnie to be taken away from the other three." Ethel heard a slight noise to her right and turned quickly. There stood Ronnie in the doorway. He looked straight into his mom's eyes and then turned and ran out the front door. The screen door slammed shut behind him. Julie, Matt, and Jerry sprung to their feet to go after Ronnie but were stopped by Ethel as she sprinted past the trio. Gramma Winnie followed close behind Ethel. She gave the trio a stern look and, with one hand, motioned them to stay inside. Gramma Winnie went out the screen door and then grabbed the large wooden door and shut it behind her.

Julie quickly climbed up onto the couch and stood on it. She peeked out the front window. She saw Gramma Winnie and her mom sitting on the swing with Ronnie between them. Ronnie had his face buried in his hands, and Julie could tell that he was crying.

"What do you see?" asked Jerry as Matt joined them.

"Ronnie's crying," Julie said slowly.

"Why?" asked Matt.

Julie shrugged her shoulders and slowly slipped down the back of the couch to sit beside Matt. She just couldn't understand all that had just happened, and by the look on her brothers' faces, they didn't either. They sat in silence for a while. Julie sat staring at her outstretched legs and nervously tapped her feet together. Matt bit his fingernails, and Jerry continually cracked his knuckles.

Shortly, Julie stood back up on the couch. "You're going to get in trouble if they catch you," Matt said. Julie turned to Matt and put her finger to her mouth signaling him to be quiet. Slowly, she touched the shade on the window and moved it just enough so that she could peek between it and the window frame. She saw Ronnie sitting on the swing. His shoulders were slouched down, and his eyes were fixed on the banister at the opposite side of the porch. He said nothing. Winnie continued to talk, and Ethel rubbed his back. Julie leaned closer to the window in the hope that she could hear something, but she could only hear the sound of muffled voices.

"Well?" asked Matt as Julie slid back down to sit on the couch. "Ronnie looks so sad," Julie answered.

Julie sat tapping her feet once again. She watched Matt and Jerry stare at the TV set, but she knew that they were not really watching it. Neither of them seemed to care that Brutus had Popeye in a death grip as his can of spinach rolled down a hill.

The loud beep of a horn broke the silence. Julie, Matt, and Jerry ran to the front door and swung it open. They saw Aunt Mary's car pull off the highway and park. The car was hardly stopped before the car doors had swung open wide and Aunt Mary's five children poured out of the car. Julie squeezed past her brothers who were blocking the doorway. Julie hoped that maybe Tonya was with Aunt Mary, but she soon noticed that she had not come with her.

Winnie arose reluctantly to meet them. Ethel sat with her arm still around Ronnie. Shortly, she gave Ronnie a gentle squeeze and leaned down to kiss him on the head before she also reluctantly stood up to meet Mary. "We'll talk more, honey," she said to Ronnie. Ronnie sat quietly on the swing as his siblings joined him. He didn't speak and seemed oblivious to everyone that was around him.

Aunt Mary's children gathered around and beckoned them to come play in the yard. Julie was glad when Jerry told them to go ahead and play and that they would come over in a little while. Julie didn't feel like playing, and she could tell that neither did Jerry or Matt. They all sat quietly on the swing. Julie gave the swing a slight push with her foot and let it carry them lightly through the air. None of them spoke. Even Julie had no desire to say a word or to even ask a question. It was enough to know that Ronnie's heart was broken. The reason why did not seem to matter. All that mattered was that Ronnie knew that they loved him and that they would stick by his side and that somehow they would all get through it together.

The sound of their cousins playing in the backyard drifted to the porch. After awhile, Ronnie stirred. "I'll talk to you later, okay?" he said sadly. "Let's just go play with them for now," he said and pointed to their cousins. "I don't want them to come over and start asking us a bunch of questions." Ronnie slowly got off the swing as Jerry, Matt, and Julie followed him off the porch and to the backyard.

It wasn't until later that evening after Aunt Mary and her children had gone and when it was time for them to go home that Julie began to realize the seriousness of the situation. It was time for her and her brothers to go home, but Julie hoped against hope that maybe they could stay overnight.

To Julie's dismay, Ethel told them to get their things together and that she would walk them back to their house. Ethel knew that it meant facing Ron again, but this was just the way that it would have to be. As they got ready to go, Julie noticed that Ronnie was still sitting in the chair in the living room. He sat in a daze as he stared aimlessly out the front screened door.

"Ronnie, come on," Julie called out to him. "We're ready to go home!"

"Ronnie's going to stay here with me for a few days," Gramma Winnie said and then turned to face Ethel and the three children.

Ethel stood and looked at Ronnie sitting in the chair in the far room. She then turned and looked down at the three questioning faces that stared up at her for an answer. She was just too tired to argue with Winnie, and she knew that it was too soon to send Ronnie back home with what he had learned that day.

"Come on," Ethel said as she herded Jerry, Matt, and Julie toward the back door.

"But, Mom," Julie wailed.

"Not now, Julie!" Ethel said firmly and opened the back door and walked out.

Jerry, Matt, and Julie followed slowly behind. One by one, they turned as they went out the door and sadly glanced back at Ronnie. Gramma Winnie quickly stepped behind them and blocked their view as she hurriedly ushered them out the back door to join their mom.

✳

The next morning, Julie was awakened as Matt shook her gently and told her to get up. Slowly, they all got up and got dressed for church. They hardly said a word to one another as they ate their wheat puffs with canned milk.

They had all gone straight to the boys' bedroom when they came home the night before. They all missed Ronnie so much, and no one would tell them what was wrong. They closed the door not even having a desire to listen in on their mom and dad's conversation that erupted immediately into a loud argument. Even with the bedroom door closed, they heard their dad's words go from sober to the familiar slurred speech they had grown accustomed to hearing when he was drinking. Since their mom had left, it was not unusual for their dad, when he was drinking, to call them to come back downstairs to talk to him after they had already gone to bed. He would go on and on telling them of the family dilemma. Sometimes, he would make sense, and other times, he would make no sense at all. They would wait until he tired out and then ask him if they could go to bed. Sometimes, he would wave his hand for them to go on upstairs, but at other times, he would say, "No, you need to know this," and would continue on for another round of the same. So after they had heard their mom leave, Jerry quietly got down from his bed and locked the bedroom door. It did not seem to matter nor did he seem to care if they got in trouble for locking it. Even Julie didn't seem to care if she was yelled at for being in her brothers' room.

It was now the next morning as Julie hurried and put her cereal bowl into the sink that was full of dirty dishes. She ran to catch up with Jerry and Matt as they headed out of the front door. Jerry locked the door and then ran to hide the key on the back porch while Julie and Matt waited at the front gate. To Julie's surprise, Mamie came running around the corner of the house with Jerry following her. Mamie quickly ran to Julie and Matt and nudged them with her nose. Julie and Matt knelt down and hugged her and then patted her on the head. As they all started to go out the gate, Mamie remained behind. "Come on, girl," Matt called out to her. But Mamie seemed confused and turned to look back at the front door of the house before reluctantly joining them.

"She knows that Ronnie's missing," Jerry said sadly.

"She misses him," Matt said in a low voice.

"I do too," Julie said in a hushed whisper.

Julie sat through Sunday school in a daze. Her brothers were in a different classroom, and Julie felt lonelier than ever as she sat by herself.

"Hey! You want to sit with me?" a friendly voice asked Julie.

Julie looked up to see her friend Sarah. They were in the same class at school and were beginning to become good friends. Actually, Sarah was one of the first friends Julie had ever had outside of her cousins.

Julie stood up and went to sit beside Sarah but continued to sit quietly. She sat and listened as Mrs. White taught them about Peter's faith to walk on the water and how he had begun to sink when he doubted. Julie thought she knew how Peter must have felt. She too doubted if God would put her mom and dad back together again, and without Ronnie, she too felt that she was sinking. She felt that she would burst out crying at any moment. Julie shifted in her seat to hold back the tears and to regain her composure.

It was later in the day after church that they walked up to Gramma Winnie's house to spend the rest of the day with their mom. Everyone seemed so much quieter than the day before. Julie kissed her mom and then ran into the living room to find Ronnie. She slid up on the couch with him. He looked at her and gave her a faint smile.

"I miss you, Ronnie," she said. Julie turned and peered up into Ronnie's eyes. Matt and Jerry sat down quietly beside them.

"Let's go outside," Ronnie said and then glanced over at the doorway. He wasn't supposed to tell anyone about what he had learned, but he knew that he had to tell them.

Quietly, they slipped out of the front door. Matt followed last and quickly grabbed the screen door so that it wouldn't slam shut. Ronnie took them past the horseshoe pegs and around to the back of the long, narrow red shed that sat off to the side in Gramma Winnie's yard. They all plopped down and leaned their backs against the red insulbrick siding.

Jerry pulled a reed of grass and sipped it like a straw as he waited for Ronnie to speak. Matt sat still, his bright blue eyes slowly moving from one sibling to the other. Julie wiggled uncomfortably waiting for her brother to talk to them.

Ronnie began to speak, hesitantly at first, "Do you know why I have to stay at Gramma's?"

"No," the three voices answered in unison as they shook their heads back and forth.

"Well," Ronnie paused. He looked sadder than Julie had ever seen him. She reached and took his hand as Matt and Jerry turned to face Ronnie. "I don't know how you'll feel about me after I tell you," Ronnie continued, his voice cracking as he spoke. "They're saying that I'm not your whole brother," he blurted out as he stared at the ground.

"You are so my brother!" Julie yelled.

"They're nuts!" cried Matt.

"Who told you that?" Jerry yelled.

"Well, they say that Dad isn't my real father," Ronnie answered.

"I don't understand," said Matt.

"That makes no sense!" Jerry interjected. Julie sat quiet, totally confused.

"Well, that's what they're saying," Ronnie answered as he threw his hands up in the air helplessly and then let them fall to his side.

Julie grabbed Ronnie's hand and held it tight as if to never let it go. Jerry and Matt jumped up and circled around Ronnie and then sat down Indian style in front of him.

"You will always be our brother, Ronnie," Jerry and Matt said almost in unison.

"Always," Julie said as she squeezed Ronnie's hand tightly. Tears creased out of each of their tiny eyelids and ran down their faces as they sat in silence.

Ronnie was still not allowed to go home with them that night. Once again, they walked down the winding road to home. Julie cried quietly all the way home as she walked between Matt and Jerry. They had no sooner entered the door when their dad told them to go up to Gramma Emma's. Julie was actually relieved because she could see that her dad was in a very bad mood.

It was the last week of school. Nothing had changed. They continued on in the routine that they were trying to adjust to. They met Ronnie every morning at Gramma Winnie's and walked to school together.

Everyone said that things would all work out when the divorce was final. But Julie didn't believe anyone anymore. It was even becoming difficult for her to believe in Jesus. *Maybe he was just like Santa Claus*, Julie thought as she remembered overhearing her brothers talking one day that Santa was just make-believe. *Maybe, Jesus is just make-believe too.* But Julie shook the thought from her head. Surely, she'd go to hell just for thinking that. She knew that Jesus was real because she had felt him in her heart. *No, Santa Claus had never done that. But why wouldn't God answer their prayers*, she thought sadly.

On the last day of school, they stopped at Gramma Winnie's. They were anxious to show their mom their report cards, ribbons, and prizes. Julie noticed that Gramma Winnie was very quiet as she fed them their dinner and had not answered their question as to why their mom was late from work. As the evening wore on, they dared not ask her again. Finally, Winnie came into the living room after she had cleaned up the dishes. Still holding the dish towel, she wrung it nervously in her hands. "Your mom and dad went for a ride together. They'll be back in a little while."

Julie could hardly believe her ears. Dare she even hope that her mom and dad might be on a date? She glanced at her brothers to attempt to read their faces. They too had an amazed look on their faces. She looked at Ronnie who seemed to at first light up and then seemed sad as if he wasn't sure how he fit into their family. For Julie, nothing had changed between them, but she could only imagine how bad Ronnie felt. She could see it on his sad face.

As they waited for their parents to return, they fell asleep on the couch and in the chairs. John soon left for work. Winnie took several light blankets and covered each of the sleeping children and then went to lay down in the adjoining room. It was early the next morning while they were eating breakfast that they heard their mom and dad come in the front door.

They walked into the kitchen. Julie searched their faces. Her mom looked tired and worn. Her dad looked serious but not angry. Winnie turned from the kitchen stove and looked at both of them but did not say a word. She turned and sat down at the kitchen table. Julie glanced at her brothers and then at the adults.

Ethel approached the table and looked at her children. Their eyes met hers. They didn't move. Ethel then turned toward Winnie who was looking straight ahead. "Mom, we're going to try and work things out." Ethel leaned forward and put a hand on her mom's shoulder. Winnie looked up into Ethel's weary face but didn't say a word. Ethel gave Winnie a kiss on her cheek and then turned to face the children. "Get your things, kids, so we can go home."

Go home, Julie thought. All of them were going to go home. All that Julie could hear in her mind were the words "go home".

Matt, Jerry, and Ronnie rushed through the house to gather their things. All four of them ran for the door. "Shotgun," yelled Matt. Julie hurried to catch up. She thought that maybe she even saw her dad smile at Ronnie. *Maybe things were going to be okay*, Julie thought as she jumped into the backseat of the car.

They sat in the car and waited for their parents to join them. Julie wondered if she could even dare dream it to be real. Here they were, all four of them, in the backseat of the car, and their mom and dad were walking hand in hand toward the car. They were all going home.

Pap Pap John and Gramma Winnie

CHAPTER

16

Julie was surprised at the quietness of the drive home. No one said a word, not even Julie's brothers. Julie wanted to shout and sing and release the joy that she felt in her heart but knew that she should be quiet. It was enough that they were all together again. God had answered her prayer, and she didn't want to do anything to ruin it.

Ron parked the car in the alley behind the old barn. Julie waited for her parents to say something, anything, but they didn't say a word.

Jerry glanced cautiously at his mom and dad and then at the others and then quietly opened his car door. Matt followed his example and opened the other car door. They gathered their things and, then one by one, climbed out of the car. They walked across the little footbridge that crossed over the little stream and then rounded the corner of the barn. Julie followed her brothers and then paused and looked back at the green Chevy. She wasn't sure what to think.

Julie ran to catch up with her brothers. "I knew it! I just knew it!" Julie said as she released her pent up excitement for the first time.

"Knew what?" Matt asked with apprehension in his voice.

"I knew that God would answer our prayers," Julie answered and then began to skip slowly up the sidewalk. "Aren't you happy?" she asked. She stopped and glanced at all three of her brothers. She was puzzled at their silence.

"They're too quiet," Jerry mumbled.

"Well, it's better than yelling," Matt interjected.

Julie ran and grabbed Ronnie's hand. She could hardly believe that he was back home with them again. She waited for his input. However, Ronnie remained quiet. Julie had seen him grow very quiet and withdrawn in the last weeks. She gave his hand a little squeeze and looked up into his eyes.

"I don't know, Julie," he said as he seemed to read her questioning gaze.

Julie refused to be discouraged. She broke away from Ronnie and ran to the back porch. She opened the old metal cabinet and braced her foot on the lowest shelf. She balanced herself and, then with a quick heave, grabbed for the top shelf with her left hand. The metal cabinet swayed for a moment, and Julie thought for sure that it might topple forward with her in it. She balanced herself and hung on tightly with her left hand and then groped the shelf with her right hand. Finally, she felt the thin metal key that had slid to the back of the shelf. She grabbed the key and, with one jump, landed on the floor. She shut the cabinet door and ran out the screen door and quickly down the steps. Julie stopped abruptly when she almost knocked Matt down as he approached the steps. She gave the key to Ronnie and then glanced past him as Mamie had come out of the crawl space and was running to greet them. Julie ran to meet Mamie and knelt down beside her and wrapped her arms around her furry neck. "You good girl, you," Julie whispered in her ear. "You hungry?" she said as she stroked Mamie's reddish-brown hair as if she was waiting for an answer. Mamie turned and gave Julie a quick unexpected lick across her face. Julie quickly took her arm and wiped it across her mouth and laughed. "Come on," she called out to Mamie as she walked to the front porch. "You get to come inside tonight. Mom's home."

Julie paused at the front porch and looked down the long sidewalk. The peonies that lined the sidewalk were in full bloom now. Julie looked as far as she could see down the sidewalk, past the clothesline, to the old barn, but her mom and dad were still not to be seen. Julie turned and saw that her brothers had already gone into their home. She ran to go into the house with Mamie following right behind her.

Ethel sat in the car and fidgeted as she waited for Ron to talk. He had called her nearly every night that week. Surprisingly, he had sounded sober each time. She reluctantly agreed to meet him at lunch. She refused to meet with him in front of the kids. She couldn't bear for them to be upset again. They had talked that day and agreed to meet in the evening. Ethel was surprised at the change in Ron. He was sober every time that they had met. Ethel couldn't help but think of how it reminded her of when they had first gotten together. He was like the old Ron that used to stop by at the little red house. This was the man that had fathered her children, yes, even Ronnie. If only, she could erase all the pain that he had caused. If she could just turn back the clock and prevent what had happened to Tonya. If things could just have been different.

Ron sat quietly across the seat from Ethel. He slowly puffed at his cigarette. He didn't want to rush Ethel or start an argument. He knew that she had come back to him because of the kids. She had as much as told him so. He had promised her that he would change. He didn't really know if he could. He didn't think he was really so bad of a guy. Yes, he had made a few mistakes, but he was a good provider. He never missed a day's work, not even when he drank. He never corrected the kids unless they needed it. He never smacked them around like Tony Mesner's father. *Now that was a real drunk*, Ron thought to himself. Old man Mesner drank, didn't work, and beat up on his wife and kids all the time and for no good reason. *No*, he thought to himself, *I'm not such a bad guy. Ethel should be thankful that I'm not like that. Then she'd have something to complain about.* Ron lowered his window and flicked his cigarette butt into the little stream.

Ethel could not help but think about her last conversation with Bob. They had gotten very close since Ron and her had separated. *It was true*, Ethel thought. *Misery loves company. And between the two of them, they had shared a lot about the misery of their two failed marriages.* Ethel broke down and cried when she told him about what Ron had said about her being just like Nina. She told Bob that she could never do to her kids what Nina had done to his. "Even if I can't have them live with me every day, I'll get them on weekends. I'll make sure that they have clean clothes and the things that they need. I just don't know what to do." She sobbed.

Bob quickly responded, "Ethel, Nina was a drunk. She left Bobby and has never called him or tried to find out how he is. The girls are sleeping in the storage rooms of taverns on dirty mattresses. That's why I'm trying to get custody of them. You're nothing like Nina," he said as he tried to comfort her.

"But…how can I provide for them, Bob?" she asked. "What kind of mother leaves her children?"

"Ethel, you're not leaving your children. You're leaving your husband," Bob replied back.

But Ethel struggled with her situation every day. She struggled every time that she saw her children and every day when she could not see them. No matter how she tried to figure it all out, she couldn't find any answer. So when Ron had called her, she agreed to meet with him. She saw that he was really trying to change. *When Ron doesn't have a beer for a week, he really is trying to change*, she thought. He had begged her to come back. He told her to think of how happy it would make the kids. Ethel had told him no at first. Surely, it would never work. He had asked her why she couldn't forgive him. She had answered that it wasn't that she could not forgive him but just that she didn't feel that she could love or trust him anymore.

The next evening, they talked again. Ron promised that he would continue to change. He reminded her of how happy they had been before and of how happy the children would be if they could be a family again. But Ethel couldn't remember being happy for a long time. Yes, she had been happy with the children, but as for her and Ron, she had just accepted their relationship as a way of life. Ron saw that Ethel was slowly weakening, and when they had met Wednesday night, she reluctantly agreed to maybe try to come back. She said that she would let him know on Friday.

On Thursday, she met with Bob and told him of her decision. Bob sat quietly and listened. He didn't agree with Ethel at all but knew that this was something that she would have to decide on her own.

And so on Friday when Ron had met with her after work, she reluctantly agreed to come back home. They spent the night together.

If it was supposed to get easier, it wasn't, Ethel thought. She squirmed uncomfortably in the car and waited for Ron to say something. She looked at Ron who sat and tapped his fingers nervously on the steering wheel. She wanted to feel love for this man, but in her heart, he had become a stranger to her.

She turned to look away. Ron reached out and took her hand. "It'll be different this time," he said. And then he added, "We better go on up."

"Here they come," Julie said. She ran from the bathroom, where she had been looking out the window at the backyard where the barn sat and where her parents' car was parked. Quickly, she pounced into her brothers' room. "Hurry, you guys! Come see! Dad's got his arm around her," Julie squealed with delight. They all jumped up and tripped over each other as they ran into the bathroom and peeked out the window.

❁

Julie ran down the hill as fast as she could. She rushed past the lilac bush that stood by Gramma Emma's front porch. She took a deep breath and let the fragrance fill her senses.

School was out for the year, and Julie felt free. Julie could not remember when she had felt so happy. Julie and her brothers were staying with Gramma Emma until their parents got back from their trip. Julie had grown accustomed to going to Gramma Emma's in the weeks that had followed her parents' separation. Julie loved visiting Gramma Emma. Unlike her Gramma Winnie who hugged you with her arms, Gramma Emma seemed to hug you with her eyes. Still the same, Gramma Emma always made her feel welcome no matter how tired she was after work.

Julie loved running up and down the hill with her brothers. Sometimes, they would take a hike in the woods or play at the horseshoe pegs. No one lived in the little white house with the red shutters. Julie thought it looked sad as it sat there all alone. Often they would stop and peek in the windows. But somehow, Julie felt sad when she visited the little house. It seemed to remind her of happier times from the past that had somehow gotten lost along the way.

At Gramma Emma's, Julie wasn't allowed to go downstairs with her brothers to the basement kitchen. Ronnie, Jerry, and Matt would often go downstairs and talk with Grandpap James and listen to country music. Julie didn't quite think it was fair that she wasn't allowed to go with them. No one would tell her why or give her a reason. But Julie didn't mind that much. Except for Sunday dinners, Julie always felt uneasy in the basement kitchen. Even more so, she could not bear to go back into the coal bin or Grandpap James' workshop. She wasn't sure why she felt that way, but she was more than content to stay upstairs with Gramma Emma and watch the *Perry Mason* show with her.

Julie continued to run down the hill to Aunt Lisa's house. She extended her arms like an airplane and pretended to fly, soaring to the right and to the left. She slowed her pace as she rounded the bend. The large, green hand pump stood beside the small wooden porch. Julie hopped up on the small wooden porch and knocked on the wooden door. Aunt Lisa opened the door.

Julie loved to visit her younger cousin. They played together until Julie heard her Gramma Emma call for her. Julie ran up the hill and took a shortcut through Grandpap James' rose garden and hurried to the back door.

Later that evening, Gramma Emma gave them all a box of Cracker Jacks to eat while they sat and watched TV. "Thank you, Gramma," Julie said as she reached out for her snack. She then asked, "When are Mom and Dad coming back?"

"Tomorrow, I think," Emma answered. She patted Julie's shoulders and gave her a smile and then went back to her favorite chair that sat in the corner of the small room. Emma didn't mind watching the children. They listened to her and were no trouble. She had actually offered to watch them for a few days so that Ron and Ethel could get away. She had grown to love Ethel dearly. She loved Ron too of course. But she could not understand how he could behave the way he did and why he treated Ethel so badly. She only hoped that they could somehow work through their problems.

James came up later that evening to watch *Gunsmoke* on TV. He sat down in the worn velvet chair. Grandpap James was always so quiet. Julie thought that maybe it was because he stuttered. But he was never at a lack for words if Gramma Emma asked him to do something. This would usually cause quite a squabble between the two of them. It was the only time that Julie really ever heard them interact. They didn't yell and scream and rant or rave. They just seemed to fuss with each other. Julie thought they seemed to almost enjoy having this form of conversation of sorts.

At bedtime, Julie climbed over her gramma to get onto the side of the bed that was up against the wall. This was where she slept when she stayed there. At first, Gramma Emma had made a bed for her on the couch in the living room, but for some reason, she had decided that it would be best if Julie slept in her room. Julie slid beneath the covers and glanced over at her gramma. She wanted to ask her if she would like to come to church with her tomorrow. Julie turned and looked at her gramma. Emma was propped high in a sitting position with her pillows behind her. Julie wondered how her gramma could sleep propped so high up, but often, she had seen her sound asleep, her glasses resting on the end of her nose and her *True Story* magazine still in her lap. Julie liked that her gramma read in bed because the light stayed on all night. Julie was never afraid when she slept with her gramma. Her brothers all slept in the spare room on the pull-out sofa. Julie could hear them in the next room talking and giggling. She wondered what they were talking about.

"Gramma?" Julie asked.

"I thought you were asleep," Emma answered. She was surprised to hear Julie's voice.

"You want to go to Sunday school with us tomorrow?" Julie asked.

"I can't, Julie," Emma said kindly. "Maybe another time."

"Okay," Julie said. She yawned and then turned over to face the wall. Julie lay awake. She couldn't help but think of what was going to happen to her family. She hoped they could get to be happy again. She resolved that she would pray about it tomorrow at church and then fell asleep.

Somehow, things were not quite the same. Julie's mom and dad had come home the next day. Julie kept waiting for the laughter to return to their house.

Julie awoke one morning and heard her mom downstairs in the kitchen. She knew that her dad had already left for work. Julie swung her feet over the bed and pushed her dolls aside. She tiptoed down the landing and peeked into her brothers' room. They all were still sleeping. Julie was tempted to go in and jump on them but changed her mind. She crept quietly down the stairway, and about halfway down the steps, she paused and sat down. She leaned her head up against the rails and watched her mom clean up the kitchen. Julie could not explain the feelings that she felt. They did not even compare to Christmas morning. Julie was happier than she had ever been. Nothing could compare to having her mom at home with them, not even Christmas. This was the first day since her mom and dad had gotten back together again that they would have her to themselves. Julie peered through the stair rails and continued to watch her mom. Julie noticed her mom didn't sing or whistle anymore. It was as if she had lost her song. Julie knew that her mom loved them. But Julie could not help feel that her mom was unhappy. She knew that it wasn't them. The only time Julie would see her mom smile at all was when she was with Julie and her brothers. Julie had never seen her mom so sad. She wished there was something she could do to make her happy.

Ethel turned and saw the young face peering at her from the stairway and smiled up at Julie. Julie ran down the steps and into the kitchen.

"What would you like for breakfast?" Ethel asked.

It had been awhile since anyone had asked her that. "Can I have anything except rice puffs or wheat puffs?" Julie asked.

Julie sat and ate her Rice Krispies. Shortly, her brothers joined her. Julie watched her mom pull the garbage out from beside the stove. It had overflowed onto the floor, and Ethel had grabbed another bag to put it into. As she did, Julie saw her mom wince as the beer cans toppled to the floor. Julie wondered if her mom could stay if her dad would not change.

"Mom, can we go up the alley and play some baseball with the guys?" Ronnie asked.

"Well," Ethel said and gestured with her hand to all four of them. "First, we clean up the house, and then we can play ball."

Matt started to say something but caught himself as Jerry gave him a quick kick under the table. They had all talked and agreed that they would do everything they could to help their mom and to make her happy. They thought if they could make their mom happy that maybe she would never leave no matter what their dad did.

They all jumped in at once after they had finished eating to help clean the house. Julie went to clean her bedroom. Matt went to clean the boys room and Jerry and Ronnie worked on the living room together because there were a lot of little knickknacks to dust. Ethel told them she would clean the rest.

Ethel finished the kitchen and bathroom and went to clean up her and Ron's bedroom last. The room seemed to vex her. She felt so empty inside. She thought she could never feel the same toward Ron again. She made their bed slowly. The marriage bed had been defiled, and no matter how hard she tried, she could not help feeling herself cringe when she was near Ron. It was as if every last bit of love that she had for him was totally gone. She was sucked dry.

The boys hurried down the steps and swung past their parents' bedroom. They stopped short when they saw their mom making the bed.

"We'll be back in a little bit, okay, Mom?" Matt asked.

"We're all done," Jerry said.

"I got the ball and bat," Ronnie said with a broad smile.

This was the first time Ethel had seen her children truly happy for quite a while. "You have fun," Ethel said. "Just be back in time for supper."

"We will, Mom." They called out in unison and then hurried out the door.

Ethel went back to making the bed. "Mom," Julie said. Ethel startled at hearing Julie's voice.

Julie stood in the bedroom doorway. "I put all of our dirty clothes out in the washroom."

"Well, thank you, honey," Ethel said as she tucked in the corner of the bedspread. "I thought you had gone with your brothers to play ball."

Julie came in the bedroom and squeezed to the far side of the bed that was up against the wall. She pulled on the spread and helped smooth it out. "Nah, I thought I'd stay here and help you do the wash."

"Well, let's see how fast we can get it all done, and then maybe we'll have time to play some Jacks before I fix dinner."

Julie smiled and followed her mom to the big washroom. Julie started to sort the clothes as she had seen her mom do so many times before. Ethel reminded her of the ones that would fade and told her to put them into a separate pile. It took them about two hours to wash all of the clothes and to hang them out on the clothesline, but Julie had enjoyed it.

"Now can we play Jacks?" Julie asked. She dropped the empty clothes basket onto the summer porch and then followed her mom through the back door and into the kitchen.

"We sure can," Ethel said. She pulled out a pack of hamburger to make a meat loaf later. Julie pushed back the little crocheted tablecloth and poured the jacks onto the table. She handed the little red ball to her mom. Julie loved playing Jacks with her mom. There were ten little metal spikes, almost star-like, and the little red ball. The object was to pick up the jacks in sequence while catching the ball without dropping either the jacks or the ball. Julie thought that her mom was probably the best Jack player of all times. They played until they heard the screen door of the back porch open. Ron was home from work. Julie picked up the jacks and ball and went to put them away as her dad entered the kitchen.

Ron nodded a hello to Ethel and then pulled out a kitchen chair to sit down. He lit a cigarette. Ethel took the hamburger and began to make the meat loaf. She called to Julie and told her to go and get her brothers for supper.

Julie started to run past her dad and was ready to dart out the back door. "Hey, hey, hey," Ron said. He caught her arm and pulled her toward him. "Don't you say hi or give your dad a kiss anymore?" he asked. This caught Julie by surprise, and she stopped quickly. Slowly, Julie leaned forward and gave him a kiss on the cheek and gave him a hug around his neck. He reached and picked her up and sat her on his lap. He started to talk to Ethel about work. Julie sat still. This was the first time that her dad had treated her so nice since before Tonya had left. Julie sat and listened to her dad talk and watched her mom pat the meat into a loaf, put it into the pan, and then into the oven.

After awhile, Ron started to get up, and Julie slid off his lap. She met her mom's gaze and wink and then headed out the back door to go get her brothers. She stopped at the corner of the house and looked up under the crawl space to see if Mamie was there. She wasn't there. *She probably already went with the boys*, Julie thought as she turned and ran down the sidewalk. She darted under the dry sheets that still hung on the clothesline. She ran around the old barn, crossed the little bridge, and then darted up the alley.

Julie stood and watched her brothers playing ball. She was so proud of them. Ronnie pitched a fastball, but the batter nabbed it. Jerry caught the grounder on the second bounce and then fired it to Matt at first base. In one quick motion, Matt snagged the ball in midair, turned, and tagged the base. Gloves flew in the air signaling the game was over. Julie beamed with pride as she ran to greet her brothers and to tell them that supper was ready.

After dinner, Jerry and Matt brought the game of *Sorry!* downstairs to play in the living room. Ron had asked Ronnie to join him in listening to the Pirates baseball game on the radio. Julie sat with her mom and was helping her fold the laundry that they had brought in from outside. Julie sat quietly watching her family. She looked over at her dad and Ronnie. They were talking about the game. Earlier, she had heard Ronnie laughing and kidding with Matt and Jerry at the ball game. It was so good to be a family again. Julie noticed that her dad had gotten a beer earlier and that he seemed to be taking all night to drink it. She was glad.

Julie picked up the last towel from the pile of clothes and held it to her face and breathed in its freshness. She shook the towel and then folded it neatly and then placed it on the top of the pile.

One by one, they took their baths and got ready for bed. Ethel had come up to tuck them in and tell them good night. Julie had crawled in bed with Ronnie and hoped that she could spend the night with her brothers. Ethel sat down on the edge of Ronnie's bed, but she said nothing. Julie and her brothers remained quiet. They all waited for their mom to say something. They did not know what silence meant anymore. They had all learned that the silence could be more disturbing than the loud arguments.

"Julie, why don't you sleep in your bed tonight, honey?" Ethel asked.

Julie sat up and looked at her mom. She thought that her mom looked so sad. She couldn't understand why she would be so sad now that they were all back together again. Julie didn't want to make things any harder on her mom. She hesitated, and then in a low voice, she asked, "Can Ronnie sleep with me tonight, Mom? Please."

"Go ahead you two. But don't be up all night talking," Ethel said with a weak smile. She shooed them out of the room and then turned to tuck Matt and Jerry in. Julie paused at the doorway and watched her mom lean down and kiss them on the cheek. In the dim light, she could see Matt's and Jerry's mixed expression of joy and sorrow. Julie turned quickly and ran off to her room to join Ronnie.

Ethel stood on the landing at the stairs. She glanced from the one bedroom to the other. *If they could only understand*, Ethel thought. *But how could they?* She didn't understand herself how their family could have gotten so torn apart.

Ethel turned and went down the stairs slowly. She felt so tired. Ron sat on the couch watching TV. She went to walk past him to go into the kitchen, but he reached up and took her arm. He pulled her toward him. Ethel knew better than to resist Ron and sat down beside him. She crossed her arms and rested them lightly on her lap and pretended to watch the movie. Ron put his arm around her and leaned over to kiss her neck. Ethel could feel her blood run cold but sat motionless. She was so unhappy. The love was just not there. *If only things could have been different*, Ethel thought as Ron kissed her again.

Ronnie and Julie sat on the bed. They weren't ready to go sleep. It was still daylight outside, but their dad had insisted that they all go to bed early. So much had changed. Matt, Jerry, and Julie had all agreed that they would make Ronnie feel extra special. Julie knew Matt and Jerry didn't mind that she had asked Ronnie to sleep with her. She had even seen Matt give her a little wink. Julie was so glad to have Ronnie back with them. She thought that she'd never let him out of her sight again.

Ronnie motioned for Julie to come to the end of the bed where he was sitting. Julie squeezed up against Ronnie and pushed her head on the screen to look out the window with him.

Julie turned to Ronnie. "Whatcha looking at?"

"Don't you see it?" Ronnie asked.

"See what?" Julie asked and looked out the window again.

"Over there. On the top of Lindy's house. On the roof," Ronnie answered. He pointed to the pink house that sat across the street beside the tavern.

"I don't see nothing," Julie said with a puzzled look. She pressed her forehead tightly against the screen.

"Anything," Ronnie said, correcting Julie's grammar.

"What?" Julie asked. She was totally puzzled.

"Right there, Julie," Ronnie said and pointed to a piece of metal that protruded from the roof of the house. It was in the shape of a small rocket.

"Oh, yeah. I see it," Julie said smiling. "What is it?"

"Don't you know?" Ronnie turned and faced Julie and was very serious.

"*No*," Julie answered in a whisper.

"Well, it's a secret, Julie," Ronnie said.

"Tell me, Ronnie," Julie started to squeal with excitement, but Ronnie quickly put his hand over her mouth.

"*Sh!*" Ronnie whispered into her ear. Slowly, he released his hand from her mouth. "We'll get in trouble for talking if Dad hears us. Promise that you won't tell anyone."

"No, I promise. Cross my heart and hope to die," Julie whispered. "You know I've never told a secret."

"But you can't even tell Mom and Dad."

"Not even Mom or Dad?" Julie asked, surprised at the magnitude of the secret that her brother was going to share with just her.

"Not even Mom or Dad," Ronnie echoed back. "Promise?"

"I promise!" Julie said emphatically. She stared at the pointy object on the roof and then back at Ronnie.

"Okay," Ronnie said. He took in a deep breath and then paused.

Julie turned once again and, with great wonder, studied the object and waited patiently for his answer.

"It's a spaceship!"

Julie turned quickly from the window and looked Ronnie straight in the eyes to see if he was joking. Her eyes were as big as saucers, and her mouth hung open. She struggled to form her words. "Uh-uh, Ronnie. You're just teasing me."

"No, I'm not," Ronnie answered without cracking a smile. He gave Julie a worried look and then said, "They've come to take over the world." Ronnie knew that he had Julie believing him.

"Oh, Ronnie!" Julie said as she leaned close to him. "We've got to tell someone."

"No, Julie, we can't," Ronnie said. "Once you know and if you tell, they'll capture you."

"Oh no, Ronnie!" Julie looked at the pointy object, picturing it to be a spaceship and then looked back at Ronnie. "What are we going to do?"

"Well, I don't know," Ronnie answered. He wasn't sure if he had taken his story too far with Julie, but he just couldn't tell her the truth, not yet.

"Here comes Dad," Ronnie whispered and pulled Julie down onto the bed. "Pretend you are asleep."

"How can you always hear his knees cracking when he comes up the steps?" Julie whispered.

"*Sh!*" Ronnie answered. They heard the bathroom door close.

"Ronnie, don't you think we should tell Dad?"

"Tell Dad what?" Ronnie asked. His mind was not on Julie's question or the story he had just told her. All Ronnie could think about was that if their dad heard them talking, he would make Ronnie go back to his room. Ronnie enjoyed being with his little sister more than she knew, and he had missed her and his brothers. He never wanted to ever leave them again.

"Ronnie," Julie whispered. She tugged on his shirt to get his attention. "Should we tell Dad about the spaceship?"

"Oh, no, we can't!" Ronnie said. He continued to listen intently for the bathroom door to open and their dad to appear.

Julie started to cry. "I'm scared, Ronnie."

"No, Julie. It's okay, honest. Listen I was just kidding. *Sh!* We have to be quiet or…"

"I think it's time for you both to stop talking and go to sleep," came the stern voice of their dad.

Julie and Ronnie startled at the sound of their dad's voice. They both looked up and saw him standing in the doorway.

"Okay, Dad," Ronnie answered.

"Good night, Dad," Julie chimed in. "We'll go right to sleep."

Julie sat up in bed beside Ronnie and listened. "I hear Dad's knees cracking." Julie knew it was now safe to talk. She turned to

Ronnie and plowed him with a hard punch in the arm. "That's not funny, Ronnie."

"Ouch," Ronnie called out and pretended to hold his arm in pain. He started to laugh quietly.

Julie couldn't help it. She burst out laughing and then gave Ronnie a big hug. She turned to Ronnie and asked, "So what is that thing if it's not a spaceship?"

"It's just an old exhaust vent," Ronnie told her. "We better go to sleep."

Julie thought that life could never be happier than it had been that day. Christmas had not even made her this happy. She grabbed her Thumbelina doll and lay down beside Ronnie. She wound the knob on the back of the doll and listened to the lullaby. Ronnie put his arm protectively around her as they looked out the window and watched the people coming and going from the tavern. A gentle breeze blew across their faces, and soon, they fell peacefully asleep.

Growing up: Julie—age eight and one half, Matt—
age nine and one half, Jerry—age ten and one half,
and Ronnie—age eleven and one half.

CHAPTER

17

Julie put her brother's baseball glove on her hand. She patted it with the fist of her other hand like she had seen her brothers do and guarded the base. Ronnie, Jerry, and Matt were going to play in the little league soon. Ronnie had suggested that they practice playing ball while they waited for their mom to come home from work. Ronnie was now eleven and one-half years old and was left in charge when they were alone. They knew that they were not allowed to leave their yard nor were they allowed to have any visits from the neighborhood kids when their parents were not home.

Julie couldn't help wonder why her mom was so late. She stooped down and watched Jerry with the bat in his hand. Ronnie was about to throw the ball when Jerry stood straight and put the bat down. "Hey, Dad's home!" he called out. They all turned and saw their dad's car parked at Lindy's. Julie put her hand to her brow to block the sun from her eyes and watched as her dad got out of the car. She wondered why he was parking there. Usually, if he was staying home, he would park his car down in the alley at the barn. Julie continued to watch and noticed that as her dad crossed the street, he wasn't walking straight. She had learned a long time ago that these were signs of trouble. She had seen it coming all week. Ronnie, Jerry, Matt, and she had talked about it. Their dad started to come home late from work. He had said that he had to wait for the woman who rode home with him. They had heard their mom asking him about this woman. She had asked Ron if he was having an affair with her. He had denied it and said that she paid him gas money for driving her to work. The drinking had started up again and so had the arguments.

Julie watched her mom grow sadder and sadder. The children had tried to make things better. They took out the garbage and cleaned up the kitchen. They picked up their rooms and helped do the cleaning on Saturdays. When they were alone with their mom, she seemed like her old self, but as soon as their dad came home, everything would change.

Ron let out his rage one night, "You, think I'm so bad, Ethel! I guess you'd rather be with Bob!"

"Ron, I'm trying," Ethel said frustrated.

"Yeah, you just can't get past the incident with Tonya!" Ron screamed.

Julie awakened at the sound of their arguing. She tiptoed out of her bedroom. She was surprised to see that her brothers were all sitting on the landing at the top of the stairs. Matt hung his head sadly when their dad brought his name up. Julie knew that he felt somehow responsible when he told their mom that their dad had kissed Tonya. They sat quietly and peeked down the stairs into the living room.

"Well, Ron," Ethel continued sadly. "It's a pretty hard incident to forget."

"Look, Ethel," Ron said. His words slurred as he tried to put his arm around her. "Maybe we could raise the baby as our own."

They could see the expression on their mom's face. Ethel stood in pure shock. She pushed past Ron.

"What?" Ron asked. "What? What did I say?"

"What?" Ethel asked, her voice raising. She thought that it seemed incredulous that Ron could not know the impact that his words would have on her. It would be senseless to even try to reason with him when he was drinking, but he just would not let it go. "You say it's not your baby!" Ethel screamed as she broke into tears. "But you want us to raise it as if it's our own?" She had broken into tears and ran into the bedroom and slammed the door.

Ron headed after her but stopped short seeing the children watching from the top of the stairs. Julie quickly followed her brothers as they rushed into their bedroom. Julie turned to shut the door, but Jerry motioned to her not to shut it. Julie practically leaped into Matt's bed. Shortly, they heard their dad's knees cracking as he came up the stairs. All four pretended to be asleep even though they knew that he had seen them. Julie heard her dad's footsteps stop on top of the landing. There was a long pause, and then Julie heard him go into the bathroom.

None of them had talked anymore that night. They didn't want to take a chance that they'd upset their dad. Julie lay in the bed quietly next to Matt. In the stillness of the night, the only sound that she heard was the sound of her brothers' breathing. Julie couldn't sleep. She was too stunned by the words that she had heard. She now knew why everyone was so upset at Tonya having a baby, and she also knew that the father was not the Winston boy.

Julie sat in the living room with her brothers. Their dad had told them all to come in from playing ball. He said that he needed to talk to them.

They grabbed their gloves, bat, and ball. "Are we in trouble?" Julie asked Jerry as they walked toward the backdoor.

"I don't think we did anything wrong," Jerry said as they neared the house.

"Why isn't Mom here?" Matt asked Ronnie.

"I don't know," Ronnie answered as they entered the back porch and let the back screen door slam shut. One by one, they put their baseball equipment in the corner of the porch and then went into the house.

Ronnie slowly led the way. They went into the living room and sat down on the floor. Ron sat on the couch. He cleared his throat and then popped the lid off the Iron City beer can.

"Your mom's not coming back home," he blurted out. He tipped the can to his mouth and took a long drink.

Julie looked at each of her brothers and then broke down and started to cry. Julie could see through her tears that her brothers looked shocked. Ronnie immediately began to bite his lower lip. Julie knew that he was wondering, as she was, where he would live. She couldn't bear to lose him again. Jerry tightened his face in anger and with a stern determination. Julie knew that he was trying to be grown up and not to cry, but the tears ran down the side of his face anyway. Matt buried his head in his lap so that the others couldn't see that he was crying. But Julie could see his back heaving up and down and heard his quiet sobs. She knew that he blamed himself.

"Well," Ron continued, unmoved by his children's reaction. "Let me read you the letter that your mom left with me." As he read the letter, Julie scarcely heard a word of it. The words just did not register in her mind. She tried to sort it all out but couldn't make any sense of it. All she heard was that their mom would come by tomorrow sometime and pick them up. One by one, they slowly got up and went upstairs, leaving their dad sitting on the couch.

Julie climbed into her own bed as her brothers went into their room. *There was nothing left to be afraid of*, she thought. She grabbed her Thumbelina doll and clenched it to her chest. *What did it matter if the light was on or not? What did anything matter?* She rolled over in her bed and sobbed into her pillow. She didn't say her prayers that night. She couldn't help but think that even prayers didn't matter anymore.

Julie was surprised the next morning when she woke up hearing someone down in the kitchen. She ran down thinking that maybe her mom had come back home. Julie was surprised to see Jerry.

"What are you doing?" she asked. She searched his face and wondered if he was okay.

"Dad asked me if I'd fry him an egg for breakfast," he answered slowly.

"Do you know how to do it?" Julie asked.

"Well, it broke a little bit, but it turned out pretty good," Jerry said. He turned and went into the living room. Julie knew that he didn't want to talk. That's the way Jerry was. When something was too painful to talk about, he would just go off to himself and be quiet. Julie followed Jerry into the room and sat down beside him on the couch and watched the cartoons that were playing on the TV. Shortly, Matt and Ronnie joined them. None of them spoke. They went to the kitchen later and ate some cereal and just kind of went through the motions of what they normally did.

Julie went to wash her face and hands and comb her hair. She wanted to be ready when her mom came to pick them up. One by one, her brothers did the same. They cleaned up the dishes and picked up the house just in case their mom would change her mind and decide to stay.

It was in the early afternoon when they heard the beep of a horn. They all ran out the front door. Ronnie locked the door and ran the key around to the back porch and then joined the others at the gate. As they all went out the gate, Jerry told Mamie to stay and to go lie down. Matt closed the gate tightly behind them. Across the street was Aunt Mary's car. Julie could see that their mom was sitting in the front seat. Carefully, they crossed the road and climbed into the backseat of the car.

Aunt Mary said hi to them and then turned the car around in the parking lot and then turned left and headed toward Grantville. Julie could only guess that they were going to her house and not to Gramma Winnie's. Julie wondered why but didn't ask. She knew that Tonya would not be at Aunt Mary's house. She longed to see her. She had heard Gramma Emma tell her mom that Tonya had moved in with her older sister.

Julie had never seen her mom look so bad. Her face was puffy, and her eyes were red and swollen.

At Aunt Mary's house, they went to the kitchen with their mom while Aunt Mary herded her children outside to play. Ethel made peanut butter and jelly sandwiches for them and poured out some Kool-Aid. They sat quietly at the table and waited for their mom to talk to them.

"I am so sorry," Ethel started. She tried not to cry. I'm going to get an apartment so that you can be with me on the weekends. We'll still eat at Gramma Winnie's on Tuesday, and I'll pick up your clothes and wash them for you. Ethel paused and looked at the four motionless children that sat quietly staring back at her. "I'll bring you your clean clothes on Thursdays so that you don't have to wear anything dirty. "I'll see you on Tuesdays and Thursdays, and you'll come with me on Fridays, Saturdays, and Sundays. Mondays and Wednesdays are the only days that I won't see you. I've been trying to save some money to get an old car so that I can pick you up and drive you myself. You can always go over to Goldie's store and call me any time that you want once I get a phone. It's going to be hard. I know it is…" Ethel's voice trailed off as she rushed to their sides and knelt down beside them. She hugged all of them and kissed them as the four of them remained still. They didn't know how to absorb her words or how to accept the reality that their mom was never coming home again. Jerry sat stiffly, letting his hurt turn to anger. Ronnie hung his head, confused and still at a loss as to where he would be instructed to live. Matt put his head down hopelessly on his outstretched arm that rested on the table. Julie buried her head in her folded arms and cried softly.

Ethel knelt down beside Ronnie. "I've spoken to your dad, and it's up to you where you want to live."

Ronnie looked up at his mom. He was confused. All three of his siblings looked at him intently. He could see that they were confused also.

A mixture of emotions raged through Julie. *How could they give Ronnie a choice*, she thought. *Doesn't anyone understand that they are brothers and sister, all of them?* They just couldn't take Ronnie from them again. Julie began to cry harder. She wanted to scream out loud.

Ronnie looked up at his mom without even glancing at the others and said, "Mom, I want to stay wherever Jerry, Matt, and Julie stay. I want to be with them."

"I know," Ethel said softly. "I know." Ethel took each one of them by the hand and drew them from their chairs and into her arms. She broke down and cried. *How could she ever make it up to them for the pain that they were bearing?*

Jerry, Matt, Julie, Ronnie, Aunt Tassy behind
Julie, and Mamie in the forefront.

CHAPTER

18

Julie sat on the back porch steps while Mamie sat between her straddled legs. The long, red-haired spaniel looked up at her with unmovable eyes and listened to Julie's every word. Julie poured her heart out and then buried her face onto Mamie's neck and cried. Mamie didn't move, not even to wag her tail. Now more than ever Mamie stayed close to the children she loved so dearly.

It had been a sad summer, and Julie was actually glad that school would start soon. Her mom had told her that they would all go shopping and get new school clothes.

Things were going pretty much like her mom had told her. She had gotten a little apartment over a store and bought an older, used car. After cleaning the little store on Saturday mornings, she would treat them to an ice cream. Julie could hardly stand it when she dropped them off. Julie would walk across the road lagging behind her brothers. She would turn around and wave good-bye to her mom and walk a few more steps and then turn around again and wave reluctantly again to her mom. The house seemed so sad. The laughter was gone. Even between the four of them, it seemed that all they did was argue.

Julie had found a refuge in her little, furry friend. She stretched her legs and climbed down to the last step and leaned her back against the shingled wall. Mamie climbed up the step and inched close to Julie. She nudged Julie's arm with her cold, wet nose. Julie lifted her arm, and Mamie laid her head in Julie's lap. Julie sat thinking as she gently stroked Mamie's fur.

Her dad was drinking more now than she had ever seen him drink. Julie felt like she was walking on eggs, never sure what mood he would be in. She longed for the old dad that she would once in a while get a glimpse of. *He seemed further and further away, maybe lost forever,* she thought. He hardly said a word to any of them. They routinely gave him a kiss good night when they were home. Most nights, they spent up at Gramma Emma's house. At times, Aunt Tassy would come over and stay with them. Julie liked Aunt Tassy. She was Gramma Emma's sister, and Julie thought that she was such a nice lady. But Julie liked staying up at Gramma Emma's. She had always felt loved at Gramma Emma's, and she loved sleeping by her side at night. It was better than hearing her dad come in late after taking Aunt Tassy home and listening to him stumble into bed.

Sadly, they were getting used to the routine. Julie petted her friend's head and scratched her big, floppy ears. Mamie rolled her eyes and looked up at her little friend. "Come on, girl," Julie said as she stood up and stretched. Her brothers were inside the house watching the *I Love Lucy* show, but Julie just couldn't get into it today. Being in the house just seemed to make her sad. Julie walked across the yard to where two lilac bushes had grown together as one. There was a small opening barely in between them. Julie squeezed into the opening and was able to walk between the branches where it opened up into a little private cove. Julie sat down and leaned against a hidden fence that separated their yard from their neighbors. Mamie followed and squeezed into the little cove and sat down beside Julie. This had become her special hideaway. Julie sat quietly and crossed her legs and tapped her feet together as she sat and thought about how much their lives had changed. At least if she started to cry here, no one would see her.

They took turns among the four of them doing the dishes and trying to cook supper, which usually was a can of Dinty Moore Beef Stew or Campbell's Chicken Noodle Soup. Breakfast had become a routine of canned milk and rice or wheat puffs as their dad had told them that the eggs were for his breakfast with the exception that on Sundays they could have eggs. Lunch was usually comprised of mayonnaise and ketchup on slices of bread as there was never any peanut butter. Their dad would get upset if they ate all of the bread, so they would eat crackers, but then all the crackers would be gone too. Julie counted the days until she would see her mom. They would go with her on Fridays and come home Saturdays and clean the house. Sunday after church, they would wait for their mom to pick them up again.

They learned to settle their differences with a deck of cards. Whoever pulled the highest card would get to choose what they wanted. Sometimes, Julie would get so upset that she'd just let a big punch go to her brothers' arm if she didn't agree with them. Which in turn, if she didn't run fast enough, she would receive a bigger punch back. They were lost in this new life, but through it all, Julie didn't know what she would do if she didn't have her brothers. They had become her heroes.

Julie heard Matt calling her name and jumped up and ran to meet him.

"Hurry up!" Matt said. "We gotta get cleaned up before Mom gets here! Where were you anyway?"

"Oh, I was just in the lilac bushes," Julie answered as she bent down and scratched her legs and then her arms.

"Why were you in the lilac bushes?" Matt asked.

"It's my special fort," Julie answered. She felt grown up explaining it to Matt.

They washed up and dried off, but Julie lingered behind. She rubbed her legs and arms over and over again with the towel.

"What are you doing, Julie?" he asked.

"I itch real bad, Matt."

"Wow," he said. "You better be staying out of the lilac bushes for a while and find yourselves another fort."

"Why?" Julie asked and looked up at Matt puzzled.

Matt reached out and took Julie's hand and turned her arm up and down and back and forth. He took the towel from her and threw it on the edge of the tub and took her other hand and turned it back and forth. "Because you got poison ivy real bad."

Julie picked up the towel and continued to rub her arms and legs.

"Try not to scratch it, Jul. Mom will take care of it when she gets here."

Later, Ethel picked them up and stopped to get Julie some calamine lotion for her poison ivy. When they arrived at her apartment, she sat the four of them down and talked to them. "I need to tell you all something," Ethel began.

Jerry, Matt, Ronnie, and Julie all looked at each other. Julie wasn't sure what she hated the most, when adults would sit you down to tell you something or when they didn't tell you anything at all.

"Tomorrow, we're going to go school shopping. We'll put the clothes on layaway and pay on them when I get my paychecks, and by schooltime, I'll pick them up for you."

Julie looked at her brothers and gave them a big smile as if to say, "See, sometimes there is good news."

"But," Ethel continued.

Julie looked at her brothers, and they looked at each other. They all had the same look on their face as if to say, "Here we go."

"The landlord told me that the apartment is too small for me to have all four of you here at one time."

Jerry kicked the chair in front of him to let out his anger. Matt got up to walk away. Ronnie and Julie sat still and just stared down at the floor.

"Wait," Ethel said to all of them. "I'm still going to pick you all up on Fridays. We'll spend the evening together, and then I'll take two of you over to Aunt Mary's to stay the night while two of you stay here. Each week we'll take turns until I can get a bigger place. Next week, I'll pick you up on Saturday, and we're going to go to the skating rink and learn how to skate."

"Really?" Matt asked as he walked back into the small living room with Jerry behind him.

"You think we can really learn how to skate?" Jerry asked as Julie and Ronnie joined in the conversation excitedly.

Julie laid in bed that night with her brothers and mom and wished that the night would never end. She knew that this would be their last night together this way. She tried not to toss and turn as she continued to scratch her poison ivy. Ethel gently reached over and took Julie's hand, patted it gently, and pulled it away from her scratching. Julie thought, *At least she would still get to see her mom, and Aunt Mary was always so nice to them. No matter how many cousins, Aunt Mary always had room for one more.*

Julie awoke the next morning and smelled the pancakes and chipped beef gravy. They had real milk from the carton, the kind that Julie loved. Matt, Jerry, and Ronnie were having a contest to see who could eat the most. "Hey, save me some!" Julie said as she squeezed up to the small kitchen table.

They quickly hurried and cleaned up to get ready to go school shopping. Julie loved the smell of hot cashews roasting as they walked into the old Murphy Store. The wooden floor creaked as she ran across it to the racks of dresses. Ethel took what she could afford and signed the layaway papers.

It was a quiet ride home. Julie hated for the day to end but knew that she would get to see her mom again tomorrow.

Julie knew that the house was really messed up this week. It would take them a long time to clean it up before their dad came home from work. She knew that if they hurried too quickly and didn't do it correctly that their dad would make them do it over again the next day.

Julie's thoughts were interrupted by her mom's voice. "So who wants to go to Coney Island for a hot dog and a chocolate coke?" Ethel asked. All four of them let out a loud squeal.

"Broom first!" Julie called out as they crossed the rickety, wooden bridge that connected the two little towns.

"Shucks!" said Jerry. "She beat us to it."

"You're getting pretty good at remembering that," Ronnie said as he tousled her curly hair.

Ethel waited for them to cross the street and get the house key before starting to pull out. She lingered as Julie entered the front door and turned once more to wave a slow wave good-bye to her mom and then disappeared behind the closed door.

The tears streamed down Ethel's face as she quickly pulled out onto the highway. She couldn't bear to go into the house; it was too painful. There were just too many memories, and she thought that if she went in, she might not be able to leave her children. She was never sure when Ron was home, and she knew that she wasn't up to dealing with him. They talked often enough about the children and the divorce proceedings, but Ethel refused to argue with him and to talk to him when he was drinking.

Julie opened the heavy front door and ran back out onto the porch to wave one more time to her mom. But it was too late. She stood on the porch and continued to wave as the big, old yellow Hudson went down the highway.

Julie sat down on the long, wooden bench in the Sunday school classroom beside her friend, Sarah. Sarah and her sister, Molly, were nice to her. They were not like some of the other girls in the neighborhood. Julie had just gotten promoted to Mrs. Nelson's class. Everyone liked Mrs. Nelson. She would really make one feel that Jesus loved them. She would take the class on trips and give out prizes for learning their memory verses. Most of all, she was friends with her Gramma Emma. They worked at the same factory. Julie had hoped that maybe Mrs. Nelson could talk her Gramma into coming to church.

Mrs. Nelson began to teach them the lesson after they had sung some songs. Julie listened intently as she told them about how the disciples didn't understand why Jesus had died on the cross. Julie thought that it was strange how the disciples didn't understand. Even she understood why Jesus died on the cross. She had learned how that on Easter, Jesus died so that we could have our sins forgiven and that we could be cleansed and be able to go to heaven. Julie looked at Mrs. Nelson puzzled and then over at Sarah. Sarah had straight, brown hair and blue eyes. She had a great sense of humor and could make Julie laugh at anything. Sarah looked over at Julie and gave her a big smile.

Julie wondered if Mrs. Nelson had read the story correctly. Surely, the disciples understood why Jesus had died. Mrs. Nelson continued on saying, "They didn't understand why Jesus would let the soldiers take him away or why Jesus didn't defend himself or do some kind of a miracle like he always had done when they really needed him too. Julie thought about that too. *I guess they did wonder why*, she thought, *but didn't they know that He died because He loved them?* As if reading her mind, Mrs. Nelson said, "They didn't understand that He died to save them. They just thought He had failed them. Later, they understood it, but not that day." "And," Mrs. Nelson continued; she talked slowly and looked at each of them individually, making each one of them feel so special. "Sometimes, we think Jesus doesn't love us when our prayers aren't answered the way we want Him too. We think that He doesn't love us. But He does love us." Mrs. Nelson paused for a moment and looked directly into Julie's eyes. "And we may not always understand why bad things happen to us…but always, always remember that Jesus loves you," she said. As she finished, she looked deep into Julie's eyes.

As they closed in prayer, Julie asked Jesus to forgive her for being angry at Him. She was like the disciples, and she didn't understand, but she promised Him that she would never again forget that He loved her.

Julie hurried for the stairs with Sarah as the second bell rang. Julie stood in the line waiting for the others to go forward. She glanced back at Mrs. Nelson who was still picking up the crayons and papers. She hoped that Mrs. Nelson would tell her Gramma Emma that story at work.

Jerry in little league uniform

Ronnie in little league uniform

Matt in little league uniform

CHAPTER

19

Julie sat on the floor in front of the television with her brothers as they watched the Walt Disney show. Aunt Tassy sat quietly in the big armchair that sat beside the gas space heater. Julie heard her dad upstairs in the bathroom getting ready to go out for the evening.

She didn't know why they just couldn't have stayed up at Gramma Emma's tonight. They were having so much fun playing with their cousins. Gramma Emma had said, "Oh, Ron, just let them stay over tonight." But he had insisted on taking them home. He said it was because they all needed baths, but Julie didn't think that was really the reason. Julie thought it was because her dad was upset at Gramma Emma for telling him that he was drinking too much. She had mentioned it to him when Ron had said that he was going out later that night. Julie had heard their conversation while she stood outside the screened door. When Emma pressed him telling him that he should stay home more with the children, he motioned with his hand for her to stop and told her that it was none of her business.

Julie squirmed to get comfortable and sat on top of her hands hoping to keep them from scratching her poison ivy. She had coated herself with the calamine lotion that her mom had given her. Aunt Tassy had said that she looked like a painted Indian. Julie liked Aunt Tassy. She didn't say much. She would just sit quietly with them and watch whatever program they were watching. She never yelled at them and had the warmest smile. Julie thought that she radiated what Julie called silent love.

Julie turned as she heard her dad speak. He told them to be good and to listen to Aunt Tassy. He then turned and went out the door, closing it behind him as he left.

They went to bed when Aunt Tassy told them it was bedtime. Julie wished that one of her brothers could sleep in her room or that she could go to their room, but her dad had yelled at them one night and said that they could no longer sleep together. He said that they were getting too old to sleep together. Julie didn't feel any older than when her mom had lived with them. He also said that they couldn't lock their doors at night. They usually all kept their doors open except for when sometimes they would all be together, they might close and lock the door. Julie couldn't understand her dad. Although he didn't beat them or hit them, it just seemed like he didn't want to be bothered with them.

Her grammas, mom, and brothers were concerned about how bad the poison ivy had gotten, but her dad was totally indifferent. It was like this even when their mom had lived with them; her dad had always acted that way. Julie remembered when at one time Matt had wrecked the neighbors bicycle, was thrown over the handlebars, and was hurt very badly. Her mom took care of Matt and fixed him up, but her dad had said, "He'll be okay, Ethel! Come on, or we'll be late for bowling." Julie just couldn't understand her dad. He wasn't at all like her uncle Tom. He was a quiet man, but you could tell he really loved his kids. She visited her friend Sarah and Molly's house to play a few times, and though their dad was strict, he would always tease them and make them all laugh. Julie missed those simple things of life, and it made her heart sad to think that their dad didn't care for them.

Julie rolled over in her bed and grabbed her favorite Thumbelina doll. She crawled to the foot of the bed and laid in front of the screened window to feel the gentle breeze. Never had she felt so alone as she watched the continual blink in the sky. The beacon light from the distant airport that was behind their home, circled and shined its faint light into the dark sky. Julie watched it circle over and over again, bringing her little comfort as she began to cry. She cried until she fell asleep.

It was late that night when she heard her dad come home. She wondered why he was raising his voice. She didn't see how anyone could get mad at Aunt Tassy. "Well, I didn't think you'd mind sleeping on the couch one night," he said in his slurred voice. "Fine, fine!" he yelled. "I'll take you home." Aunt Tassy's voice was so soft that Julie couldn't hear her muffled words. "I won't ask you to watch them anymore! Yeah, I'm just the poor sap trying to raise four kids by myself!" he complained as Julie heard the door slam and the venetian blind rattle loudly. Julie lay back down and pulled the sheet up over her, only wishing that she could close the world out. Shortly, she fell into a deep sleep.

Julie rubbed her eyes, confused as she woke up to see that her light was turned on. Julie had left the door open and hoped that somehow she might not feel so alone if she could hear her brothers' voices across the hallway. She blinked her eyes and saw that her dad had shut her bedroom door and locked it. He walked over and sat on the edge of her bed. Julie sat up and rubbed her eyes again and tried to wake up. She felt confused as to why her dad was sitting on her bed.

She could smell the alcohol radiating from him. His eyes were all puffy and cloudy, and he smelt like cigarette smoke. He had a beer in his hand that tilted wildly as if it would spill at any moment. "Well, honey," he said slowly as he tried to form his words. He looked at her and smiled. It was a crooked smile. It was as if it was too heavy from his drinking to be a real smile.

Julie sat quietly as her dad set his beer down carefully onto the floor. "You better let me take a look at that poison ivy of yours," he said as he pulled back the sheet. Julie studied her dad's face. It sounded like the old daddy that used to take her on his lap, but Julie had never seen her daddy act that nicely when he was drinking. She didn't know why, but for some reason, she felt afraid as he pulled the sheet off her. Julie wanted to believe that her daddy really was concerned about her poison ivy, but she felt afraid as he drew near to her. He took her hand and briefly looked at her arms. He then proceeded to touch her whole body. Her heart began to race in terror. She didn't know what was happening to her. She did not know why her daddy was touching her in places that she knew were not to be touched in that way. An old terror arose in her. She somehow felt that she had felt this way once before, but the fear and shame she felt encompassed her and blocked out everything except for the present, which she longed to escape. Julie stared at the dresser. She squirmed and wanted to scream out loud *stop*! Her dad's eyes met hers and commanded her to submit. He continued to touch her, and Julie felt as if all the blood was rushing from her body. She felt nauseated. Her dad then got up, turned out the light, and left her room. Julie sat motionless in the darkness and stared into the blackness as she heard his knee crack when he proceeded to go down the stairs to his bedroom.

Julie threw herself back into the bed and grabbed her blankets and dolls. She placed the dolls tightly around her as if they could protect her. She clutched her Thumbelina doll to her chest so tightly that she could hardly breathe. The world seemed to spin around her. She didn't understand what had happened. All she knew was that for the first time in her life she wanted to die and go to heaven.

✳

Julie heard her dad's voice calling to her from the bathroom. She saw the early morning light flicker across her bed. She lay in her bed in a daze as she slowly woke up. Confused, she wondered if the night before had been a bad dream. But the more she awoke, the more she knew that it wasn't a dream. She still had her blankets and dolls clutched close to her side.

As she lay in bed and faced the wall, she heard her dad in the bathroom getting ready for work. She could hardly believe her ears when she heard him leave the bathroom and pause in her doorway. She could feel his presence without even turning over. "I need my lunch packed," he said and then walked back into the bathroom.

Julie remained still and felt every emotion possible. The one that surfaced above all the others was anger. Julie had never felt such anger in her heart before. She would often get upset with her brothers when she didn't get her way, but she had never felt this kind of anger. She thought to herself, *I'm never, never fixing his lunch or breakfast again. Never!* She laid still and stared at the wall. She wanted to kick it. But as she laid there and her thoughts raced, her heart changed from anger to fear. She knew how her dad thought, at least in part. She remembered the many times of how her dad had treated her mom. She knew that he would make her get up anyway and fix his breakfast and lunch. He could have called Jerry to do it. It was actually Jerry's turn, she remembered. So he wanted her to be in the kitchen when he came downstairs. She couldn't face him. She just couldn't. She didn't want him to talk to her. She didn't want to be near him. Julie threw her sheet aside with her dolls and darted out of her door and down the steps as quickly and quietly as she could so her dad wouldn't hear or see her.

She quickly put a pot of water on for his tea and turned the burner on for his eggs. She grabbed the little iron skillet and put it on the burner. She quickly put the bread in the toaster and threw two more pieces on the table. She ran to the refrigerator and grabbed a piece of ham out of the wrapper and the mustard. She smeared it on so quickly that it oozed over the bread onto her hand. She could hear the grease in the little skillet pop as she ran the mustard back to the refrigerator and grabbed one single egg in one hand and shut the door with her foot. She cracked the egg into the sputtering grease, not caring if the yolk broke or not. She covered it with a lid as she ran to get the toast and butter it quickly. She took the plate from the dish rack and carefully flopped the egg onto it and carried it to the table. She ran to the cupboard to get a teabag and left the cupboard door wide open. She practically flung the tea bag into the cup before turning off all the burners and then took the boiling water and slowly poured it over the tea bag. Some spilled on the toast, and Julie could see that it was a little soggy, but she didn't care. Julie actually felt glad that it was wet. Finally, she yanked open the drawer at the sink and took out the wax paper and a paper sack. With a quick jerk, she tore off a piece of paper, flung the sandwich onto it, and wrapped it tightly. She threw it into the paper sack along with a banana and rolled the bag up. Julie ran up the stairs on tiptoes. She was glad that the bathroom door was still closed. She ran and leaped onto her bed and plunged completely under the sheet and covered her face. Seconds later, she heard the bathroom door open and heard her dad go down the stairs. Julie knew he thought that she was downstairs and that he hadn't seen her under the sheet.

Now what could he do? she thought. He's got his breakfast and lunch. If he calls me, I'll just ignore him or run over to the boys room. Julie stayed under the covers until she heard the front door open and close. She lay there a long time, not realizing that she was trembling and, then after awhile, fell asleep.

"Wake up, Julie," Matt called as he entered Julie's room. But Julie didn't turn over. He went over to her bed and climbed up onto it and shook Julie gently, but she still wouldn't stir. He pulled the sheet back and saw Julie's face plastered with wet curls from sweat. Julie jerked and bolted straight up in bed. "Hey, what's wrong, Jul? You have a bad dream or something?" Matt asked.

Julie just sat still with a look of confusion on her face. "Did you know it's noon? Ronnie wants us to go outside and play ball with him so that he can practice for his Little League game tonight."

"I don't want to," Julie murmured softly.

"How come?" Matt pressed Julie for an answer. "You always beg us to play."

Julie just shrugged her shoulders not wanting to answer. Matt got up slowly and went to leave. He stopped and looked back several times hoping Julie would say something, but she didn't.

Julie got dressed and went downstairs. She grabbed two pieces of bread and went to the refrigerator. There was no peanut butter left. She pulled open the drawers to see if there were any leftovers, but all that was in the drawer was her dad's ham. Below the drawer on the shelf was a case of beer, which was half gone. Julie bent down and looked way back into the refrigerator to see if maybe she was missing something. Finally, she grabbed the mayonnaise jar and the ketchup bottle and made herself a sandwich. *It really was not so bad*, Julie thought as she grabbed a plastic cup out of the cupboard and got a glass of water. She walked to the back porch steps and sat down and watched her brothers play ball.

After awhile, Jerry came running over and said, "Come on, Jul. We need a fourth player."

Julie finished her sandwich and looked up at Jerry. "Come on!" he coaxed her. Julie didn't feel like playing ball, but she didn't want to tell her brother no, so she got up and wiped her hands on her clothes and followed slowly after him.

They finished on time to get cleaned up for Ronnie's ball game. Matt had learned how to make a pot of soup beans from their mom. Julie sat down and tried to butter some bread without tearing holes in it while Matt and Jerry took turns scooping out the soup into bowls for them. They sat quietly and dipped their buttered bread into the hot soup.

Julie went upstairs to wait in her room until it was time for her dad to come home. She sat on the edge of her bed and twitched her fingers nervously. She pulled one finger and then the others and listened to them pop. She glanced out the window over at Lindy's and watched for her dad's car to pull in. Julie felt a resurgence of anger begin to rise within her heart. She felt herself becoming angrier and angrier the more that she thought about her dad coming home. *I wish he would get killed in a bad car accident*, Julie thought as the hate rose in her heart. She knew it had to be wrong to feel that way, and she felt so badly for even thinking it. She grabbed her wrists and dug her fingernails deep into the skin as her emotions welled up within her. She reached for her head and rubbed it and rubbed it as if to rub the memories away. But the more Julie tried to forget, the more they intensified. She hit her forehead with her rolled up fist lightly at first as if to help her to think good thoughts, but soon, she was hitting her head with both of her fists as if she could pound the thoughts out of her head. Julie began to cry. She lay down on her bed and grabbed her big doll and held it close to her and fell asleep.

Ronnie woke her up when they were ready to go. Julie got up quickly and followed Ronnie out of the room. She stopped for a minute to try to tidy up her hair, which was flat on one side.

The four of them climbed into the backseat of the big, green Chevy. Julie clung close to Ronnie who looked so grown up in his baseball uniform. She stared at the floor past her grass-stained sneakers. She couldn't bear to look up at her dad who was now getting into the driver's seat.

As they got to the ball field, Julie started to feel excited for the first time that day. It was only Monday night, but Julie knew that her mom would be at the ballgame. She ran ahead with her brothers and ignored her dad. As soon as she reached the bleachers, she saw her mom and ran to her.

Ethel saw Julie coming and moved her purse so that she could sit down beside her. She wrapped her arm around her little girl, and Julie laid her head in her mom's lap. Ethel gently stroked Julie's curls as she watched the ballgame. Julie was glad when her dad didn't come up and sit with them.

"Look, Julie!" Ethel said and pointed to home base. "Ronnie's up to bat!"

Julie sat up and looked over at her brother. She could see Matt and Jerry in the dugout in the distance. The umpire called strike one as the ball flew past. The next two were balls. Julie crossed her fingers for good luck for her brother as the pitcher released the ball. Julie heard the crack of wood as the ball went flying out into left field. Ronnie took off and ran the bases, stopping at second. Julie clapped her hands as she watched her brother. She was so proud of him.

After the game was over, Julie ran down the bleachers to avoid her dad who was coming up the bleachers to talk to her mom. Julie ran to the chain-linked fence and pressed her face against it as she looked through the crowd of uniforms trying to find her brothers. She stood there waiting as the crowd began to thin. She turned and saw that her mom and dad were talking and looking down at her. She knew that they were probably talking about her. Her mind raced as she wondered what her dad was saying about her to her mom. She didn't understand anything that had happened. She didn't want to talk about it or even think about it. It made her feel ashamed and dirty, and she didn't know why. She didn't know what she had done to feel so awful. She didn't want anyone to ever, ever know what had happened to her.

Matt joined her and interrupted her thoughts as he put his arm around her shoulder. "You won," Julie said and looked up at him with a big smile.

"Did you see Ronnie's big hit?" Jerry asked as he came running up to join them.

"I sure did," Julie answered. She could see Jerry just beaming with pride for their big brother.

Ronnie pressed past his team players and joined his brothers and sister. He sheepishly received the praise that they poured out upon him. Ethel joined them and gave them all a hug and kiss. "I'll see you up at Gramma's tomorrow." Julie grabbed her mom's hand tightly and listened to her talk to Ronnie about the ballgame. She never wanted to let go of her mom's hand. Ethel gave them one more kiss good-bye and then broke away slowly to leave. Julie could see the tears in her mom's eyes. She hid her own tears deeply within her heart where no one could ever see them and ask her why.

They raced to the car and hopped in to wait for their dad. He slammed the door very hard as he got in. Julie glanced from side to side at her brothers. They looked as puzzled as she felt. She couldn't help wonder why he was so upset now. They drove slowly back to their home.

After awhile, Ron glanced into the rearview mirror at Ronnie. "That was a good hit you made today."

Ronnie beamed with pride at his dad's approval. But Julie couldn't help but wonder if her dad came to the ballgames to see Ronnie play or just to get a chance to talk to their mom. She didn't trust her dad. She knew that she would never be able to trust him again.

Julie wasn't surprised when they drove right past their home without stopping. Jerry leaned over and whispered quietly, "We're going to get a soda." But Julie didn't care about getting a soda. She knew that it was just an excuse for her dad to go into the beer tavern to drink. They drove down the small dirt lane into the parking lot at Barker's Tavern. Their dad went into the small bar and came out with four orange sodas. He leaned into the car and handed them to Ronnie and Jerry and said that he would be back out in a little bit.

Julie liked the feel of the cold bottle clasped between her hands. She sipped her soda slowly to make it last longer because she knew from the times past that her dad would be inside the bar for a long time. It was dark when they saw their dad come out of the bar. Julie saw him stumble as he fumbled in his pockets looking for his car keys.

Julie hurried up the stairs as soon as they got home. She washed up quickly and put more lotion on her poison ivy that was starting to dry up. She ran and jumped onto Ronnie's bed and waited for her brothers to come upstairs.

Matt looked at Julie as he entered the room. "Julie, Dad said that you couldn't sleep in here anymore." Julie didn't answer Matt but stayed glued to Ronnie's bed. Ronnie and Jerry heard Matt's conversation as they entered the room.

"You'll get in trouble, Jul," Ronnie said as he sat down on the edge of his bed and took his shoes off.

"I don't care," Julie said defiantly as she lay down and leaned against Ronnie's wall. Matt and Jerry and Ronnie all glanced at one another. Never had they seen their little sister so defiant to their dad's rules.

Julie remained awake in the darkness. She could hear her brothers breathing as they quietly slept. Julie stilled her thoughts and shut out the memories of the night before. *At least tonight, she would be safe*, she thought.

The weeks began to pass quickly. The leaves on the trees speckled the mountainside in an array of fall colors of oranges and yellows. The cooler breezes beckoned in a new season. Julie could almost forget that terrible night at times, but then at other times, it seemed to come back upon her, terrifying her in the night. They were spending most of their evenings up at Gramma Emma's house. Aunt Tassy had never watched them again.

Julie was in the third grade now. Matt was in the fifth; Jerry, the sixth; and Ronnie, the seventh. They still walked to school every day although Julie had heard that they were soon going to have a school bus pick them up. Julie tried to focus on the new school year. This was the year that if she didn't miss any school days, she would be asked to be the school queen of the spring May Day. Julie was determined in her mind that no matter what, she would not miss any school days that year. There was a new girl at school this year. Julie thought that she looked like a little China doll. Every curl was in place, and she wore the nicest clothes that Julie had ever seen. Julie thought at first that she was shy but learned quickly that she was just plain mean. She wouldn't let Julie play with her or the other girls at recess. So Julie was left to play alone. She would make fun of Julie's wrinkled clothes and her frizzled curls. Julie couldn't figure out what was wrong with her that made people dislike her. She couldn't figure out why her dad treated her the way he did. There must be something wrong with her, but she couldn't figure it out. She couldn't talk to anyone about it, not even her brothers. The shame and reproach and fear that she felt kept her quiet. Julie thought at first that maybe she had imagined that night with her dad. But all too soon, she realized that nothing that she was experiencing was imagined.

Julie kept the blinds up so that the streetlight would dance across her room in the dark night and comfort her. But one night, when she was awakened in the middle of the night, Julie thought that she saw a shadow in the faint light of her bedroom. She then felt her baby dolls and pillow being pulled away from her. She could smell in the darkness the odor of alcohol and lingering cigarette smoke. She bolted up in her bed. She heard the bathroom door close and then saw her bedroom door open. She saw the outline of her dad's figure leave the room and heard his knee creak as he went down the stairs. Shortly, she heard the bathroom door reopen and heard one of her brothers go back to bed. She lay awake a long time. She listened carefully to see if she could hear her dad's steps return. She felt herself trembling and pulled her dolls close to her side and clutched them tightly. She wound the Thumbelina doll and let the tingle of its music calm her fears. Her mind raced in confusion and fear. Her emotions surged within her. *Why? Why?* she thought. *What is wrong with me? Why doesn't anyone want to play with me? Be my friend? What am I doing wrong that my dad wants to do these things to me? Who can I tell? Who would believe me?* No one ever believed Tonya. She had even heard people talking and blaming Tonya for breaking up their family.

One day, Julie came home and changed her school clothes and hung them up so that they wouldn't get wrinkled. She was glad that they were going up to Gramma Emma's house that night. There she would be safe.

"You'd better hang your clothes up so they don't get wrinkled," Julie told her brothers as she entered their room. They were all trying to get their homework done before they went up to their Gramma's house.

"We will later," Matt said.

"You'll get made fun of if you don't hang them up and they get all wrinkled," Julie continued.

"By who?" Jerry laid down his pencil and looked up at Julie.

"By the kids at school," Julie answered. She picked up a shirt and hung it on the doorknob.

"Someone making fun of you, Julie?" Ronnie asked concerned.

"Yeah, when I wore my dress to school one day, it was all wrinkled," Julie replied as she picked up a pair of their jeans.

"Well, we will beat them up next time," Jerry assured her.

"You can't beat up girls, Jerry," Julie said. "You'll get in trouble with the principal."

"Well, they shouldn't be making fun of you," Jerry said defiantly.

For weeks, they had been staying with their grandma most nights. On weekends, they were with their mom. Recently, they had met Bob, their mom's new friend. Julie was disheartened as she now knew with the divorce becoming final and Bob being in the picture, there was no hope of her mom and dad ever getting back together again.

Julie cast all her cares aside as much as she could. Today was Tuesday, and they were going to get to see their mom at Gramma Winnie's house. Julie entered the back door and could see the condensation on the kitchen windows. She could smell the fried potatoes and pork chops cooking. Julie grabbed the plates and began to set the table. She then ran into the living room to watch television with her brothers while watching for her mom.

Julie saw the car pull up in front of the house and darted out the front door. "Hi, Mom!" Julie yelled as she ran to meet Ethel at her car.

"Hi, sweetheart," Ethel said and leaned down to give Julie a big hug and kiss.

Julie thought that her mom looked tired tonight. "Hey, I've got something for you," Ethel said excitedly and gave Julie a bag that she held in her hand. Julie saw the bag was from Murphy's and smiled up at her mom. She then pulled out the Crayola crayons that were in the bag.

"Mom, this is the big crayon box I needed for art class!" Julie squealed with delight. "Now I can draw nice pictures!" Ethel was so glad to see Julie's smile. She knew for some reason that Julie had not been herself lately. Ethel was greeted at the door by the boys and gave them all a big hug. She then went to help Winnie with supper while Julie lingered behind with her brothers.

"It doesn't take much to make Julie happy," Winnie said to Ethel as she flipped the pork chops in the old cast iron skillet.

"No, Mom, it doesn't," Ethel replied.

"Will the boys mind that they didn't get something?" Winnie asked.

"I mentioned it in passing the other day to them when Julie wasn't around, and they said they didn't mind. They seem to understand one another that way, Mom. I can't explain it."

"How are the kids adjusting to everything, Ethel?" Winnie asked as she scraped the fried potatoes into a large crock bowl.

"I don't know, Mom. I worry about them so much." Ethel went to get glasses for their water.

"Give them some of the milk in the fridge, Ethel," Winnie said pointing to the refrigerator door.

"Ronnie gets very withdrawn at times. Jerry reacts with such hurt and anger, and Matt seems to always be trying to find his niche and help everyone. Julie seems deeply troubled about something, but she won't talk to me about anything."

"What do they think of Bob?"

"I'm not sure," Ethel said slowly. She poured the milk into their glasses. "I introduced them the other day, and they just took it in stride and tried to shrug it off. I hear through their small, little grapevine that Julie calls him a bald-headed eagle, if that gives you any idea. I don't think they like the idea of Bob coming into my life especially since he has three children. They aren't ready to share me with them, I'm sure. I believe they're still hoping that their daddy and I will get back together. They hear too much and understand too little."

"Well, if Ron had not—" Winnie continued.

But Ethel interrupted her and said, "No, Mom, let it go." Ethel patted Winnie's broad shoulders and went into the living room. "Let's eat," she said to the foursome. They jumped up from in front of the television and ran past their mom into the kitchen.

Julie ran as fast as she could run to try to catch up with Matt who lingered behind Jerry and Ronnie. "Wait up!" Julie called out. The cool wind blew against Julie's face and tossed her hair in all directions. Matt called out for Ronnie and Jerry to wait. "Wait for me!" Julie pleaded as she panted, almost out of breath, at Matt's side. "I can't walk up the hill that fast." Julie walked in silence beside her three brothers as they approached the school building. They had all noticed Julie's quiet spells. They were all trying to cope the best way that they knew how.

But no one could ever know what Julie was trying to cope with. Julie had not been successful in her latest attempts to fend off her dad. Too often, she would wake up in horror at what her dad was doing to her. She would push him away in the black of the night with the blinds pulled down tight. Julie would cry out, and he would get up and leave. Julie would lay in her bed, the terror of the night upon her. She would take her pillow and put it between her legs. She groped in the night to find her dolls and put them on either side of her. She would at first go toward the wall in an effort to feel safer. When that failed, she would try to take up the whole bed so that he wouldn't be able to sit down unless he awoke her. She would force herself to stay awake and listened for any sound of him coming into her room. But time after time, she failed. She would finally fall asleep, and then all of her plans would just fall apart as she tossed and turned. At first, Julie thought it was only because her dad was drinking. But he would continue to grab for her when he was sober at breakfast. He had grown wise to her tactics too. He would call her in the morning to make his breakfast and would deliberately make sure that he was downstairs before she could finish preparing it.

Julie tried to dodge him in every way possible. She was so tired, so exhausted, so ashamed, and so afraid. She would go to the bathroom and run the water so no one could hear her cry and cry. She would sit on the edge of the claw foot tub and wipe away her tears with a cold rag. What pleasure could her dad derive out of seeing her in so much pain? Why would he want to continually hurt her? What was wrong with her that would lead him to her? What was she doing that encouraged her dad to do what he was doing?

Who could she tell? Who would believe a nine-year-old little girl? They would blame her as they had blamed Tonya. They would hate her and say it was all her fault. They'd say that she was just trying to get attention. Worst of all, what would happen to them? Their dad had said that if he wasn't raising them, they would all be split up and go into an orphan's home. No matter what happened in her life, Julie knew she would die if she was ever taken away from her brothers. She could never risk saying anything that might cause this.

Everyone in the little valley seemed to think that her dad was a great man for taking the four of them and raising them. Julie had often heard the adults in her community run her mom down. They'd say, "How could she have left her children?"

Some would say, "Well, Ron may drink a little, but bless his heart for raising those children all by himself." Julie couldn't understand why they thought her dad was some kind of a hero. Julie could not help but think of her dear Tonya. *What about Tonya? Did anyone ever think about what had happened to her? No, that was just pushed under the rug.* Julie had heard that she had given birth to a little baby boy late that summer. Julie had not seen her since that last day when she had said good-bye. She had heard her gramma telling her mom that she was having a hard time on her own with a baby and that she was dating men that were much older than her. Julie couldn't help what others thought, and though she was just a kid, she, more than anyone else, believed Tonya.

Julie kept all of her pain inside and continually tried to think of new ways to protect herself. She prayed every night earnestly and asked Jesus to protect her and hoped that they wouldn't have to stay at home at night.

"Come on, Jul," Matt called out and interrupted her thoughts. They had reached the school's front door. Julie usually loved school. It was the one area of her life that she could stand out. She was an A student and was well-liked by the students. That was until Lindsey had come to their school. Of all the times in her life, when she needed friends the most, Lindsey would rule the classroom and playground not letting any of the kids play with Julie. If they did, they would be shunned also.

Today, nothing could change Julie's happy mood. She had her new box of crayons, and she was going to draw a great picture for art class. Julie placed the new crayons on her desk. She opened the box and pressed them to her nose smelling the waxy fragrant odor. As Mrs. Mahonie passed out the new art pages, Julie was surprised to hear her name being called softly. She looked up and across the aisle and heard Lindsey calling her name and staring at her.

"You got new crayons?" Lindsey asked.

"Yeah," Julie answered. She was not sure of Lindsey's intentions.

No matter how hard Julie had tried, Lindsey had refused to be her friend and would have nothing to do with her. She would absolutely be livid when Julie would score a higher test grade or out jump her at jump rope during recess. If Lindsey wasn't around, the other girls would play with her and be nice. But if Lindsey was around, they would tease her and make fun of her hair, her clothes, or anything they could think of just to be mean to her.

"Can I borrow your crayons?" Lindsey asked as her eyes met Julie's.

"Yeah," Julie answered a little reluctantly. She was puzzled over Lindsey's mannerisms. Lindsey reached across the aisle to take the crayons, but Julie grabbed them quickly. "Will you let me play with all of you at recess time?"

"Yeah, you can play with us," Lindsey retorted, "just give me the crayons." Lindsey placed them on her desk for Mrs. Mahonie to see.

Julie could hardly wait until lunch recess. She looked at the clock on the wall above the chalkboard. It was almost noon. Julie was so excited. She had already read the lunch menu, and they were having her favorite that day, shepherd's pie, butter bread, chocolate pudding, and a whole box of milk. Julie loved lunch.

Julie took her crayons off Lindsey's desk as the bell rang and put them carefully inside her desk. She quickly got into line to get her lunch. She ate every bite and finished on time to run and catch up with Sarah, her friend from church. But as Julie approached, Sarah turned and ran away with the other girls. Julie ran outside the school behind them. She thought that Sarah might not have seen her. But when she got outside, Julie couldn't find any of the girls. It was awhile before Julie had seen them playing jump rope over in the far ball field. Julie ran over to join them.

"What do you want?" Lindsey asked.

"I want to play." Julie answered puzzled by Lindsey's question.

"Well, you can't play!" Lindsey snickered.

Julie felt her face flush. She glanced at Sarah and the other girls from her classroom, but they all turned away from her as if they didn't know her.

"But you said I could play with you if I let you use my crayons!" Julie said defiantly. She bit her quivering lip to hold back the tears.

"Well, I changed my mind!" Lindsey returned tartly. She turned her back on Julie and motioned to the other girls to swing the rope. Julie stood outside the circle of girls and looked at her friends. She could feel her eyes starting to glisten as the tears rushed forward. She turned to run away. "Go ahead, crybaby!" Lindsey's words taunted Julie. Julie could hear the other girls, even her friends, laugh and ridicule her as she ran away.

The weeks continued, and nothing changed at home or at school. Julie began to wonder if it would be wrong to take your own life and to die. She had heard that it was wrong and that you could go to hell for doing that. Julie didn't want to go to hell. Her only hope was that someday she could go to heaven and that someday she wouldn't feel the sorrow that she felt now. But would Jesus even want her now? Maybe she wouldn't go to heaven now? Maybe that's why no one would play with her? Maybe she was just a bad person?

Every day she went to school, and every night, she cried herself to sleep, terrified that her dad would come into her room at night. She didn't know why Jesus wouldn't just take her up to heaven. Julie felt that she couldn't go on living this way. She felt so tired and so hopeless. She was tired of sitting alone on the swing by herself and watching everyone else play. She was tired of being afraid at night. She was tired of hoping for life to change. She was just tired of everything. She didn't have the strength to care about anything anymore.

Julie, second grade princess; Julie, first grade
flower girl; and Julie, third grade queen.

CHAPTER

20

Julie hurried to get her share of the cleaning done. She had yelled "broom first" feeling good to finally be in charge of something. She was in a foul mood and knew it, but she just didn't care anymore. What little she could feel in her heart felt icy cold. Julie stopped to sit down and rest a minute. She rested her aching head on her hands that still held the broom. Slowly, she let the broom slip from her hands while rubbing her head and hoping that her headache would go away. Julie knew that there weren't any aspirins downstairs for she had seen the empty bottle in the cabinet earlier.

As Julie sat wringing her hands and staring at the wall, she dug her fingernails into her wrists and wished that she could claw through herself but didn't know why. She felt her heart harden into a tight knot as she refused to cry and let any tears break out. Crying was for babies, and she would never let anyone call her a cry baby again.

"Julie, can I use the broom?" Ronnie called up from the kitchen.

"No!" Julie screamed back.

Ronnie came up the steps and sat down beside Julie. "How come you won't let any of us use the broom?"

"'Cause I'm in charge!" Julie snapped harshly.

"Well, if you're not using it, then that's not fair," Ronnie growled back and went to take the broom from Julie.

Julie stood straight up and grabbed the broom quickly. She placed her hands behind her back and held onto the broom with a tight grip.

"Let go, Jul," Ronnie said softly.

"Make me!" Julie shouted.

Ronnie had had enough. He raised his fist and was ready to let go but stopped short. He could plow into Matt or Jerry, but it was harder for him to hit Julie. "What is your problem?" he asked. "What is wrong with you lately?"

Julie bit her lip and felt the tears coming but refused to cry. "Nothing's the matter with me!" she yelled. "You hear me… there's nothing wrong with me!" she screamed at the top of her voice and then gave Ronnie a hard push. Ronnie was caught off guard and stumbled against the stair rail. Julie knew that she had crossed the line with Ronnie. She ran as fast as she could into the bathroom, slammed the door shut behind her and threw the lock in place. Here she would sit until she knew that her brother had cooled off. She couldn't help thinking, *What was wrong with her?*

Julie joined her brothers later while they were watching television. They gave her a sad glance. Julie knew that she had hurt all of their feelings. She felt so badly inside thinking that it would've been better that they hit her than to feel this kind of pain from hurting them.

The next morning, they all got up early. They had stayed all night at Gramma Emma's house. Quickly, they hurried to leave and get down to their house to get ready for Sunday school. "Do you want to come with us, Gramma?" Julie asked as she grabbed for her jacket.

"Not this time, Julie," Gramma Emma answered softly. "I'll come sometime." Emma smiled at her little granddaughter as she watched her dart out the door to follow her brothers.

Julie paused as she went out onto the porch and looked up the hill where the little white house stood. It's red shutters were fading, and it was deserted. The bushes had overgrown the property, and the grass was tall. Julie thought the house looked as lonely and sad as she felt.

She hurried down the hill and almost tripped over her untied shoestrings. She didn't call out to her brothers. She wasn't sure if they would even want to wait up for her. She ran as quickly as she could to catch up with Ronnie who was walking off by himself. Matt and Jerry were walking ahead. She finally caught up with Ronnie and walked slowly by his side. He didn't look up. Julie thought he looked sad. His head was hung down, his shirt tail hung out untucked, and his hair was uncombed. She reached for his hand. Ronnie raised his head and looked at her and searched her face. "I'm sorry, Ronnie," Julie said softly. She looked into her big brother's dark-brown eyes. Her eyes pleaded with him to forgive her. "I'm so sorry." Ronnie gave Julie a faint smile and squeezed her hand as they walked down the hill.

The tiny church was full of people that morning as they entered the building. There was a guest preacher, and they were all told to stay upstairs today. Julie had never heard the singing so vibrant. When the guest preacher got up to preach, Julie listened intently as the man spoke. She was surprised at all that he was saying. It was as if he knew every thought and hurt of her heart. Julie had always loved Sunday school. But lately, she couldn't understand God. Why wouldn't he help her? Was he mad at her? Was she a bad person because of what her dad was doing? How could God love her and let her life be the way it was? Surely God must not love her.

Maybe, God was not real, Julie had thought one day. She had overheard her brothers talking about Santa and how he was just make-believe. *Well, maybe Jesus was make-believe too*, she had thought.

The more her thoughts raced through her mind and heart, the more on target the preacher preached. It scared Julie a little. It was as if the preacher could read her mind and thoughts. She had made up her mind that she would be angry at God. If God didn't love her and wouldn't help her, then she wouldn't love God either. The preacher just continued on.

"But Jesus knows how you feel. He knows your secret hurts. He knows all the pain you have inside. No matter how you feel toward Jesus…He loves you. He will always love you. He has never left you. He will never forsake you. He died on the cross just for you because you matter to Him. He knows how it feels to be hurt, forsaken, and rejected by the people you love. Just come to Him and give Him your heart."

It was more than the words that the man spoke. It was the feeling that Julie felt all around her. She had felt it in the songs, the music, and now the preaching. Julie had never felt such a strong presence of love as she did that day. Julie let the words settle in her heart. She wanted so much to go up to the altar as the preacher had asked but felt too shy. If only her brothers that were sitting beside her would go up, then she would follow them. Julie peeked out of her eyes at her brothers as the preacher led in prayer and beckoned people to come. She held on so tightly to the pew in front of her that her knuckles turned white. She could see that her brothers also were holding on tightly to the pew. Julie wondered if they were feeling what she was feeling. Suddenly, Julie saw movement beside her, and as she looked up, she saw her Ronnie going into the aisle to go up to the altar. Jerry followed closely behind him and then Matt. Julie hurried behind them. As tears came down her face, she didn't care who saw her. She didn't care if everyone called her a crybaby. Somehow, she knew that she was feeling Jesus' love. Somehow, that was all that mattered to her. None of her questions were answered, but as she knelt at the little wooden altar beside her three big brothers and saw the tears on their faces, she knew that something wonderful was happening on that day as she asked Jesus to come in and stay in her heart. She didn't understand all that the preacher had said, but one thing she knew for sure, Jesus was real and that He loved her very much.

The cold winter seemed to pass quickly. Julie loved the thought of spring coming. She had a newfound hope that she could not explain. Maybe it was just knowing that she was not alone anymore, for at night, she could still feel that same presence of love that she had felt that day at Sunday school. She had won a picture of Jesus as a prize in Sunday school. It glowed in the dark. Every night, Julie would take the cardboard picture of Jesus knocking on the door and hold it up to her bedroom light for a few minutes. Then, when she would turn off the light, the little cross on the picture would shine brightly through the dark night.

Because her blind was broken, she had it rolled up causing the streetlight to shine brightly into her room. She knew that her dad couldn't sneak in and pull it down now because it would fall down onto him if he did. God was helping her. There were still nights that she didn't succeed at thwarting off her dad's plans, and the night terrors would begin all over again. But Julie could only try to get through each day and hoped that somehow something in her life would change.

Julie now had two friends. Sarah and her sister Molly had given their hearts to Jesus also. They had gotten to be good friends at Sunday school. The three vowed that they would always be friends and that they would not let anyone separate them ever again.

At about this same time, Julie learned that her mom and dad's divorce was soon to be final. She now knew that her mom and dad would never get back together again. She didn't like her mom's new friend Bob who had come into their life. She felt that he took her away from them with what little time they had with their mom. Julie was not willing to share her mom. And Julie wasn't sure what to make of her dad's behavior. He was dating a woman who sometimes stayed overnight with them at their home. It seemed that the more that she was there, the more that her dad left her alone in the night. Julie began to sleep better as the abuse subsided. She now had two friends to play with at school. Julie began to smile again, and slowly, she began to return to her old self.

Julie began to look forward to the spring May Day that was held every year. On the first year of school, she had not missed any school days and was honored to be a flower girl. Though Julie loved being a tomboy, she was thrilled to be asked to wear the beautiful, flower girl dress. It was a beautiful gown of lace and ribbon, and Julie felt like a princess. The second year in school, Julie again had gone all year without missing a single school day. This year, her mom had told her that she would get to be a princess in the May Day program. Julie could hardly believe it when she got to wear the beautifully laced and ribboned gown of the princess. It was a beautiful pastel pink and was much fuller and prettier than the flower girl dress. But this year, being her third year in school, her mom had said that anyone who went three years and didn't miss a single school day would be chosen to be the queen of the May Day. Julie was sure that there could be no greater honor than to be the May Day queen. As the year went on and spring neared, Julie began to wonder if she would be asked. She had not missed a single day. Even when she had the flu, she went to school sick. But when they began to practice for the May Day program, Mrs. Mahonie had her practice the maypole dance with the rest of the children. Mrs. Mahonie really liked Lindsey, and Julie began to wonder if she might just ask her to be the May Day queen. Maybe her mom was wrong, maybe they just picked who they wanted to pick.

One day before school let out, Mrs. Mahonie asked Julie to stay after school. Julie felt so embarrassed. Lindsey waited until Mrs. Mahonie had turned her back and then said, "Whoa… you're in trouble now! Probably because your desk is such a mess." Lindsey laughed, and the other girls joined in until Mrs.

Mahonie turned around and gave them a look to be quiet. Julie thought that maybe Lindsey was right. She had never known anyone to be asked to stay after school unless they were in some kind of trouble. Sarah whispered to Julie, "Don't worry, Julie. I'll wait for you outside, and we'll walk home from school together." Julie gave Sarah a quick faint smile and then looked at the papers sticking out of her desk. She tried to stuff them in better as she heard the bell ring. Julie sat quietly at her desk and waited for Mrs. Mahonie to get done writing on the chalkboard.

Mrs. Mahonie put down the chalk and went back to her desk. Julie thought that maybe she had forgotten that she was there. Julie waited patiently. Under her shallow breath, she whispered a prayer, "Please, Jesus…don't let me be in trouble."

Mrs. Mahonie took her glasses off and let them hang dangling from the gold chain that she wore around her neck. She motioned with her hand for Julie to come up to her desk.

"Julie, what do you think of the maypole dance that we're doing?" Mrs. Mahonie asked.

Julie was caught totally off guard with Mrs. Mahonie's question about the maypole dance. All that she could still think about were the papers that were still sticking out of her desk.

Mrs. Mahonie saw the puzzled look on Julie's face. "Do you like doing the maypole dance?" she asked.

Julie was about to say, yes, she loved doing the maypole dance. But she remained quiet. She felt confused and unsure of how to answer the question. Her young mind raced. If she said yes, maybe she would not be asked to be the queen. She couldn't understand why Mrs. Mahonie was only asking her about the maypole dance and not asking the rest of the class.

Julie could see Mrs. Mahonie's big, blue eyes still locked on her as she waited for her answer. "The maypole dance is very nice," Julie answered slowly.

"But do you like doing it?" Mrs. Mahonie pressed.

Julie was now becoming bothered by Mrs. Mahonie's persistence. She couldn't help thinking that everyone, especially adults, seemed to think that kids were just plain stupid. Julie didn't trust adults, and she especially didn't trust Mrs. Mahonie.

"It's okay," Julie answered firmly and looked directly into Mrs. Mahonie's big, blue eyes. Julie didn't want to jeopardize her chances of not being asked to be the May Day queen. Julie knew that all of the other girls in her class had missed many days of school, especially Lindsey.

Mrs. Mahonie sat quietly and tapped her pencil on the desk and stared at Julie and didn't say a word. Julie began to feel very awkward. She put her hands behind her back, hiding her scratched arms and broken fingernails. She knew that her hair was probably a mess. It always was a mess at the end of the day. And of all days, she had dropped her bread on her lap and dirtied her blouse. She knew that she didn't look like a queen, but she had worked so hard to become one.

Mrs. Mahonie leaned back in her chair and studied the young girl. After a long pause, Mrs. Mahonie began to speak, "Julie, you do know that the third grade must choose a queen for the May Day?"

Julie had been staring down at her feet, unable, in her nervousness, to look up at Mrs. Mahonie. She inched closer to Mrs. Mahonie's big oak desk to hide her worn-out shoes. Julie couldn't believe what her ears were hearing. Julie felt her heart begin to race, and she could feel her face flush. She could hardly contain her excitement. She could not look up or form any words to speak.

"Would you like to be the queen of the May Day?" Mrs. Mahonie asked.

Julie jerked her head up and looked at Mrs. Mahonie. She tried to read her expression to see if she was playing some cruel joke. But Julie was too shocked to answer. The word yes just clung to the roof of her mouth.

Mrs. Mahonie sat up straight in her chair and drew closer to the child. The young girl puzzled her. She waited for Julie's answer. She leaned forward in the big chair across the desk toward Julie. "Would you like to be the May Day queen?" she asked again.

Julie quickly shook her head and answered, "Yes, ma'am."

"Yes, ma'am," she repeated again, afraid that she might not have been heard. She stood frozen and tried to read Mrs. Mahonie's expressionless face. Julie was so unsure of what was happening.

"Then from now on, you'll not be practicing the maypole dance, and you'll be joining the other classes to practice for the queen's court."

Julie stood there quietly, waiting for Mrs. Mahonie to continue to speak; however, she just reached for her glasses and turned back to work on the papers on her desk.

"Thank you, Mrs. Mahonie," Julie said. She paused to see if Mrs. Mahonie would reply. Mrs. Mahonie continued to look down at the papers on her desk. Julie quickly turned and went to her desk to get her books and coat and then hurried from the classroom. Her heart was still racing, and she couldn't wait to get some fresh air. She couldn't wait to catch up with her brothers and tell them the good news.

As Julie entered the hallway, she was surprised to see Sarah. She had forgotten that Sarah had told her that she would wait for her. Sarah gave her a quick nod and then shot Julie a warning look as she glanced to the group that stood behind her. Julie stood holding her books in her arms and stared at Lindsey and the other girls.

"So what did you do to get kept after class?" Lindsey asked. She gloated and looked at the other girls. The girls giggled and waited for Lindsey to continue. Lindsey could hardly conceal her joy of wanting to embarrass Julie in front of her classmates.

Sarah shifted her feet nervously, not knowing what to expect. Julie stood quietly as she watched Lindsey and the girls giggle.

Lindsey walked up to Julie. "So what did Mrs. Mahonie want?" she asked again as she taunted Julie.

"Well," Julie started. She hung her head as if she had done some terrible thing.

"Yeah," Lindsey edged her on.

Julie stood quietly. Now it was her turn to play the game. Sarah protectively drew closer to Julie. She was not going to let Julie stand alone against Lindsey this time.

"So?" Lindsey continued.

"So?" the other girls chorused in.

"Well," Julie spoke slowly and seriously. She turned her head ever so slightly and gave a subtle wink to Sarah. Julie turned to Lindsey and continued, "Mrs. Mahonie wanted to ask me a question. That's all." Julie bit her lip and looked straight into Lindsey's eyes. She knew that the answer was just enough to peak her curiosity.

"What kind of question?" Lindsey asked. She was caught off guard by Julie's confident manner.

"Oh, it's nothing that would interest you," Julie answered. She looked at the other girls' puzzled faces. Her eyes met Sarah's, and Julie gave her a quick smile. Sarah smiled back. She had gotten to know that her little friend could be a force to be reckoned with.

"Yeah, you just don't want to tell us that you got into trouble," Lindsey said smugly.

"Yeah," the other girls joined in."

Julie turned to Sarah. "We better get going, don't you think, Sarah?"

The duo started to walk away. Julie knew that Lindsey wouldn't give up so quickly. Lindsey and the girls followed closely behind Sarah and Julie. Lindsey gave Sarah a cross look and pushed in between her and Julie.

"Scaredy cat," Lindsey said. "Just tell us. We'll find out on Monday anyway."

Julie stopped and turned to face Lindsey and the other girls. Sarah rejoined Julie and stood beside her. "You're right," Julie said. "You'll find out Monday anyway."

Lindsey and the girls stood smugly in front of Julie. They could hardly wait to hear what Julie had to say.

"Mrs. Mahonie asked if I would like to be the queen for the May Day, and I answered yes." Julie smiled a big smile as she watched Lindsey and the other girls' faces, the one that made her smile the most was that of her good friend Sarah.

"No way!" Lindsey said loudly and looked at Julie in disbelief. "You're lying!"

Sarah turned to Julie and gave her a big smile. Julie smiled back and turned with her friend and walked down the hallway leaving the stunned girls to themselves.

"You're just making that all up!" Lindsey yelled down the hallway after them. But Julie and Sarah just kept on walking. They saw Molly, Sarah's older sister, coming toward them in the other direction and joined her to tell her the good news.

Julie walked home slowly after Sarah and Molly had parted ways with her at the fork in the road. She felt the spring breeze against her face as it rustled through her curly hair. The air was fresh; the breeze, warm. Julie could feel the warmth of the sun's rays upon the back of her neck. She heard the birds in the treetops singing happily. She watched two bunnies nibble at a newly planted garden. Julie could not help feeling that life was like the seasons—some brought sunshine, some brought rain.

Julie pounced through the front gate and went to run into the house. She stopped quickly to pet Mamie who was waiting patiently for her at the front door. "Hi, ole girl!" she chirped. "I get to be the May Day queen!" Mamie wagged her tail and licked her little friend's hand.

Julie ran into the house and plopped down in front of the television and blocked her brothers' view.

"Hey, move, Jul!" the three of them chimed in. "We can't see!"

"I got to tell you something!" Julie exclaimed.

There was a shared happiness as Julie shared her whole story to her brothers.

They had become a family, the four of them. They shared their joys. They shared their sorrows.

The summer came, and Julie played ball with her brothers. They went on hikes together and played in the old barn. They climbed the old cherry tree and ate as many cherries as they could without getting a bellyache.

Julie lived for the times they could be with their mom. They had seemed to grow into a routine of life. She knew that her mom loved them desperately. She tried to make sure that they were eating right. She would buy them clothes and wash and iron them every week. She would take them skating and to the drive-in to see a movie. She cared if they had been sick or got a cut. *Oh, if she could just live with them,* Julie thought. She wished that her dad would move out and her mom would live with them. Then her dad could visit them and she would be safe from him.

But summer brought many new surprises for Julie. Julie could never get used to how fast life could change. She tried to hold on to the new hope that she had found in Jesus. Vacation Bible school would start soon, and she was excited to be in the junior class with her brothers and Sarah and Molly. They were going to make beautiful arts and crafts out of match and popsicle sticks. On the days that they didn't have Bible school, they went to Matt's, Jerry's, and Ronnie's baseball games. She was so proud of her brothers. They were so good at ball that the coach played all of them, and Ronnie had been chosen for the all-star league.

Julie could not help noticing the changes in her life and couldn't help wondering at how they would affect her life. Her dad had begun to leave her alone at night since he had met a woman named Rhonda. Sometimes Rhonda would sleep over at their house. Julie couldn't help wondering why Rhonda and her dad slept in the same bed since they weren't married. Julie was going to say something to her dad but had learned a long time ago that it was better to just be quiet. Rhonda had two children. Peter was four years old, and Patsy was eight months old.

At first, Rhonda and her children would visit once or twice a week. Then, before Julie knew it, they were there almost every evening and night. By the time midsummer had come, Rhonda and her children had moved in. Peter slept on the couch and Patsy slept in Julie's old crib that her dad had gotten out of the attic. Julie wanted to like Rhonda. She knew that she could never like her, like her mom, but maybe it would be nice to have someone cook a dinner for them rather than just having soup beans. The more that Rhonda stayed over, the more her dad quit abusing her. Julie thought that maybe he was sorry and that he would never do it again. She even thought that maybe she had made more of it than it was, that maybe she had been mistaken. She would put it out of her mind. Maybe her dad wasn't so bad. She began to see him laugh again. Once in a while, it seemed that maybe he was more like the old dad she used to know a long time ago.

Then when Julie thought that life couldn't change anymore, it did. Their mom had gradually introduced Julie and her brothers to her friend Bob. Julie didn't like Bob. She remembered that when her mom and dad had broken up that her dad had blamed it all on Bob. How could she like someone who had taken her mom from them? If they were a couple, then for sure, her mom and dad would never get back together again. Julie also had met his three children. Julie liked them despite her desire to not like them. She even found herself liking Bob against her will. She could see that he was so different from her dad. She could tell that he really did love his children. He had fought hard to get them from their neglectful mom. Julie wished that her dad would love them the way that Bob loved his children. Bob was nice to her, extra nice. But Julie was afraid of men. She didn't think she could trust any of them except maybe Pap Pap John.

Julie sat under the cherry tree one hot summer day. She leaned up against the rough tree bark and rested her head. Mamie lay beside her, her head resting in Julie's lap. Julie stroked her dear friend's ears and rubbed her wet nose gently. The dog closed her eyes and opened them droopingly to look at Julie and to show her that she was listening.

"I just don't get it, ole girl," Julie spoke out loud. "I know Mom and Dad are never going to get back together again, but I never thought it would be like this. Well…that Rhonda won't even let you come into the house. It's like she's the boss, and Dad says we have to listen to her, or we'll get into trouble."

Julie listened to hear if Rhonda was calling her name. The boys had gone inside to get cleaned up for the ball game. Julie was waiting for her turn to get a bath. Julie sat up and listened as she heard someone coming. She glanced up the sidewalk. There was Rhonda's little boy, Peter. Julie didn't want to be mean, but she had to run and hide before he saw her. "Come on, Mamie," Julie whispered as she ran to the old barn to sit. Julie loved Rhonda's little girl, Patsy. She was like a live baby doll. Julie was learning to change her diaper and give her a bottle. She was a happy, little baby. Julie couldn't even be jealous of the attention her dad gave Patsy. The sweetness of the little girl touched Julie's heart. But Peter, he was a terror on wheels. He was always disobeying and would lie and do mean things. Julie could never forget the day that he had taken her Thumbelina doll and wound it too tightly and broke it. He didn't even get in trouble for what he had done. Nothing made sense to Julie anymore. Julie had tried to talk to Matt, Jerry, and Ronnie at different times, but they seemed as confused as Julie.

Julie sat on the worn wooden steps of the old barn. She looked around at the old barn slats. You could see the sky, right through the roof where the wood had weathered through. Mamie sat closely by her side. Julie put her arm around her furry friend and nestled her head into Mamie's fur. A tear slid down onto her face and then another. She was glad to see her mom happy again. She was glad that her dad had quit hurting her. She was glad to even see him happier. So why did she feel so sad and alone?

Julie in fourth grade.

CHAPTER

21

Another school year was about to start. Julie was looking forward to going shopping with her mom for new school clothes. Lately, she had so little private time with her mom. Ethel had married Bob. They had bought a big house. Julie was glad that her mom no longer lived in the small apartment and that all of them could spend the weekend with their mom together. Julie hated sharing her mom with Bob's children. They were nice enough, but Julie could tell that they too weren't always happy to share her mom with them either. Julie didn't care; after all, she was her mom, not theirs. Ethel had promised Julie that on Saturday, just she and her brothers would go shopping.

As the weeks passed and the new school year started, Julie had already given up the hope of getting close to Rhonda. In three short months, Julie had made up her mind that she didn't like the woman at all. Julie thought that no one could argue as much as her mom and dad had when they were together; however, Rhonda and her dad argued more than her mom and dad had ever argued. Julie couldn't figure out, that if they hated each other so much, why they even stayed together.

The more that Rhonda and her Dad argued, the more her dad began to drink. He deliberately would leave work and go directly to Lindy's bar. He wouldn't even stop at the house first. The longer that he stayed at Lindy's, the madder Rhonda became. Rhonda had decided that the best way to get back at Ron was to not let the children eat supper until he came home. This way, it would force Ron to come home so that his children could eat supper. What Rhonda didn't know, nor did she care, was that Ron would not be told by anyone what to do. And what surprised Rhonda was that it didn't matter to Ron if his children got to eat supper or not.

Julie sat on the couch quietly by herself. She dared not breathe a word, but inside, her whole being was screaming, "Stop! Stop!" Julie could feel the tears well up in her eyes. With each loud thrashing, her eyes blinked. Jerry had his eyes closed tight. His jaw was locked sternly in place. Rhonda had grabbed him by the arm and threw him across her lap. She had the yellow plastic hammer from Peter's play tool set in her hand.

"I'll teach you!" she screamed. With each blow, she thrashed him harder than the time before. Julie didn't even know why Jerry was in trouble. He hadn't done anything wrong.

All that Julie knew was that the angrier that Rhonda was at her dad, the more she took it out on Jerry. *Maybe it's because Jerry looks so much like dad*, Julie thought.

Julie inched her way to the end of the couch and then slowly got up. She paused at the stair post and hid behind it. Jerry wouldn't open his eyes but just clinched them tightly with each passing blow.

"You're not going to cry?" Rhonda shouted angrily. "We'll see about that!" And with another smack of the hammer against Jerry, Julie softly slid up the stairs. She couldn't bear to watch. Tears poured down her cheeks as she slipped into her brothers' room. Matt and Ronnie sat quietly on Ronnie's bed. She saw them jerk with each sound of the beating. They both glanced up sadly at Julie as she sat down beside them.

"She's really beating Jerry hard," Julie sobbed.

"She always takes it out on Jerry when she's mad at dad," Ronnie spoke softly and put his arm around Julie.

"I wish someone would just throw away that old plastic hammer that she beats us with," Matt said as he twitched hearing another smack.

"I don't think I'll ever like the color yellow ever again," Julie said as she thought of the bright yellow hammer that all of them had been beaten with by Rhonda when she was upset. Julie remembered when Rhonda had first picked up the yellow hammer in a fit of anger toward her. Julie had pushed Peter because he had taken her doll again. Rhonda had seen her do it and came bellowing into the room after her. Julie could see her freckled face get as bright red as her red hair. Rhonda yelled at her, grabbed the hammer, and laid into her beating her over and over again. Julie could feel the sting of the plastic against her bare legs, and unlike Jerry, she cried horribly. Now any time that Rhonda was in a bad mood or they did the slightest thing wrong, she would grab it and start beating them. They had told their mom a few times about Rhonda beating them. It seemed that the more they would tell their mom and she would talk to their dad, the harder Rhonda would beat them the next time. All their dad would say to them was that they had better listen to Rhonda or they would get a beating from him if they caused her trouble. Julie hated the yellow hammer worse than the marine belt.

"At least when dad gives us a licking, we've usually done something pretty bad," Ronnie said.

"Sometimes," Matt said sadly. Julie could tell that Matt didn't agree with Ronnie about their dad.

The three children sat quietly and waited for the beating to stop. Finally, there was a stillness, and they heard Jerry coming slowly up the stairs.

Julie jumped off the bed and ran to the door. Matt and Ronnie followed closely behind her. Jerry opened the door before Julie could reach it. He looked at them briefly. Julie could not remember ever seeing so much pain on her brother's face. His eyes were drawn tight to hold back the tears, and his jaw pulsed tightly as he continued clinching his teeth. Before they could talk to him, Jerry ran and jumped onto his top bunk and buried his head into his pillow. Julie could hear his muffled cries and saw his back heaving from his sobs. Only now would he cry. Jerry had told them at one time that he wouldn't let Rhonda ever see him cry again. This only made Rhonda more angry, so she would beat him longer and harder. Julie had taken a different plan. As soon as Rhonda would start to beat her, she would start crying as loud as she could. She would cry and cry even after the beating just because she knew that it got on Rhonda's nerves.

The only good thing about Rhonda staying with them was that her dad had quit coming into her room at nights. Julie would much rather take the beatings than have her dad hurt her. But it was almost unbearable to see Rhonda beat her brothers.

Ronnie, Matt, and Julie sat back down onto Ronnie's bed. They looked up at Jerry and then at one another. They knew that Jerry needed this time alone. Julie wanted to jump right up into his bed and comfort him, but she knew that Jerry felt that he was too old to cry, and it would embarrass him.

"I hate her!" Matt said loudly.

"Me too!" both Ronnie and Julie chimed in. They wanted Jerry to hear them. They wanted him to know that they were there for him whenever he was ready. They had tried to tell their dad at times how Rhonda was treating them, but he would just brush it aside.

"Why does Dad let her treat us this way?" Ronnie asked.

"Because…he doesn't care," Matt answered matter-of-factly.

Julie couldn't defend her dad like she used to when she was younger. She had also begun to feel that her dad really didn't care about what really happened to them. Sometimes she even got angry at her mom. She knew that her mom loved them, but she felt so left alone at times.

"You know what Dad says," Matt continued mocking his dad's voice. "You kids better not upset Rhonda and make her leave, or it'll be all your fault."

"But she's the problem," a quiet voice spoke up softly from above them.

Julie, Matt, and Ronnie looked up to the bunk bed and saw Jerry sitting upright.

Julie paused for a minute and then climbed up the end post to the top bunk to sit beside her brother.

"Well, this time, I'm really telling Mom how bad it is!" Ronnie said defiantly. "I don't care how much we get into trouble. She can't keep beating us this way."

"Me too!" Matt chimed in.

Julie looked at Jerry. His face had relaxed. Julie pretended that she didn't see his tear-streaked face.

"What can Mom do?" Jerry asked hopelessly.

"Well, she can either talk to dad or even tell Rhonda to stop," Ronnie assured his younger siblings.

"She made Rhonda quit making us wear those dumb, ragged railroad pants," Matt jumped in.

"Yeah, but that's because Mom agreed to take all of our dirty clothes and wash and iron them herself," Jerry stated.

"I've heard her try to tell Dad to make Rhonda stop," Matt said.

"Really?" Jerry asked a little surprised.

"Yeah," Matt continued, "but Dad just says, 'Now, Ethel, the kids don't listen, and they need to be corrected.'"

"Why doesn't Dad just marry her or make her leave?" Julie asked. "She still has her apartment over in Grantville."

"Don't you know why?" Ronnie asked as he looked at each of his siblings.

"No," the trio answered in unison.

"Because then, Dad would have to support her kids. She gets welfare checks right now for both of them and some child support. If they get married and she gives up her apartment, she'll loose her welfare checks. And there is no way that Dad is gonna raise and provide for her and her kids when he barely does it for us," Ronnie's voice crescendoed as he spoke.

Julie sat quietly and listened as her brothers continued to talk. She looked at Ronnie as he expressed his frustration at wanting to protect his younger brothers and sister. She saw the discouraged look of helplessness on his brow as he spoke. She watched Matt hang his head in brokenness and sorrow, a sorrow that she had seen so often. She wanted to hug him and make it all go away. When she looked over at Jerry, she couldn't help but put her hand onto his shoulder. Oh, if she could only take their pain away. She marveled at how smart Ronnie was and how good he was at explaining the things of life and coming up with a plan. She was sure that Ronnie would always have an answer, and if he didn't, she was sure that either Jerry or Matt would know what to do.

But she had wondered if even they could explain to her why her dad had done to her what he did. She tried and tried to forget it and brushed it aside, but it always came back to haunt her. For that reason and that reason alone, she had hoped that Rhonda wouldn't leave. Julie knew that if she left, her dad would probably start to hurt her all over again. A month before, Rhonda had gone back to her apartment for a few days and threatened her dad that she wouldn't come back. Julie thought at first that their dad was relieved that she was gone. But in those few days that she had left, her dad had come into her room and abused her once again. Julie squirmed uncomfortably as the thoughts taunted her.

"You okay, Julie?" Jerry asked seeing his sister fidget.

"Yeah. I'm okay, Jerry," Julie replied softly. She could never tell anyone about her dark secret, no one, not even her dear brothers. *No one must ever know these horrible things*, Julie thought as she sat quietly.

"Well, I'm just glad that school has started again, and we don't have to be here most of the time," Matt said encouragingly.

"The other day, Mrs. Hornworth, the eighth-grade teacher, stopped me in the hallway and asked me who that woman was that was living with us," Julie said. She was glad to change the subject.

"No way!" Matt said. He was shocked at what Julie was saying.

"That's none of her business, Julie!" Ronnie said.

"She is such a busybody!" Jerry snapped.

Julie knew that her brothers didn't like Mrs. Hornworth. That's why she hadn't told them. But she knew that she would get them to laugh when she told them what had happened.

"What did you say when she asked you that?" Matt asked curiously.

Julie turned her head and looked at Matt, then Jerry, and then Ronnie. She had an impish grin on her face and broke into a big smile. "What was I supposed to say?" She threw her hands up in the air helplessly. "I just told her that Rhonda was our housekeeper."

Jerry turned to his sister, paused, and then burst into laughing. Julie started laughing and Matt joined in.

"You told her what?" Ronnie tried to ask but couldn't stop laughing.

Julie just repeated her answer and laughed all the more. She couldn't help but wonder what Mrs. Hornworth must have thought of that answer.

Ronnie age thirteen, Jerry age twelve, Matt
age eleven, and Julie age ten.

CHAPTER

22

Julie walked slowly down the hill. She wrapped her jacket tightly around her and pulled the collar up around her neck. The wind was cold and went right through her thin jacket.

"Come on Julie!" Matt called out to her. He stopped and waited for Julie to run and catch up to him.

Julie slowly lifted her head and saw Matt in the distance. She motioned to him with her hand to go ahead. Matt paused to see if she would change her mind and then turned and ran to catch up with Jerry and Ronnie.

Julie felt so sad inside. Even the thought of going to Gramma Winnie's for dinner and getting to be with her mom didn't seem to cheer her up. Julie just couldn't seem to snap out of it no matter how hard she tried.

She loved the times that she was able to spend with her mom, but it just wasn't enough. There were times when Julie felt angry at her mom for leaving them with their dad. It just didn't seem fair that Bob and his kids could have her mom and not her. She knew that they were never going to get to go live with their mom. The pattern had been set. They were able to be with their mom only on the weekends and on Tuesday evenings. The rest of the time they lived at home with their dad and Rhonda. None of the adults ever talked about changing anything. *No,* Julie thought sadly to herself as she kicked a rock aimlessly into the air with her shoe, *nothing is ever going to change.*

Julie loved the time that she spent with her mom and brothers. She had even grown to like Bob and his three children. She had actually become friends with them, and they had lots of fun together, playing games, hiking, and taking adventures through the old underground water pipe that crossed under the highway. Why couldn't they just go to live with Bob and her mom? Why couldn't they all be a family? But Julie had heard Bob talk about how their dad should do more for them, that he should buy their clothes so that their mom wouldn't have to. Julie had even heard them argue about it. Her mom had vehemently stood firm on spending her money to get them what they needed. She had said, "Bob, Ron will never buy these things for the kids. If I don't, they'll be without. I told you before I married you that I would never let my kids do without. You've got to understand." But never did Julie hear them talk about the possibility that they could come to live with them. And this broke Julie's heart. Unlike her dad, she knew that her mom truly loved them. She knew that her mom would always be there for them. She nurtured them and loved them.

A smile crossed Julie's face as she remembered the one night that they had all piled into the big, yellow Hudson that her mom owned to go to the drive-in. All of the boys had gotten into the trunk of the car, and all of the girls went inside the car. Ethel only paid for the girls. Julie knew that somehow this wasn't honest, but somehow, she thought that maybe God would understand. They pulled out a blanket and sat on the ground outside of the car as they ate the popcorn that their mom had popped at home before they came. *Those were the good times,* Julie thought. So why couldn't she be happy? Sometimes Julie had thought that things were going to get better with Rhonda and her dad. A few times her dad had taken them out to the creek to swim and have a picnic. Julie thought at times like these that her dad was really trying to make them a family again.

Every time that Julie thought that things were changing for the better, then it would start all over again. First the arguing, then her dad's drinking, and then Rhonda would leave him and then the abuse from her dad would start again. As much as Julie wanted to like Rhonda, she just couldn't. Rhonda was just too mean. But Julie was glad for the times when she would move back in with them so that the abuse from her dad would stop.

Julie stopped at the side of the road. She looked both ways and waited for the traffic to clear and then crossed the road to her gramma's house. She took off running across the dirt path. She saw her mom's car and knew that her mom was already there.

Julie barged into the back door. She was so glad to see her mom. She could smell the fried potatoes and fried chicken and the sweet smell of a freshly baked chocolate cake. Julie looked over at her gramma bustling around the little stove. She loved Gramma Winnie. Pap Pap John sat in his favorite kitchen chair at the table waiting for his supper. Julie thought that he looked very tired. He gave her a smile. Julie smiled back. She thought Pap Pap John was one of the nicest men that she knew. He would always give them Juicy Fruit chewing gum for a treat. Sometimes, he would call her over to his desk and give her a special pack of Jacks or some hair barrettes. At other times, he would whisper, "I've got some cheese in the fridge for my little mouse." Both Gramma Winnie and Pap Pap John made Julie feel so loved and so special. At times like these, Julie could forget the bad things of her life.

Julie sat down beside her mom and put her books on the table. "Mom, I've got so much homework! I don't think I can get it all done."

"Come on, honey, maybe I can help you," Ethel said. She brushed the ringlets of curls away from Julie's face. Julie just sat and stared at her geography book. She tried to read the pages, but her mind was in a blur. She reread the sentences again and again, over and over. She just couldn't focus. All she could think about was that she was never going to get it all done and that she would then be in trouble. Mrs. Smith was such a hard teacher. Julie just felt that she couldn't do all the work.

Ethel looked down at Julie and saw the tears in her eyes. "What's wrong, Julie?"

But Julie just stared at the book and at the words that made no sense to her. How could she ever tell her mom what was really wrong?

"I just keep reading the same thing over and over, Mom. I can't understand what I'm reading."

"But your getting good grades, Julie. You're doing okay, honey. It'll be all right." Ethel tried to comfort her little girl.

After supper, Julie took her books into the living room to do her homework. She wanted to sit in the kitchen and listen to her mom and Gramma talk. She wanted to be near her mom. This was their special time. Bob's children didn't come over on Tuesday's, and this was her time and hers alone with her mom. Julie hated that she had to do homework instead. She wanted to cry and cry and didn't even know why.

Ethel helped Winnie clean up the dishes. She glanced into the living room and saw the boys sitting and watching television. Julie sat in the big armchair staring down at her books. "I'm worried about Julie," Ethel said to Winnie.

"She's not herself, Ethel, and she's losing weight," Winnie replied. She grabbed a dishrag and wiped down the kitchen table.

"She's totally withdrawn, and I can't get her to open up. She says she's got way too much homework, but I think that there's more bothering her than that," Ethel said.

"Get her to bring her books out here and try to help her, Ethel," Winnie insisted. She dried the table.

Ethel went into the living room and sat down with Ronnie, Jerry, and Matt. "Mom, you ought to watch this show," Matt said.

"Yeah, Mom, this guy is running for his life," Ronnie added.

"And he's looking for a one-arm man," Jerry joined in. "It's called the *Fugitive*."

Ethel smiled and tousled Jerry's hair before getting up. "Julie, come out to the kitchen, and we'll work on your homework together."

Julie got up and followed Ethel to the kitchen. Gramma Winnie had a glass of milk and a big piece of chocolate cake for her on the table.

Julie struggled with her geography and math assignments. She then worked on her English. Julie was glad when she had finally finished it all. She leaned against her mom and rested her head onto her shoulder. She was glad that it was her turn to stay overnight with Gramma Winnie. She knew that in the morning, Gramma Winnie would fry her eggs and bacon and give her a big glass of orange juice.

Julie walked out to the porch and waved good-bye to her mom. It still made Julie sad to say good-bye. She wondered if she would ever get used to the way her life had changed.

The weeks passed, and Julie continued to struggle with her schoolwork. No one seemed to understand because she was still getting As on her report card. Julie didn't even understand how she got the good grades. But the struggle of doing the work seemed more than Julie could handle. She felt like something inside of her was breaking into little pieces, and she didn't know how to stop it.

One Sunday after they had come home from Gramma Emma's Sunday dinner, Julie was faced with the task of doing her homework. She went right up to her room to start it. She knew that if her dad had found out that she hadn't done it yet, she would be in trouble. She just couldn't do it. She had tried several times, but her mind was a blank. She did her English and math first because these were easier for her than the reading assignments. She finally opened her history book, but she just could not concentrate on the words. Her mind drifted back and forth. She knew the words and could read them, but that was all that they were, just words without meaning.

She hadn't heard her dad come up the steps. Suddenly, her door opened. "Why aren't you done your homework?" he asked.

Julie just shrugged her shoulders.

"Why didn't you do it earlier?" he asked.

Julie just sat and stared at her feet as they hung over the edge of the bed. She didn't answer.

"Well, get it done," he said as he left and shut the bedroom door behind him.

Julie could hear *The Ed Sullivan Show* playing on the television downstairs. Julie wished she could be downstairs with her brothers. She didn't want to be alone in her room. It wasn't that often that it was this peaceful. Tonight would've been a good night to be downstairs. No one was fighting or arguing. Julie knew that she wouldn't be allowed to go downstairs until her homework was done. Julie felt the tears of loneliness slide down her cheeks. She got up and opened her door to listen to the show. It seemed to help her to relax. She seemed to be able to finally get past the history reading, but she knew that next was her geography. She hated geography the most.

Julie had just picked up her geography book and opened it. When she looked up, to her surprise, she saw her dad standing in the doorway.

"Now, Julie, there is no reason that you aren't done your homework by now," he said impatiently.

"I can't help it, Dad," she said. She brushed away a tear from her eye.

"Didn't I tell you to get your homework done Friday, after school, before you went with your mom?"

"Yes." Julie could not bear her dad's anger.

"Stand up," he said as he pulled off his belt.

Julie stood up. She was surprised at her dad's actions. He wasn't drunk. He had only had a few beers. She wondered why he had taken off his belt. She knew that she hadn't done anything wrong. But as she stood there, he folded the belt in half and began to swat her with it. Tears streamed down her face as she withdrew further into her "I don't care anymore" mood. She braced herself against the impact of the leather belt.

Her dad left and went back downstairs. Julie sat on the edge of her bed and began to wonder why Jesus wouldn't help her or why he wouldn't just let her die.

Julie lifted her head slowly. She heard laughter. She went to her doorway and looked out into the stairway. There sat Peter on the steps peeking up at her. He was laughing at her because she had got a whipping. Julie looked at the young freckled face and wondered why he was laughing at her. The tears were still wet upon her face as she brushed them aside with the sleeve of her blouse. How could her tears not even faze him? How could her pain bring him joy?

Julie ran back into her room and shut the door. Oh, if she only had a door to shut out the world as well. She sat and stared at the pages of her geography book and let her eyes skim the pages. At least she could tell Mrs. Smith that she had read the assignment. She didn't care if she understood a word. She didn't care about anything anymore.

Julie continued to struggle throughout the whole school year. She knew that Jerry had talked to their mom about their dad whipping her for not doing her homework. Julie didn't know what she had said to her dad, but he didn't beat her anymore because of her homework.

Julie was actually glad when the school year came to an end. Her dad had once again let up on his drinking. She never knew how long it would last before he would plunge back into drinking full force, but for now, she was glad. These were more peaceful times.

Julie loved summer. She had learned to stay outside as much as possible. This kept her out of Rhonda's way and path of anger. Julie couldn't stop wondering about Rhonda. She couldn't figure her out. She had asked her if Peter could come to Sunday school with them, but Rhonda had refused. And yet, often when leaving for Sunday school, she would hear Rhonda listening to a preacher on the radio in the kitchen as she would do the dishes. Sometimes, she would even see Rhonda and her dad sit and watch the fiery preacher, Oral Roberts, on TV. *Why didn't they just come to church?* She wondered if they had ever felt Jesus love the way she had in church.

This gave Julie hope, hope that maybe things would continue to get better. Summer fell into a routine of sorts. Rhonda planted a garden, and Julie was tickled with the fresh vegetables. She especially liked the cucumber salad. Ronnie, Jerry, Matt, and Julie picked the cherries from their cherry tree, and Rhonda made cherry pies.

Julie was able to see her mom more often at the ballgames because the boys were playing baseball again. Most of all, Julie looked forward to the weekends. They would sit and play all kinds of games at their mom's kitchen table with Bob's kids. Julie would drink all the chocolate milk that her mom would let her drink. And then there were the picnics with Gramma Emma and the family out at the creek. Julie found herself laughing again and felt a new hope rise within her.

The new school year began with many new changes. Ronnie had told her that a school bus would now be picking them up for school instead of having to walk to school. Jerry told her that she would have a nice teacher this year.

Julie got ready for her first day in school. She put the new hair barrettes that Pap Pap John had given her in either side of her hair. Julie looked at herself in the mirror and patted her new dress. She twirled around in front of the mirror and smiled. She loved her new clothes. She looked down at her shiny, new shoes and bright, white socks. She felt so grownup. She was going into the fifth grade. Matt was going into seventh, and Jerry the eighth grade. Ronnie was going into his first year of high school. Julie could hardly believe it and was saddened that Ronnie would be going to a different school than her and her brothers. She didn't like anything that split them up.

Julie hurried out of her bedroom door and almost ran into Ronnie coming out of the bathroom. She stopped quickly and smiled up at her big brother. Julie thought, *How grown up he looks.* She reached up and straightened his collar. Ronnie smiled down at his little sister. "You look cute, sis," he said. "You'll like school this year."

Ronnie was right. Julie loved school this year. She threw herself into her studies with a new vigor. She felt a new confidence as she excelled in her schoolwork. Often, she would walk home with her friends Sarah and Molly. She had grown used to the ups and downs of her dad's relationship with Rhonda. Julie and her brothers tried to just stay out of Rhonda's way to avoid her beatings as much as possible and to make the best of it. Julie had accepted that even though she may never live with her mom, she truly did enjoy the time that she spent with her, Bob, and his children. It had sort of become a home away from home.

One day, as they sat in the boys' bedroom talking about school, Ronnie had told them how different high school was from grade school. Julie sat mesmerized with the stories that Ronnie would tell them.

"Hey, Julie, what are you going to be for trick or treat tomorrow?" Jerry asked.

"I'm going to be a hobo," Julie answered.

"I hope you guys won't get upset with me," Ronnie paused and let his eyes search his siblings' faces. "I was going to go trick or treat with some of my friends."

"Can't we come too?" Julie asked.

"Yeah," Matt echoed.

"Not this time," Ronnie said. "You know, I'm getting older now."

"Not that much older," Jerry joined in.

"Come on, guys," Ronnie pleaded.

"Oh, okay," Jerry answered first. Matt and Julie reluctantly agreed.

Julie could hardly believe, the next night, when she saw Matt and Jerry come out of their room. "You've got to be kidding!" she exclaimed.

Matt and Jerry both dressed up like girls. Jerry strutted around showing off his new style. Matt followed likewise behind him. Julie giggled out loud; her hobo smile spread across her face.

Rhonda tried to make them take Peter with them. But when all three of them vehemently protested, she gave up.

"I sure am glad we didn't have to bring Peter with us tonight," Matt said.

"Well, it just wouldn't have been fair," Jerry answered.

Julie walked behind her brothers. She was surprised at how grown up Jerry sounded. She missed Ronnie not being with them, but she understood that he wanted to be with his friends.

They walked and walked. Julie could feel her bag getting fuller and fuller with the sweet treats she cherished. They were near Gramma Winnie's house, but Julie saw that all the lights were out, and no one was home.

"Shucks," Julie said, "I really wanted to stop at Gramma's house."

"Me too," Matt said.

"Hey…watch out Julie! That car is flying up the hill!"

An old, blue-gray car pulled up beside them. Jerry whispered to Matt and Julie, "Just keep walking real fast…stay together."

Julie felt a twinge of fear as she detected the earnestness in Jerry's voice. The car pulled alongside Matt and Jerry. Julie cowered behind her brothers. Julie heard the young men in the car let out a loud wolf whistle at her brothers. She glanced at Matt and then Jerry to see their reaction. But both of them walked faster, and Julie hurried to stay near them.

"Listen, you guys," Jerry whispered to them. "It's Monkey-Wrench! We're going to take off running in a minute across that field and get over to Gramma's house."

"But Gramma's not home," Matt reminded Jerry.

"We can still hide from them there so that they can't catch us," Jerry said.

Julie had never heard Jerry sound so grown up. She hurried and stayed close to Matt's side.

"Whew, baby!" came the voice from the car that was now barely moving.

"Yeah, how about a date?" the driver called out. They were close enough now to almost grab them.

Julie heard the faint sound of the brakes on the car. Fear and terror rushed through her. She watched Jerry closely as he turned toward the driver of the car.

Julie could see the old car in the dimness of the streetlight. The gray patches of primer were spotted against the original blue, making it look like leopard patches.

Jerry turned for a brief moment to Matt and Julie and whispered, "Get ready."

Then he turned back to the young men in the car and replied slyly, "A date? In your dreams!" Jerry turned quickly to Matt and Julie. "Now!" he shouted out.

Matt and Julie took off running into the open field. Jerry took off right behind them. He grabbed his wig as it was falling from his head. His ankles turned crazily as he tried to run in the high-heeled shoes he was wearing. He didn't look back once and hoped that they had escaped the streetlight and faded into the dark. They came out of the field onto a dirt alley road. They crossed it quickly. The car vanished. They then ran past Gramma Winnie's outhouse and up onto her porch. They knocked and knocked, hoping that maybe their Gramma might be home. But no one answered.

Jerry looked up and saw a car driving slowly in the distance. "Come on, you guys!" he said. He led the way across the porch and down another flight of steps where it was darker. "Quick, in here!" he commanded.

Matt dove under the open stairs with Julie right behind him. Jerry took one more quick glance and then joined them. "Squeeze tighter in the corner so the light doesn't reflect on us!" Jerry said earnestly.

Julie was afraid. She could see that her brothers were afraid too. They were never afraid, and Julie couldn't figure out what had upset them so much.

"Who is Monkey-Wrench?" Julie asked loudly.

"*Sh!*" Matt ordered Julie to be quiet.

Julie began to cry, saying, "We're going to die!" She then felt Jerry's hand clasp around her mouth. But Julie couldn't have said another word even if she tried. There, not even fifteen feet from them, was the blue-spotted car. The young men jumped out of the car and stood beside it. "Wonder where those kids went?" asked the one that Jerry had called Monkey-Wrench.

"Well, they couldn't have gotten that far!" the other one answered. "We'll find them."

Julie had thought they would surely hear her heart beating out loud. She held her breath and didn't mind that Jerry's hand was still clamped over her mouth.

"Hey, let's knock over this outhouse!" Monkey-Wrench called out.

Julie sat between Matt and Jerry and watched as the two young men rocked the old outhouse back and forth until it fell over. They then got into their car and sped off.

Julie felt Jerry's hand release from her mouth. But she couldn't say a word.

"What are we going to do?" Matt asked.

"Well, we better get on the main road home where there are more houses than on the back way," Jerry advised.

Julie just sat still. She marveled at her two brothers and how smart and brave they were. It was as if they weren't afraid at all. Julie felt so safe with them.

"You okay, Jul?" Jerry asked.

Julie just nodded her head. "Maybe we should wait until Gramma comes home," she suggested, trying to be grown up.

"No, we can't," Jerry answered.

"Yeah, they might come back," Matt finished Jerry's statement.

"Okay, let's go," Jerry said as he ducked from under the steps.

Julie followed closely behind him. Matt followed behind Julie.

"Now, no matter what!" Jerry commanded. "We just have to stick together. Julie, you stay between Matt and me at all times."

Quickly, they ran to the main highway. Julie thought they just might make it home safe. Then out of nowhere, she heard Matt call out, "They're coming after us! They've seen us!"

They ran down the highway as fast as they could. Julie was actually outrunning her two brothers. She didn't know if it was her fear or the fact that both Matt and Jerry were having a hard time doing anything in their girly high-heeled shoes.

"Jump!" Jerry called out.

One by one, without hesitating, the trio jumped off a tall wall that surrounded the patio of a nearby house. The car raced past them.

"Ouch!" Jerry called out.

"What'd you do Jerry?" Julie asked as she ran to his side.

"I sprained my ankle on these dumb heels!" he wailed.

They sat and leaned up against the wall to catch their breath. Jerry pulled the heels off and rubbed his ankle. "How do you girls ever walk in these things?" Jerry asked as he let out a nervous laugh.

Julie wanted to laugh too, but somehow, she was still too scared.

"Come on," Matt said. He helped Jerry to his feet. "We'll have to go the back way now to throw them off." He put his arm around Jerry to help him walk.

They hurried as fast as they could. They stayed close to the houses. They walked through one backyard after another and climbed over small fences as they dodged barking dogs on long chains.

Finally, they made it home. Julie couldn't believe it, but all three of them still had their candy bags tightly clutched in their hands. Julie rushed past the front gate and pounced onto the porch with Matt and Jerry right behind her.

The door flung open wide as Ronnie met them. "I'm glad you're all home," he said excitedly. "Hey, you okay, Jerry?" he asked as he watched Jerry limping and leaning on Matt.

"Yeah," Jerry answered. "I think I just sprained my ankle on those heels."

"Well, they got all of our candy!" Ronnie continued.

"Who got your candy?" Matt asked as he helped Jerry in through the front door.

"Oh, that ole Monkey-Wrench and his friends!" Ronnie answered angrily.

"You too?" Matt asked.

"Did they get your candy?" Ronnie asked surprised.

"No," Julie whispered and turned to go upstairs. She saw Rhonda enter from the kitchen into the living room. Julie gave her brothers a quick glance. Jerry straightened up and grabbed the rail on the stairways and went upstairs. Matt, Ronnie, and Julie followed closely behind.

"Wait 'til we tell you what happened, Ronnie," Julie whispered into his ear as they hurried up the stairs.

Later that night, Julie crept out of her brothers' room across the hallway into her bedroom. She put her candy on the dresser and then laid down in her bed exhausted. It had taken her a little while to get the hobo paint off her face. They had dumped all of their candy into a pile on the floor and divided it up so that Ronnie could have some candy. They told him what had happened. Julie looked across her room into the darkness. She could see the little cross on her wall glowing in the dark. Her eyes felt heavy and flickered as she gazed at the cross. She felt a gentle peace engulf her. "Thank you, Jesus, for taking care of us tonight," she spoke out softly and then fell asleep.

Julie—age eleven

CHAPTER

23

Julie pulled the blind with a quick jerk and then let go. The blind spun wildly to the top. "Look, Jerry!" she called out. "It's snowing again!"

Jerry pounced across her bed and sat Indian-style looking out the window. "It's small flakes, so it's gonna snow for a while," he said. He rested his head against the cool windowpane.

"I love the snow," Julie said. She sat mesmerized at the white specks that flowed quickly past the window. Julie reached up and flipped the little latch on the window. She gave the window a quick jerk to open it. Jerry moved his head quickly away from the pane and gave her a queer look.

"Listen, Jerry," she said, smiling at him.

"I don't hear anything," he answered.

"Exactly! You can't hear a single thing. It's so peaceful and quiet. Isn't it wonderful?"

"Yes," Jerry said. He reached up and pulled the window closed. He gave Julie a broad smile as he wiped a snowflake off of Julie's speckled nose. "Come on. Let's play some marbles. I'll race you to the top of the bed!"

Julie laughed as she grabbed the jar of marbles. Julie loved the idea that Jerry and she had to share her bedroom until Monday.

They had both caught the measles. Julie was glad that it was Friday. By Monday, she would be better and be able to go back to school. Julie was determined, ever since the May Day, to not miss any school days. She had hoped that maybe she could go all twelve years and not miss a single day.

Julie couldn't believe when she came home from school that day that Jerry had the measles too. Rhonda had sent both of them to Julie's room. Julie was glad that she didn't have to be alone. Having Jerry in her room reminded her of old times when they were allowed to sleep with her.

Julie heard the beep of a car horn. "That's Mom! I hate that we have to stay home!"

"Me too." Jerry answered. He jumped out of bed and ran to the front window to look out. "Hey, Mom's parking her car. She's coming over to the house." Jerry ran and hopped into bed beside Julie.

The bedroom door slowly opened. Ethel stuck her head around the door. "Hey, what's this I hear…you both are sick?"

"We got the measles, Mom," Jerry and Julie said in unison.

Ethel sat down on the edge of the bed beside them. She reached up and touched their foreheads. She stood up and went into the bathroom and brought back some cool rags and placed one on each of their foreheads.

Julie felt a flood of memories race through her mind and heart. She looked into her mom's eyes and saw them cloud up with tears. Ethel got up to leave. She turned and bent down and gave each of them a hug and a kiss. "If you need anything, tell Rhonda to go over to Goldies and call me, okay? I'll see you tomorrow when I bring Matt and Ronnie home."

"Okay," answered Jerry.

Ethel turned and opened the bedroom door to leave. She lingered and leaned up against the door. She looked at her two children sitting together on the bed, both of their eyes peeled upon her. How could she leave them, she wondered. Slowly, she turned and walked away.

Julie and Jerry sat motionless on the bed. Julie looked over at Jerry, and their eyes met. Julie knew that they were both feeling and thinking the same thing. Silence hung over them like a cloud. Julie knew that it was difficult for their mom to come into the house. *All of the memories both good and bad must come flooding back*, she thought. Julie could see it in her mom's eyes as she paused at the door and watched them. She knew that her mom wanted to be with them. She knew that her mom wished they could be with her too. But neither was possible. The living arrangements had been set. It seemed a sad solution to a menagerie of complex conditions and problems.

"Come on, Julie," Jerry said as he looked at Julie's saddened face. He tossed a black marble at her and laughed. "Want a jelly bean?" he teased. Julie turned quickly toward Jerry and let the washrag on her head fall to the floor.

"I've got a good idea," Jerry said. He gathered the marbles together and placed the jar at the end of the bed against the footboard. "Let's try to toss the marbles into the jar from up here at the top of the bed."

"Great!" Julie said excitedly as she grabbed a handful of marbles. Jerry grabbed a handful too. They both started to toss the marbles at the jar, slowly and cautiously at first and then harder and faster. More marbles were hitting the outside of the jar than going inside the jar. Quickly, they grabbed handfuls and began to throw them harder and faster, harder and faster until suddenly, they heard the cracking of glass as the jar fell to the floor in pieces. Marbles rolled in all directions.

"Uh-oh!" Julie remarked. She jumped off of the bed with Jerry right behind her and hurried to gather up the marbles before Rhonda could see what they had done.

Jerry slithered across the floor on his knees and tried to pick up the jagged edges of glass. "Ouch!" Jerry yelled out loud. He reared back and rocked himself from the pain. He grabbed his knee. Julie ran to him and saw the blood oozing out from beneath his hand that held his knee.

"Jerry!" Julie cried out.

Jerry stopped rocking and slowly removed his hand from his injured knee. He looked at the cut and then gently probed it with his finger. Julie could see his clenched jaw and knew that he was in pain. Jerry pulled out a piece of glass that was in his knee and let out a loud sigh of relief as he leaned against the foot of the bed.

Julie jumped up and carefully hopped over the marbles and glass. She grabbed the washrag that was on the floor and ran into the bathroom. She ran cold water over the rag and wrung it out and then rushed over to Jerry. She dabbed the cut as gently as possible and wiped the blood away. She ran back to the bathroom as quietly as she could and wet the rag again. This time, when she put the rag onto Jerry's knee, he reached down and held it in place.

"Does it hurt real bad?" she asked. Jerry just sat holding the rag on his knee. Julie could see him gritting his teeth with his jaw muscle moving back and forth as he held back his tears. Julie ran to the bathroom with another washrag and hurried back to place a fresh rag onto Jerry's cut.

"I'm okay," Jerry said after a few minutes. "We better clean up our mess before we get into trouble."

"I better go and tell Dad," Julie said. She ran, swung the bedroom door wide open, and was ready to run downstairs but paused as she heard the voices rising from downstairs. She turned to look at Jerry.

"Never mind, Julie," Jerry said. He could hear the arguing coming from downstairs. "We'll just get into trouble if you tell them."

Julie ran back and knelt down beside Jerry. She carefully removed the wet rag stained in blood. The bleeding had stopped, but it was a nasty cut. "Did you get all of the glass out?" Julie asked. She went to touch the cut gently, but Jerry jerked his knee away.

"It'll be okay," Jerry said. Just go get the methiolate out of the bathroom, and see if there are any Band-Aids in the drawer.

Julie ran into the bathroom and gathered the medicine and Band-Aids. She wet the washrag one more time and rinsed it the best she could and grabbed a dry towel off the edge of the bathtub.

Julie dabbed Jerry's cut one more time with the warm rag and then dried it with the towel. She carefully took the dropper from the methiolate bottle and dabbed the cut gently with the medicine. Quickly, she leaned forward and blew the cut as hard as she could to ease the sting of the medicine. She looked up at Jerry and saw the pain etched on his face. She leaned over again and blew on the cut over and over again until she saw Jerry's face relax. She took the Band-Aid and, as gently as she could, placed it over the cut. Julie then, in a motherly fashion, ordered Jerry to get into bed. She helped Jerry to stand up. He grabbed the edge of the bed and hobbled onto it. Julie bent down to carefully pick up the remaining glass. She took the wet rag and wiped all the small slivers of glass into a pile, pushing them out of the way until the next day when she could sneak downstairs and get the broom.

Julie turned out the light and made sure that the door was shut tightly. She lay down beside her big brother. "You sure you're okay?"

"Yeah, I'll be okay, Jul," he answered softly. "I'm just tired. Let's get some sleep."

"Okay," Julie answered. She felt safe lying beside Jerry. She looked out the window and could see the snow still falling. The sheet of white fleeted past her window against the backdrop of the black night. She could still hear the loud voices from downstairs escalating as the arguing continued.

Rhonda and her dad had started to argue more and more again. The cycle had started again. The more they argued, the more her dad drank, and the more he drank, the more they argued.

Julie could hear bits and pieces of their argument through the closed door but could not understand what they were arguing about. Julie knew that regardless of what they were arguing about, it would end with something about "those kids."

Julie couldn't understand anything at times. At times, even Ronnie, Jerry, and Matt couldn't understand either, which made Julie not feel so bad. She couldn't imagine that they were such bad kids. She knew that they would sometimes argue and fight about things. They might even get angry and yell at each other over a game. But they didn't lie or steal, and most of the time, they listened. They weren't real mean like some kids that they knew. So why did they always feel like they were so terrible?

Julie lay in her bed and tried to understand life and people. Julie thought about earlier that day when it was lunchtime, and she wanted to play Jacks with Sarah and Betty when they had already started the game. Julie waited patiently for them to finish. Lately, Betty had joined Sarah and her in playing games. Julie didn't know Betty as well as Sarah. Betty went to the same Sunday school, and her dad taught the older boys. Julie couldn't imagine having a dad that not only went to church with you but also taught Sunday school. She thought maybe Betty's ignoring her at times was because she was shy. Surely, she couldn't be mean. No one could be mean who had a dad that taught Sunday school. But Julie had learned today that everyone who went to church was not always very nice. When Sarah and Betty had finished playing Jacks, they started another game. Julie waited to be last to take her turn. But when she went to take the Jacks, Betty said, "No, you can't play!" Julie looked at Sarah. She hoped that Sarah would remember their pact of friendship and speak up. But Sarah didn't say a word. She just looked at Julie sadly as if to say sorry.

"But why?" Julie asked. She looked past Sarah and directly at Betty.

"Because," Betty answered coolly. She flipped the jacks in her hand and continued to play. She didn't even look at Julie. She ignored her as if she wasn't even there.

"Because why?" Julie persisted. She could feel the anger rising inside of her from the hurt and rejection.

"Because our parents said we can't play with you anymore," she answered coolly.

"But why?" Julie asked sadly.

"Because of your grandpap," Betty stated firmly. She looked directly into Julie's eyes, past Julie's hurt and sorrow. "Because of what he did!"

"I don't understand," Julie said in a low voice.

Betty rolled her eyes at Sarah and bit her terse lip and ignored Julie. Julie looked over at Sarah and searched her face for an answer, but Sarah shrugged her shoulders and looked away.

Julie was glad to hear the bell ring at that very minute. Later that afternoon, she had been sent home with the measles. Julie wondered if she would ever understand people, Christians or life. Why couldn't Betty or Sarah play with her because of something that her grandpap had done? She wasn't aware of anything that her grandfather had done. And besides, what did that have to do with who Julie was? She hadn't done anything to anyone.

Julie let out a deep sigh and rubbed her forehead. Her head hurt, and she felt tired. She turned on her side and listened to Jerry's breathing as he slept. She lay quietly and watched the snowflakes fall outside of her window as they flickered in the dim streetlight. They lulled her into a peacefulness and she fell asleep.

❦

The winter passed quickly. The snow melted away. Julie could smell the freshness of spring as she sat on the front porch. A gentle breeze blew a mixed fragrance of lilacs and tulips through the air. A fresh season was coming, and soon school would be out.

Sarah had started to play with her again, but somehow, things were different and strained.

Julie still wasn't sure of all that had happened. It seemed that everyone in the valley always knew what was going on except her. But Julie had learned a cruel fact of life, that gossip is seldom spoken to the one that is being talked about.

Julie had asked her mom one Saturday, when she was visiting, what had happened with her Grandpap James. Ethel told the other children to go outside and play. Julie sat twiddling with the marbles belonging to the Wahoo game. She loved sitting in her mom's kitchen. Everything smelled so fresh, and everywhere Julie looked were signs of her mom's touch. It brought back so many memories. How Julie longed that things could be different in her life.

Ethel sat down at the table across from Julie and began to set up the game board with the remaining marbles. Julie took her marbles and placed them into the holes that were carved in the wooden board.

"Julie," Ethel began to talk and watched Julie's demeanor. "What do you know about what happened?"

Julie rolled the dice to start the game. "Not too much," Julie said slowly as she moved her marble around the board. "Just that Tina Sellers who lives below Gramma Emma told her parents that Grandpap James did something to hurt her."

Ethel waited for Julie to continue talking. She took the dice and rolled them on the table. "Mom, Tina is a nice girl. She's poor, very poor, but she's nice. All the kids make fun of her and say that she has cooties."

"Do you?" Ethel asked slowly as she moved her marble around the board.

"Well, I probably could be a better friend to her," Julie answered. Julie pictured Tina with her bowl-cut hairstyle and her bottle-thick eyeglasses. "But, Mom, I know that she wouldn't lie. Her mom, Flora, is so mean to her. She makes her cut all the wood for the wood stove, and I always see her pumping water from the pump outside or hanging out the wash all by herself. Especially since her older sister Joann died." Ethel reached across the table and touched Julie's hand. "Mom, poor Joann caught on fire and burned to death trying to start that old wood stove."

"Well, there's a lot we don't know, Julie," Ethel replied.

"I know ole Flora asked the doctor one time if malnutrition was contagious when he told her that her one baby was sick with it."

"How do you know that, Julie?" Ethel asked as she looked kindly into her little girl's eyes.

"Well, I heard it," said Julie with uncertainty, "but even Ronnie said it was true. Mom, Tina wouldn't lie, but everyone is saying that she made it all up, and they're teasing her worse than ever."

"Who's teasing her?" Ethel asked.

"You know, Mom…all the kids at school."

"Kids usually only say what they've heard at home, Julie."

"Well, Mom, everyone acts like she's just a big troublemaker, but she's not. And Gramma Emma's upset with Flora because Flora and her family told Gramma Emma that if she sells them the piece of land on the lower side of Gramma's road real cheap that they won't make Pap Pap James go to jail. Can they make him go to jail, Mom?"

Ethel watched Julie finish her turn and then picked up the dice. "Yes, he could," Ethel answered. She looked over at Julie. Ethel couldn't help but wonder if there might be some justice to it all if he did. As she looked at Julie's distraught face, the memories flashed back through her mind. Ethel was more concerned about how all of this would affect her children more than justice. They had suffered enough for things that were not their fault. She knew that if James went to jail, her kids would bear the brunt of it in the small valley. She longed to have them with her all the time.

"I hurt so bad for Tina," Julie said out loud. She let her thoughts pour out to her mom unchecked. "I know how she must feel."

Ethel dropped the marble that she was holding on the floor as Julie's words pierced her heart. *What was Julie saying?* she wondered.

Julie jumped off the chair and crawled under the table to get the marble. She climbed back up into her chair and tucked her legs under her. Quickly, she placed the marble back onto the board. She hoped that her mom didn't hear her last remark.

"Julie?" Ethel started to speak cautiously. She didn't want to upset Julie and still wasn't sure how much she should say to her eleven-year-old daughter. She thought that she was surely too young to hear or understand such things. "Your grandpap's never hurt you when you stay up at Gramma Emma's, has he?"

Julie could see her mom's face flush with emotion even as she tried to speak calmly to her. "No, Mom. Gramma Emma always has me sleep with her, and she says that I'm not allowed to go down to the basement," Julie answered. Julie twitched nervously. The conversation was too close to the subject of herself. Julie didn't know what she would do or say if her mom asked her about her dad. She didn't want to be called a liar. She didn't want her dad to go to jail. She never wanted anyone to ever know of the shame and reproach that she bore. They would think horrible things of her and think that she was just a very bad girl. No one would ever play with her or talk to her then. They didn't play with her now because of her grandpap. What would they do if they knew what had happened to her? Maybe even her mom might think that she was bad. Everyone had thought that Tonya was bad, and now Tina, and they weren't bad.

Julie wanted to ask her mom why she wasn't allowed to go down to the basement at Gramma Emma's. She wanted to know why she felt terrified of the coal bin and had nightmares about it. She even wanted to rush into her arms and tell her how her dad had hurt her. She wanted to be safe at last, but she couldn't. How could she ever tell anyone? They would take them from their dad and put them into an orphanage. They'd call her a troublemaker.

Worst of all, she would feel so dirty if people knew. She felt dirty even when people didn't know. She would be the reason that the whole family would be finally separated. *No!* Julie thought. She mustn't tell anyone ever. She would just block it out of her mind. She would try to forget all the bad things.

Julie wiped her head with her hand as if to brush the thoughts out of her mind. "You better catch up, Mom!" Julie said. "I'm beating you." Julie wanted to change the subject.

Ethel sat quietly and studied her young daughter. Her heart was troubled at Julie's apparent distress. She often wondered if Julie remembered anything about the incident with her grandfather when she was four years old. Ethel reached out to take the dice that Julie was handing to her. Her eyes met Julie's. She searched Julie's eyes and tried to understand her young daughter who sat before her. Ethel held Julie's hand tenderly for a moment as she took the dice. She gave it a gentle squeeze and smiled. It was best to drop the subject for now. She could see that it was upsetting Julie. Ethel was not a praying woman, but she prayed in her heart of hearts that no one would ever hurt her little girl again. She was afraid of what she might do to James if he ever touched Julie again.

"Mom, are you done? Is that your final move?" Julie asked.

"Yeah, honey. It's your turn," Ethel said. She pushed her troubled thoughts aside.

The sun beat down brightly on Julie as she raked the grass clippings into a large pile. The smell of fresh cut grass tickled her nose and made her sneeze. Matt followed behind her and filled a large bag with the clippings while Jerry carried the bags down to the stream behind the barn to dump them. Ronnie pushed the little power mower across the lawn in neat rows.

Julie listened to Matt whistling a tune. She loved to hear him whistle. He always whistled or sang a song unless he was extremely sad. Julie turned to look at Matt as she raked the grass. She couldn't help smiling at her big brother. Matt was oblivious to Julie's glance and continued to work. The sweat matted his blond hair to his forehead.

"We're almost done!" Jerry said as he gave Matt the empty bag and picked up the full one to take and empty.

"Maybe we'll have time to play a game of croquet before dinner," Matt called out to Jerry above the loud sound of the mower.

Jerry stopped and turned around to answer Matt. Julie thought he looked like a skinny Santa Claus with the bag tossed over his shoulder. "We may not have time. We have a ballgame this evening," Jerry yelled back. Jerry took off trying to run with the bag. It bounced on his shoulder and looked like it would topple Jerry and knock him to the ground.

"The bag is almost as big as him!" Matt said laughing. Julie laughed too as they stood and watched Jerry run.

Julie was going to go and get the croquet game as Ronnie finished the last strip. But before any of them could move, they heard Rhonda calling them to come inside.

Ronnie put away the mower and came out of the old barn. "Gosh, she must have been watching us out of the kitchen window to know that we were done," Ronnie said.

Julie looked at Ronnie. He had sweat running down his brow. His hands were streaked with oil, and he smelled like gasoline.

"Well, we better go in," Matt told the others. "No use getting her upset."

"Getting her upset?" Jerry said with an edge in his voice. "When isn't she upset?"

"Well, we'll play croquet tomorrow," Julie said as she tried to cheer up her brothers.

"Yeah, right," Ronnie said, his frustration sounding in his voice. "She already said that tomorrow we're going to have to pull weeds."

"Why doesn't Peter ever have to help?" Julie asked.

"She never makes him do anything!" Ronnie said. "All he does is watch us and try to get us into trouble!"

"Like we need his help to get into trouble," Jerry said. "We're always in trouble with Rhonda."

"The angrier that she gets with Dad, the madder she gets at us," Matt added.

"Which is all the time lately," Jerry stated matter-of-factly.

"Well, she wants Dad to marry her, and it's just not going to happen," Ronnie said.

"What makes you so sure, Ronnie?" Julie asked. She turned to look at her big brother as they all walked up the sidewalk to the house.

Ronnie turned to Julie and then made eye contact with his brothers and said, "I heard Dad say one day when he was drinking, 'Why buy the cow when the milk is free.'"

Matt and Jerry started to laugh as they all entered the back door. Julie let the words repeat in her mind, but she still couldn't understand what was so funny. What did cows and milk have to do with their dad marrying Rhonda?

They passed Rhonda as they went through the kitchen. She didn't say a word to them. Julie was glad. Rhonda had been in a foul mood all day. Julie hurried up the stairs with her brothers to get cleaned up for the ballgame. She hurriedly darted into the bathroom before her brothers.

"Hurry up, Jul!" Matt called through the door. "We've got to be ready in time to catch our ride."

Julie hurried out of the bathroom and told Matt that she was done. She went into her bedroom and put on clean clothes, brushed her hair, and flopped down onto her bed. Julie loved to watch her brothers play ball. She felt a little sad that her mom wouldn't be there tonight. She had told them that she had to work late.

The boys quickly ate and darted out the door to catch their ride to the game. Their dad had said that they would meet them there later. There was a knock on the door, and Julie ran to answer it. She hoped that it was her dad because he was over an hour late. But Julie knew that he wouldn't knock. She opened the door, and Pap Pap James was standing there. He had come down to go to the game with them. Julie shut the door behind him. He went and sat down on the chair in the corner without saying a word. Julie sat on the couch. She glanced into the kitchen. She could hear Rhonda banging the pots and pans. She knew that the longer that her dad didn't come home, the madder that Rhonda would become. She knew that Rhonda's quiet demeanor was not patience or even tolerance, it was a pure insolence mixed with an unquenchable anger.

The door swung open wildly. Julie watched her dad enter. He was not completely drunk, but Julie could see that he had been drinking. Rhonda turned and glared at him.

"What's your problem?" he said as he entered the kitchen.

Julie jumped up and went out the front door. She climbed up on the banister to sit and wait. She could hear Rhonda and her dad arguing from inside the house. She had learned to not get caught in the middle of their arguments. Julie dangled her legs from the banister and looked out at the yard. The smell of the freshly mowed grass mingled in the air with the smell of the rose bush that sat near the house. The sun was slowly going down and she wondered if they were going to go to the ballgame. Her mind wondered as she waited. She was glad that Pap Pap James had not gone to jail. She had overheard her Gramma Emma one day talking to him about how she would have to sell the property for nearly nothing. Julie could tell that she was upset and that she seemed very sad. The valley tired of the gossip and soon dropped the matter. Julie couldn't help but wonder how Tina must feel. It made her sad to think of the pain that she must still be bearing.

Julie heard the door open and looked up to see everyone coming out of the house.

Rhonda's face was as red as her hair. Julie glanced at her dad and could see that he was upset too. Julie jumped off the banister and followed them to the car. She walked beside Peter and said, "Shotgun!" Peter turned to her and made a face. She opened the car door, but Peter wouldn't get in. "Go on," she said firmly.

"No!" he answered. "I'm sitting by the window!"

"But you can't," Julie said back. "You didn't call it first." Julie was determined not to give in this time. Peter started to cry and throw a fit. This caused Patsy to start crying. Julie stood firm holding the doorknob and waited for Peter to get into the car.

"Get in the damn car!" Ron yelled at Julie. Julie hesitated until Rhonda turned and glared back at her. Julie got into the car and scooted to the middle. She could feel her anger rise within her. She wanted to cry and punch Peter all at the same time. Grandpap James didn't say a word. Julie wondered if he probably wished he had stayed home.

By the time that they had pulled into the parking lot for the ballgame, Julie could tell that everyone was on edge. No one spoke or said a word as Ron parked the car. Julie wanted to get out of the car as soon as possible. She waited for her dad and Rhonda to open their doors. Everyone just sat still. Julie looked over at Pap Pap James and hoped that he would get out so that she could also. But no one moved or said a word. "Let me out," she said to Peter. But he only made a face at her, crossed his arms, and refused to move.

"Let me out!" Julie said again in a hushed command. But Peter refused to budge. Julie paused a minute as the adults sat and stared. Julie felt her anger rising. "Peter, get out!" she said and gave him a quick poke to move. But this time, he poked her back hard. Julie had had enough, and with her fist, she gave him a punch in the arm. Peter let out a yell as if Julie had half-killed him. Rhonda turned around and placed Patsy on the seat beside her. She yelled at Peter to get out of the car and then leaned over the seat and grabbed hold of Julie. Peter saw the anger on his mom's face as he quickly opened the door, scrambled out of the car, and slammed the door behind him. Julie sat in horror as she saw the fury on Rhonda's face and felt the firm grip she had on her. Julie had never seen Rhonda this angry. She couldn't imagine what she was going to do to her. She had never shown so much anger at her, ever, especially in front of her dad. Julie winced and hoped that she would let go of her and that her anger would subside. She waited for her dad or grandpap to say or do something.

Suddenly, without any warning, Rhonda flung herself over the backseat of the car. The force of her body knocked Julie across the backseat. Julie's head rested toward the closed back door. Shocked, Julie watched as Rhonda plummeted over the car seat and on top of her. Rhonda straddled Julie's tiny frame and held her down. Julie squirmed and kicked her legs under Rhonda's body and tried to get away, but she knew that she couldn't escape from beneath her weight. She felt her feet kick Pap Pap James who was still sitting beside her. She wondered why no one was helping her. In the confusion, Julie heard the back door of the car open and heard her dad yelling at Pap Pap James to get out of the car. But Julie could only see Rhonda's large frame towering above her. Her face was full of a rage which Julie had never seen before in her life. Rhonda's one hand held her down while the other one was raised in the air. Julie saw the fist coming down toward her face and closed her eyes tightly. Julie felt the pain go through her body. She then felt Rhonda's weight lift off of her. Through the blood, Julie could see her dad pulling Rhonda off her. Julie tried to sit up as the blood poured from her nose. She grasped for the doorknob with her bloody hand while cupping the other hand near her nose to catch the steady stream. She had to get out of the car before she would get blood onto the seats.

Her dad came over and helped her out of the car. He grabbed his handkerchief and put it onto her nose to stop the bleeding. Julie felt for a minute that maybe her dad really did care. It was the first time that she could remember her dad ever showing her any kind of nurturing. He told her to hold the handkerchief tightly to her nose and to lean her head back. He then went back to talk to Rhonda and to help quiet her crying children. Julie let the tears stream down her face as the white handkerchief turned completely red and dripped onto Julie's lap. How she wished that her mom could be here with her. Julie could see the stares of other people as they parked their cars and walked past them to go down to the ball field. She looked up at her dad as he lit a cigarette and turned back to talk to Rhonda. Julie wanted to ask for another hanky or napkin. She pulled the bloody handkerchief from her nose, but the blood continued to flow. There was no sign of the bleeding stopping. Julie's hand was crusted with the sticky mess.

"Dad, I need another hanky," Julie called quietly to her dad interrupting his conversation. He rummaged in the car and tried to find another cloth. Julie thought that he looked a little concerned that the bleeding had not stopped. Rhonda had her back toward her and refused to even look at her. Patsy and Peter sat in the front seat with the doors swung open.

After a long time, the bleeding began to slow and finally stopped. Julie tried to take the soaked cloth and wipe the crusted blood off her face and hands the best that she could. They didn't stay for the game. Shortly, they went back into the car, and they drove back home. No one said a word. Pap Pap James got out of the car at their home and walked back to his house.

Julie ran up the stairs and into the bathroom to clean herself up. She put her pajamas on and went to bed and waited for her brothers to come home. She lay silently and listened for her brothers but fell into a deep sleep before they ever came home.

Our Dearest Mom

CHAPTER

24

"Come on, Jul!" Ronnie called upstairs. "We're waiting for you… you're my teammate for croquet."

Julie came running down the stairs and followed Ronnie out the front door to avoid Rhonda in the kitchen at the back door.

Earlier, they had pulled out all of the weeds in the yard and also in the garden. Julie was sure that Rhonda would make them do more chores, but to her surprise, she gave them a bologna sandwich and told them to go play. Rhonda had not said a word to her about the previous evening. She had actually been extra nice to them today.

Ronnie grabbed his favorite blue mallet. Julie grabbed the red one; Jerry, the orange; and Matt, the black one. No one wanted the yellow one.

"Boy, Rhonda sure is nice to us today," Matt said as he waited his turn.

"She better be," Ronnie mumbled as he swung his mallet slowly, carefully aiming at his ball.

"Yeah, when Mom finds out what she did to Julie, she's going to be in a lot of trouble," Jerry added.

Julie didn't say a word. All that she could think about was all of the trouble that she had caused. Her brothers had found the blood-soaked handkerchief in the bathroom trash can after they had gotten home the night before.

Jerry ran down the stairs with the handkerchief in his hand to ask their dad about it. Aware of the deadly silence with the look on Rhonda's face and seeing that his dad was drinking beer, he thought it best to not ask. He tossed the handkerchief into the kitchen garbage can on top of the pile of beer cans and slipped back upstairs.

They waited until the next morning while they were pulling weeds to ask Julie what had happened.

"It's your turn," Matt called to Julie.

"Take your time, Julie," Ronnie called out from the center croquet arch. He smiled a big smile at Julie. "We're winning, Jul!"

Julie hit the ball slowly and made it through the first two arches.

"Way to go!" Ronnie said. "Go for the next one!"

Julie gleamed with pride from her brother's praise. Even Matt and Jerry smiled at her even though they were behind in the game.

Julie couldn't stop thinking about the last evening. She would feel the anger rise within her every time she thought about Peter and how he was always trying to get them into trouble. Julie reached and touched her sore nose tenderly. The very thought of Peter and Rhonda made her blood boil.

They continued to play their game. Julie listened to her brothers talk about taking the right shots. Slowly, her anger began to fade. She remembered her Sunday school lesson from the week before about Saul killing the Christians. *He was such a mean man until Jesus came into his heart and changed his life forever.* They were taught how important it is to forgive others. Julie's thoughts went back to Peter. *Maybe, the reason that he was so mean like his mom was that he was lonely.* Julie remembered how terrified he had looked after he had seen what his mom had done to her. Julie began to think that she should forgive him and that she had been as much of the problem as he had been. *He's only six years old*, she thought sadly. *He's stuck with his mom and her lifestyle. He has no weekends or anywhere to go to get a break from it all. He doesn't even know his dad. He must feel so lost and all alone.*

As they continued to play their game, they came to the final arches. Ronnie was set for the final winning shot. Julie slowly walked over to the cherry tree.

Ronnie stopped aiming his ball and gave Julie a look of victory as he winked at her. Jerry dropped his mallet and ran his fingers through his hair. Matt just muttered, "Oh brother."

Ronnie went back to taking his turn, aimed, and hit the ball. Julie heard the ball smack the peg signaling their triumphant win.

It was later that evening when all four of them piled into their mom's car. Julie had never been so glad to see her mom. She was so excited when their mom told them that they were going to get ice cream and take them to the drive-in theater. Bob was sleeping because he had to work the night shift.

While they were eating their ice cream, Ronnie told their mom what Rhonda had done to Julie. Julie looked down at her butter pecan ice cream. She dreaded the subject. She thought it would be best to just forget it. She knew it would upset her mom, and Julie just wanted to have a happy time tonight. But it was too late to stop the conversation as Ethel listened to Matt, Jerry, and Ronnie tell her about what had happened to Julie.

"Julie, is this true…what happened?" Ethel asked. Ethel tenderly took Julie's face into her hand and tilted it up to look at her nose and into her eyes.

"Yeah, Mom, but I shouldn't have punched Peter. It was my fault," Julie answered. She felt for sure that she would disappoint her mom.

"Julie, it's not your fault," Ethel spoke kindly but firmly. "No one should ever correct you by hitting you in the face with their fist."

"I'm okay now," Julie assured her.

"Yeah, well you should've seen the handkerchief," Jerry continued, interrupting Julie.

"They had a hard time getting it to stop bleeding," Julie explained and then looked away.

"What did your daddy do?" Ethel continued determined to get to the bottom of it.

"He gave me his hanky and told me to hold it on my nose," Julie answered.

"I mean, what did he do to Rhonda?" Ethel asked.

"Well, he pulled her off of me so she couldn't hit me again," Julie answered, trying to defend her dad.

"Well, why in the hell did he let her hit you in the first place?" Ethel yelled.

Julie was surprised at her mom. She had hardly ever heard her say any curse words.

"Well, he had to get Pap Pap James out of the car first before he could pull her off of me," Julie explained as she tried to make it sound not so bad.

Ethel shook her head as she started the engine of the car and pulled out of the dairy's parking lot. "Let's just go to our movie for now. I'll talk to your dad later." Ethel put her arm around Julie as they drove out onto the highway.

The next day, Julie was playing outside with her brothers and Bob's children. She broke away and ran into the basement of her mom's house to use the bathroom. As Julie entered the downstairs, she could hear her mom and Bob talking louder than usual. Julie paused to listen.

"Bob, I can't let my kids be treated this way," Ethel said with desperation in her voice.

"Well, Ethel, what can we do?" Bob answered back. "We can't take all four of them to live with us. I can't support seven kids."

"Maybe, Ron would help out," Ethel pleaded.

"He won't even help now!" Bob said with his voice rising. "We work at the same factory, and he should be buying the things that they need, their clothes and shoes. Why do you have to buy them everything?"

"Yeah, Bob," Ethel said with sarcasm in her voice. "Do your kids go without? No! They have everything they need…a home, food, clothes, and me. I told you before, when I married you, that my kids would come first, and that they wouldn't do without!"

"I'm just saying that Ron should do more. That's all," Bob said wearily.

"Well, maybe he should, Bob," Ethel retorted back. "But guess what? That's never going to happen. I told you that I was always going to be there for my children. But I'm not! I was always going to be there for them. I should've been there for Julie. Now where am I? Here, taking care of your kids while my kids suffer."

Julie heard her mom's voice grow silent and heard her crying. Julie opened the basement door and went back outside. *How could she have caused so much trouble?*

The big, yellow car pulled into Lindy's parking lot. Ethel didn't know if Ron was home or not. Ethel put the car into park, pulled the emergency brake, and turned off the engine.

Jerry looked at Matt as Matt looked at Julie and then Ronnie. Julie looked at Ronnie too. She hoped that maybe Ronnie knew what was happening. Their mom never parked and turned off the engine. Ronnie looked at his three siblings and shrugged his shoulders in an "I don't know what's going on" fashion.

As they got out of the car, they were surprised to see that their mom had stepped out of the car also. None of them said a word. Julie could feel her stomach churn with mixed emotions. Her mom had not been in their home since Jerry and her had been sick with the measles. Ethel walked through the gate and up to the front door with her children behind her. She knocked on the door.

Rhonda did not answer the door. Julie thought it seemed so strange seeing her mom knock on the door of their home. *She shouldn't be knocking*, Julie thought. *She's not a stranger. This was her home, our home, she belongs here with us.* Julie wanted to cry but bit her lip instead. Ronnie pushed past his mom and opened the closed door. As they entered, they saw Rhonda sitting at the kitchen table drinking a cup of coffee.

Ethel followed behind her children. Julie could see that her mom's face was flushed. They all sat down in the living room and watched their mom march toward the kitchen. Rhonda stood up from her chair and met Ethel in the living room. Julie cringed seeing the two women meet face-to-face. Rhonda was twice the size of her mom.

"Ron's not home yet if that's who you're looking for," Rhonda said with a gesture of her hand to the air while holding her coffee cup in the other one.

"Well, to tell you the truth," Ethel said in a defiant tone, "you're the one I really want to talk to!"

"I think you should just wait and talk to Ron," Rhonda said. She slammed her cup down so hard on the end table that the coffee bounced out of the cup and spilled onto the floor.

"What right do you think that you have to beat up my kids the way you do?" Ethel snapped back.

"I have every right!" Rhonda shot back. Julie could see Rhonda's face turn bright red. "I'm the one living here, and I'm the one raising them!"

Julie felt her stomach sicken as she watched the two women continue to argue. She glanced over at her brothers as they sat on the couch across the room. But they looked as shocked as she felt. This was one time that she wished that her dad would come home early. She knew the capacity of Rhonda's fury, and she knew the determination of her mom's heart. There was going to be trouble, and she was the cause.

"You're the one who walked out and left them for Ron to raise!" Rhonda continued. Rhonda felt her words slap Ethel and she gloated as her words hit the intended mark.

Ethel paused as Rhonda approached the front door and looked through the venetian blinds to see if Ron was arriving home yet.

Ethel approached Rhonda slowly at first and then boldly stepped up to her and looked her straight in the eyes. "Let me tell you one thing, and one thing only!" Ethel said.

Ethel spoke in a tone that Julie had never heard her use, not even with her dad. Ethel pointed her finger directly into Rhonda's face. Julie had never seen her mom this angry before, never! As Julie looked at Rhonda's face, she realized this was the first time she had ever seen Rhonda afraid. Julie watched Rhonda walk backward toward the bedroom door as her mom continued and followed after her.

"You say anything you want about me, I don't care!" Ethel continued. "But, you redheaded son of a b— if you ever lay another hand on my kids, I'll kill you!" Ethel pressed Rhonda up against the bedroom door. Rhonda reached behind her and opened the door so quickly that both women almost fell down. Rhonda slammed the door shut in Ethel's face. Julie heard the lock snap into place and then the sound of the venetian blinds rattle, the sound of the window opening and closing, and then footsteps on the front porch as Rhonda ran away.

Ethel paused to gain her composure. Julie and her brothers ran to their mom. She was crying now as she put her arms around the four of them. She glanced around the room and saw Rhonda's children crying. *How could life be so complicated*, Ethel thought. *How could she ever make it up to her children for what she had done by leaving them?* She kissed them good-bye and brushed her tears aside with her hand. "I'll pick you up tomorrow after church," she said as she turned to leave. "Ronnie, you let me know if Rhonda does anything." Ronnie nodded his head in understanding. Ethel opened the door, turned, and looked back and then shut the door behind her.

Julie ran over to pick up Patsy. Peter ran through the house and called for his mom. Julie didn't want to imagine or think about what tomorrow would bring.

Ronnie age fifteen; Jerry age fourteen, Julie
age twelve; and Matt age thirteen

CHAPTER

25

The wind blew through Julie's thin sweater as she walked down the hill from Gramma Emma's house. Ronnie ran ahead to get the key that was hidden on the summer porch. The house was calm and quiet as they walked in, almost ghostlike. "Set the alarm clock, Jerry, so we can sleep for another hour before we have to get ready for school," Matt said as he slowly walked up the stairs.

Julie crawled into her bed, beneath the covers, to warm up. It was late fall, and their lives had changed as quickly as the season. Julie lay in bed as her mind wandered and evaded the sleep that she so desired. She took her pillow and dolls and placed them around her for protection and then snuggled under the covers. It had become a force of habit for her to sleep this way. Julie stared up at the ceiling tile and then rolled over restlessly. She thought hopelessly that it did little good to do all of this to protect her from her dad's abuse.

Rhonda had moved out permanently over to Mount Zion. Julie and her brothers enjoyed the peacefulness. They no longer had to walk on edge and wait for Rhonda to explode. She was out of their lives, they had thought; however, it wasn't long before their dad was taking them over to Rhonda's new apartment for visits. Julie knew that by Rhonda moving out that their dad was now under no pressure to have to marry her. But that didn't last long. Rhonda soon became less tolerant of Ron as he promised her nothing and gave her little to cling to. She soon grew tired of the situation and permanently broke up with him.

The abuse from Julie's dad started all over again. She could only hope for the nights that their dad would send them up to Gramma Emma's to spend the night. Julie knew that then and only then would she be safe.

It became a routine that their dad would come home, sit on the couch, and begin to drink his beer. Julie would go out into the kitchen and do her homework. After they would go to bed and fall asleep, her dad would wake her up and call her to come downstairs. It was always worse when her dad would sneak into her room and sit on the edge of her bed. Julie would awaken and clutch onto her pillows telling him to leave. Sometimes he would say, "I only want to talk." Julie knew that he knew that he couldn't do anything to her when she was awake. Her protests were too great, and he seemed to fear that her brothers might wake up. Julie would beg him to leave her room, but he would just sit on the edge of her bed with his head drooping down, his legs spread apart with his hand holding a beer can on his wavering knee. "I just need someone to talk to," he'd say as he struggled to get his words out.

When Julie would protest, he'd continue anyway as if Julie owed him as much. "You know, Julie, no woman is going to want to be with a man who already has four kids to raise. Maybe you'd be better off without your old man, but who would you live with then?" he would quiz her. "No one," he'd continue. "You'd all have to go live in an orphanage. Is that what you want?" Julie would sit quietly and bide the time. Sometimes, he would try to pull away the dolls and pillows that she held close to her side, but Julie would just clutch them tighter. Finally, he would give up, get up, and stagger out of her room.

Worst of all was when she didn't awake in time to stop him. Julie would wake up to the horror of his touch. When she would forcefully stop him, he would get angry and say, "Well, you know, Julie, if you hadn't been the reason that Rhonda left, I wouldn't be all alone." The words would pierce through Julie's heart causing her mind to race in confusion.

Julie heard the alarm clock go off in her brothers' bedroom. She wearily sat up in her bed. Would her life ever change? she thought. She rubbed her head as the troubled thoughts tumbled in her mind. She glanced over at the small picture of Jesus that still hung on her wall. She looked at the man with the long, wavy brown hair and the short-trimmed beard. She thought that his eyes looked so kind, and she peered at them steadily as if they could show her some sign of hope. "Why don't you care?" she angrily whispered out loud. Julie then walked away and refused to let a single tear fall.

Surely, life could not get any worse. The only thing that she could look forward to was going with her mom and visiting her grammas, aunts, and uncles. But Julie soon discovered that things did get worse.

Lindsey had moved back to the area and was in her class again. Julie cringed as she recalled the hardships that Lindsey had caused her in the third grade. But this time, the girls had all teamed up together and wouldn't let Lindsey take over the class again. Julie was unaware of the influence that she had gained with her fellow classmates. She found them looking to her for leadership. But Julie was changing. She was angry at God for not helping her. She went to Sunday school every week, but it didn't seem to matter anymore. Nothing seemed to matter anymore. Julie felt so helpless in her situation that she adopted the attitude of not caring about anything or anyone. She let her heart harden to stop the pain. The more she hardened her heart, the less pain she felt. But what she didn't know was that the more she hardened her heart, the less love she would also feel. She became distant to everyone, even with her mom and her brothers. The least little thing would set her off. Even her brothers weren't sure of how to reach her at times.

As Julie gained popularity, Lindsey tried to become her friend. Unlike in the third grade when Lindsey had shut her out. Julie's friendship with Sarah had never really healed, and Julie didn't care anymore to even try. Julie became a tyrant as she joined in with Lindsey. All the girls went along with the duo so that each wouldn't be shut out. Julie began to make fun of a girl in class that stuttered. She began to order the other girls around. She reviled in this new power and control that she had gained. She vowed that no one would ever hurt her again.

Lindsey wasn't interested in Sunday school. Julie continued to go because her dad made her go. She began to feel that Sunday school was just for kids, now being that she was in the seventh grade and would soon be thirteen years old. It was becoming harder and harder for her to believe in a God who seemed to love and care for everyone else except her. Somehow, she just wasn't important enough for God, for her mom, for her brothers, and especially for even herself.

❀

"Julie! What in the world is the matter with you?" Ethel scolded her as she sat at the kitchen table.

There was no use trying to hide it. They had all seen her do it. Her head rested hopelessly in her cupped hands as she listened to her mom's question. She couldn't answer.

"I asked you a question, Julie!" Ethel continued. Julie only shrugged her shoulders. Julie didn't know what was wrong with her. She had been trying to figure it out all her life. Why was she such a troublemaker? What did she do to make her dad treat her that way? Why was she so unlovable? What was it about her that aggravated everyone? Lately, she was even driving her brothers crazy with her mood swings. Even her mom's questions didn't really bother her. *What did it matter?* she thought. *What did anything matter?*

"Julie," Ethel said. She pulled out a chair and sat down beside Julie. "Please tell me what's wrong. It's not like you to be mean to other children." Ethel put her hand gently on Julie's back. She was surprised to see Julie recoil as her hand touched her. Julie had never reacted that way to her touch. Ethel gently rubbed her daughter's back and watched as Julie sat straight up. She stared ahead in a daze and said nothing.

Ethel slowly stood up and went to the sink to do the dishes. She had to think of how she should handle this problem with Julie.

"Mom," Julie said sadly as she turned in her chair to look up at her mom. "Mom, I am so sorry, truly I am."

Ethel patted her daughter lovingly on her shoulder and ran her fingers through her tight curls. She then turned back to do the dishes.

Julie continued sitting at the table and looked out the window watching her brothers play outside with the others. Julie was too ashamed to go out and play. Julie felt ashamed all the time lately. She felt sad and lonely. She felt guilty and fearful. But most of all, she felt angry. She was angry at herself, her dad, and anyone who got in her way. It had been so long since Julie remembered feeling good feelings or any feelings at all. The whole world seemed happy but her.

Julie didn't know how she could have been so cruel to the neighbor girl. She was angry that her brothers had thought that she was cute. She was angry that she wouldn't be her friend. Julie was tired of being shut out, so she launched out to hurt her. Julie knew that the girl's father had been sent away to prison. Julie cringed sitting in her chair as she remembered what she had done. "So where is your dad?" she had asked. She saw the girl's lip quiver, and her eyes fill with tears. Way deep inside of Julie, she heard a still, small voice say, "Don't!" But Julie had felt a new sense of power in hurting someone else instead of being hurt. She ignored the still, small voice as she had been ignoring everything in her life that mattered. "I bet I know where he is," she had continued. Julie pushed on as the young girl's eyes filled with tears. She got up and went to run into her house. But Julie hollered after her. "He's in prison!"

Ronnie came running up to her and yelled, "Julie, how could you say that to her?" Shortly thereafter, her mother had come out and asked them all to go home.

Julie hated what she had done, but yet there was a part of her that felt empowered and still another part of her that just didn't care. Julie sat motionless in the chair and continued to watch everyone play outside. She laid her head down on her folded arms and watched her mom do the dishes. How could she ever make it right? How could she have ever hurt someone so badly? Julie hated what she had done, and more so, she hated herself and what she had become.

As the days passed, both Julie and Lindsey became inseparable. They both took charge of the games they played at recess, making sure that they both were on the same team so that no one could beat them. If the other girls thought that Lindsey was a tyrant before, they were now fully aware of how impossible it would be to stop both Lindsey and Julie acting together. Both were liked by their teachers and were top A students. Both were feared more than respected. Sarah had tried to tell Julie in Sunday school that Lindsey was changing Julie. But Julie insisted that she wasn't and thought to herself that Sarah was just jealous of them. *Well*, Julie thought, *no one is going to hurt me anymore.* Julie was determined in her heart. *No one!*

One day after school, Julie decided to walk with Lindsey on the way to Gramma Winnie's house. They kidded around as some of the boys in their class flirted with them. Boys were starting to notice them, and Julie enjoyed the attention. As they walked on, Julie gleefully kicked the stones along the way.

"Hey, look at your shoes!" Lindsey said as she pointed to Julie's worn and dusty shoes and let out a cruel laugh.

Julie looked down at her ragged penny loafers. They were covered with dust from kicking the rocks, but the worst was that almost all the stringed laces had popped at the seams, leaving large gaps. Julie felt embarrassed as she looked over at Lindsey's polished loafers with bright, shiny pennies in the front. Julie didn't answer. What could she say? Her mom had noticed how bad her shoes were and had tried to clean them up. "I'll buy you some new ones, honey, as soon as I can get more hours in at work," Julie's mom had promised.

"Well, I'll see you tomorrow," Julie said to Lindsey as she neared Gramma Winnie's house. But Lindsey had already turned and ran down the road to catch up with another girl.

Julie entered the back door of her Gramma's house and laid her books on the table. She could hear her brothers' laughter coming from the living room as they watched television. "Hi, Mom! Hi, Gramma!" Julie said.

"How's school?" Ethel asked and reached out to give Julie a hug.

"Oh, it's pretty good," Julie answered and shrugged her shoulders.

"And how is Lindsey?" Ethel pressed a little further.

"She's fine," Julie murmured. She wanted to drop the whole subject of Lindsey.

"Julie, I think that Lindsey can be a little cruel at times, and I think it's affecting you," Ethel continued.

"No! She's okay, Mom," Julie answered defending her friend.

"Julie, she is the kind of person that can really hurt you," Ethel said, wanting to warn Julie.

Julie pulled out her books and started doing her homework. She half-listened to her mom and Gramma talk. The words that her mom had said echoed in her mind. She remembered how cruel Lindsey had just been in making fun of her shoes.

The next morning, Julie woke up to the aroma of bacon and eggs cooking. She loved it when she was able to stay over at Gramma Winnie's house. As Julie quickly got ready for school, she couldn't remember where she had left her shoes.

"Julie, your breakfast is ready!" Gramma Winnie called from the kitchen.

"Gramma, I can't find my shoes! I've looked everywhere."

"They're under the china hutch," Gramma Winnie called back.

"No, Gramma…I've already looked there," Julie said.

"Look again," Gramma Winnie answered back.

"Gramma, they're not there! I'm looking and looking!" Julie yelled back. "I'll be late for school if I don't hurry!"

Julie was down on all fours, crunched to the floor under Gramma Winnie's china hutch. She turned and saw Gramma Winnie come into the room. Her broad frame was covered with an apron, and she held a cake turner in her hand. She had a broad smile on her face as she approached and said, "Well, there they are, Julie, right beside your hand."

Julie looked at the shoes under the hutch by her hand. She already had seen that pair of shoes. "But, Gramma, these aren't mine. They're someone's new shoes, mine are old ones."

"Oh, honey, they're not new shoes. I just restitched and polished them for you."

"But, Gramma, they look brand-new!" Julie exclaimed. "You even put brand new pennies in them." Julie slipped them onto her feet. She stood looking down at her shoes, pointing them to the right and to the left. She looked up at her Gramma who was still standing beside her. Julie reached out her arms and wrapped them around Gramma Winnie's large frame. "Thank you, Gramma! Thank you so much!"

"Your welcome, honey. Come eat your breakfast."

Julie sat down at the table as Gramma Winnie poured Julie a large glass of orange juice and set a plate full of eggs, bacon, and home fries down in front of her. Julie noticed the many pricks on her Gramma's fingers that Julie knew were from sewing her shoes. Julie thought that she could never feel any more special than she did right now. *Wait until Lindsey sees my new shoes*, Julie thought.

Julie age thirteen.

CHAPTER

26

Julie pounced down the steps, skipping every other one and rushed to the front door. Matt and Jerry sat in the living room watching television. Julie slid the venetian blind up slightly and peered out into the night. She looked up at the streetlight across the street. "It's really snowing outside," she said. "Ronnie should be home from church by now." Julie stood, mesmerized by the falling snow; its reflection in the light was like speckles of shimmering gold dust against the black night.

"I think I see Ronnie coming," Julie called out. She pushed her face closer to the cold windowpane. In the far distance, she could see her brother coming past Lindy's bar in the faint light. The collar of his coat was up to cover his bare neck, and his hatless head was covered with snow. When Ronnie crossed the street, Julie opened the door as he stomped his shoes on the front porch. "Where you been? It's getting late?"

Ronnie took his coat off and shook it gently before hanging it on the stair post.

"You guys should've come with me tonight. We had a guest speaker, and it was really good."

"We will sometime," Matt and Jerry answered back almost in unison.

"Come join us, Ronnie," Matt called out.

"Yeah, you gotta see this crazy new show. It's called the *Beverly Hillbillies*," Jerry added.

"I don't like it!" Julie said as she dusted the snow from Ronnie's hair with her hand. "It makes all southern people look stupid."

"I've got homework to do," Ronnie answered his siblings and left to go upstairs.

"Julie, promise me you'll go to church with me some night." Ronnie paused and looked deep into his young sister's eyes.

"I will, Ronnie. I promise," Julie answered. She looked back into her brother's deep, brown eyes. His love for her moved her, and she could feel her hardened heart begin to melt under his loving gaze. "I promise," she said again with a big smile.

That night, Julie lay in bed thinking. She was actually afraid to go to sleep. Her dad had been out all night and wasn't home yet. She could hear her brothers' rhythmic breathing from the next room and knew that they were already asleep. She was growing up and taking on the form of a young woman. She had begun her cycles; however, the joy of becoming a woman was lost in the turmoil of fending off her dad's secret advances and remarks about her changing body.

Julie glanced across the room and could see the little cross that still hung on her wall. It gave a faint glow in the dark night. Julie lay in the quiet night thinking. She could still see her brother's piercing and loving eyes pleading with her to go to church with him. Ronnie had started to go to church on Wednesday and Sunday nights. Julie couldn't get over the change she had seen in Ronnie. Even when their dad would tease him for going to church, Ronnie seemed to not be deterred. He went through the house singing in his deep base voice. He gave Julie hope and reminded Julie of a hope that she also once had.

Julie had lost that hope and the joy she had once felt. She was full of despair. She was not happy with the person that she was becoming. She didn't like the cruelty that was becoming a part of her. Lately, Lindsey had been very cruel to her. She would deliberately make fun of her in front of others or ignore her altogether. Julie felt all alone. She was tired and exhausted of being angry. Mostly, she missed the love and peace that she had once felt, like her brother Ronnie, with Jesus. The glowing cross began to dim in the dark night but seemed to flicker as if to beckon her to return to the one who truly loved her. *I really do want to change, dear Jesus,* she prayed quietly. *Please help me, dear Jesus,* she prayed. Julie purposed in her heart that she would try to go to church with Ronnie at the evening service. She felt a peace come over her, a peace that she had not felt for a long time and drifted off into a deep sleep.

Julie found herself dragging in school. She wanted to get closer to Sarah, but she had hurt Sarah's feelings too many times, and she knew that Sarah didn't trust her. Julie couldn't blame her. Lately, Sarah had joined with Lindsey. Julie knew that things were changing by the cruel things that Lindsey was saying about her to others.

One day, Mr. Sanders called out their grade scores from a test they had taken. Julie hated when teachers did this. She received good grades, but it could be very humiliating to those who didn't. Julie was surprised when Mr. Sanders called out her name and then paused. Julie waited anxiously to hear her score. He continued on saying "98, you must have gotten lucky or studied hard." The words smacked at Julie's heart. So why was it not possible for her to get good grades without luck or studying hard? Determined, she would show Mr. Sanders that she was not lucky but that she could do whatever she put her mind to.

Lindsey looked over at her and smirked. Julie smiled back at her in spite of her cruelty. Julie was proud to get her grade. No one else had scored any higher. As time passed, Julie noticed that Mr. Sanders was impressed by her grades and was no longer surprised. She had earned his respect, and with it, she had also earned some respect for herself.

Julie kept her promise to Ronnie and started to go to church with him in the evenings. They hadn't convinced Jerry and Matt yet, but they continued to pester them to come. Julie knew that it was just a matter of time that they would also come.

Julie sat in the little country church beside Ronnie. The music resounded in the little building as if carried on angels' wings. Julie's eyes flittered from side to side and came to rest on the stained glass window. There Jesus knelt with the cross on his back, pain etched on his face. Julie heard the pastor's plea to come forward. She felt a tug at her heart to go up to the altar. She remembered the first time that she had yielded to that call. She wanted to go up in the worst way, but everything from her shyness to her guilt held her back. It only took one loving look from her big brother to tear down her reserves. Julie slowly stood up and went to the altar. Somehow, she knew that her life would never be the same. She sobbed into her folded arms as she knelt at the altar and poured her heart out to God to forgive her. She surrendered her hardened heart and asked Jesus to come into her life. Julie walked home that night in the dark with Ronnie. She was happier than she had been for a long time.

Julie knew as soon as they had walked in the front door that night that there was a problem. Their dad sat on the couch in a slumped fashion with his beer can in his hand. Matt and Jerry shot both Ronnie and her a quick glance. Ronnie and Julie started to go up the steps quietly and quickly.

"Come on back down here!" Ron called out to them.

Slowly, Ronnie and Julie came back down.

"You two too good to say hi to your old man?" he asked in a slurred voice.

"I've got some homework to do yet," Ronnie answered, ignoring his dad's remark. Ronnie was having a hard time lately with his dad's remarks, and Julie could see that at times, he became very discouraged.

"I have to get ready for school tomorrow," Julie answered, wanting to just go upstairs. Jerry and Matt jumped up cautiously to join them before their dad could say anymore.

"Go ahead!" their dad said as he motioned with his arm, flinging it hopelessly into the air toward the stairway. "Go ahead," he murmured as they went up the stairs.

It didn't take long for Julie's newfound faith to be tested. Julie no longer felt empowered to hurt others. On the contrary, when she did, a deep conviction would flood her heart. She saw how wrong she had been in bullying others to try to relieve her own pain. She grieved at the pain that she had caused others, and as she did, she grieved again at the pain that others had inflicted upon her. Julie began to slowly change without realizing it herself. But Lindsey realized that she was losing her control and hold on Julie.

One day, Julie was waiting in the hallway for her bus to come. She stood with her back away from the restrooms watching out of the glass doors. When her friends had gone to the bathroom, Julie had wondered what was taking them so long. Suddenly, without notice, she felt two arms wrap around her waist, which held her very tightly. She squirmed to get loose but couldn't break their hold. Julie glanced over her shoulders and saw that it was Lindsey who had grabbed her. "Let go of me!" Julie said with a slight laugh. She thought Lindsey was kidding with her. But Lindsey didn't let go.

"Let go of me!" Julie said again in a firmer voice.

"Make me," Lindsey whispered in her ear as she held Julie firmly.

Julie tried to wiggle loose and once again tried to glance back at Lindsey. She couldn't help wondering what was going on. "Come on, Lindsey. Let go of me!" Julie said. But Lindsey said nothing, held her tightly, and laughed. Julie could see that the other girls had gathered to watch them. Julie hesitated but then began to feel Lindsey's grasp tighten around her once again. Julie now realized that Lindsey was serious. With one hard thrust and a quick twist, Julie broke loose just as the bus pulled up. Julie rode home on the bus deep in thought. It was times like these that she missed her brothers the most. Now that they were all in high school, she rode the bus alone. She couldn't believe that Lindsey could have been serious. She tried to think of what might have provoked the incident but could think of nothing.

Julie waited until the bus had stopped and then quickly jumped up from her seat. She climbed down the stairwell of the bus and hopped off. All she wanted was to hurry home. The noise of the bus pulling out had muffled the scurrying of the footsteps that had crept silently up behind Julie without her knowing it. Suddenly without warning, Julie felt an unexpected arm lock around her neck, which swung her to the ground. Julie immediately saw a gold chain from Lindsey's watch dangle in front of her face. "What are you doing?" Julie yelled out at Lindsey. But Lindsey said nothing and tried to push Julie toward the bank that abutted a ditch.

This had gone too far, and Julie had had enough. It was too much, and Julie switched to a different mode. Her elbow let loose with a force that shot into Lindsey's ribs like a switchblade. As Lindsey let out a gasp, her grasp on Julie loosened. Julie took her other hand and grabbed Lindsey's arm and yanked it loose from around her neck. Julie felt her finger catch on the golden chain of the watch and felt it snap. With one more quick thrust, Julie broke loose from Lindsey's firm grip.

"What in the world is your problem?" Julie asked as she tried to catch her breath. She reached down and quickly picked up her books, keeping one eye on Lindsey who stood shocked at what had just happened.

"You broke my watch!" Lindsey yelled out at Julie. She then turned with her head in the air and stomped away angrily. The other girls that had gathered to watch turned and followed quickly behind Lindsey.

Julie slowly walked home by herself. She was so confused and could not understand what had provoked the commotion. She had hoped that she could work it all out the next day.

Julie breathed a deep sigh as she reached the iron gate. She paused and looked over at Lindy's to see if her dad's car was there. It wasn't there, and Julie took another sigh of relief because her dad wasn't home. She paused for a moment thinking that he might have parked his car down back. She never knew what to expect or what she was going to walk into when she entered the house.

As Julie opened the front door, she was glad to see that her brothers were home. Jerry was in the kitchen cooking supper while Ronnie and Matt were sprawled out on the living room floor watching the four-o'clock movie.

Matt looked up at Julie as she entered. "Gee, what happened to you?"

"Yeah," Ronnie echoed.

"Nothing," Julie mumbled softly and walked toward the kitchen to help Jerry. She tucked in her blouse, which was hanging out over her skirt. She placed her books onto a kitchen chair and then walked to the sink. She wrung out a dishrag and wiped the table clean before putting her books up onto the table. "Jerry, can you help me with my math?"

"You better ask Matt, Jul," Jerry answered with a chuckle. "You know he's better at math than I am."

"Matt!" Julie called out.

"On a commercial. I'll be out to help you," Matt answered before Julie could even ask.

Julie sat and watched Jerry stirring the pot of chili that he had made. They had gotten used to coming home and taking turns cooking supper. They had actually become pretty good at it. Matt entered the kitchen and swung open the refrigerator door. "Here, add some of this," he said. He handed Jerry the bottle of ketchup.

"You and your ketchup," Jerry said as he reached for the bottle.

Julie smiled as she watched and listened to her brothers talk.

"I hope that we get to go up to Gramma's tonight!" she said out loud.

"Yeah, me too," Jerry said as he dipped a spoon into the chili to taste it.

"Well, we'll soon find out," Ronnie interjected as he came into the kitchen to join them.

The front door had opened and their dad walked in. He didn't say a word but came right into the kitchen and went to the refrigerator. Matt leaned down to help Julie with her math problem, and Ronnie went back into the living room to watch the movie.

Jerry stirred the chili once more and said that it would soon be ready. Julie watched her dad get a can of beer and pop the lid off the can. She tried to study him to know his mood. Sometimes, he could be nice and even though she was older now, she longed to get a glimpse of the old dad that she had once known so long ago. Sometimes, Julie wondered if the nice dad had ever really existed or if he was just an imagination of her childhood.

She wondered, as she watched him, if he remembered, at all, the things that he had done to her and others, drunk or sober. He had come home today, like any other day, and acted as if nothing had ever happened as if everything was normal. The only thing that Julie couldn't figure out though, in her own life, was "What is normal?"

Julie sat flicking her pencil on her math book, pretending to concentrate on a math problem that Matt had explained to her. But her mind went back to her dad. In the last two weeks, the abuse had grown worse. The older she was getting, the worse it was becoming. No matter how hard she had tried to avoid him, he always seemed to find a time when either she was sleeping or when he would try to catch her alone in the house. He had gotten bolder with his attempts even when he was sober and she was awake.

Julie took her books into the living room and helped Jerry set the table. They finished their dinner and went into the living room and left their dad to sit at the table alone. Julie opened her science book and began to read it in the dim light. She paused and rubbed her head as she looked up from the book. Her mind drifted in its tiredness from the day. *No matter what, God,* she prayed in thought to herself, *I won't doubt you this time.* She rubbed her tired eyes. *I may not understand why God doesn't answer my prayer, but I know it's not God's fault that my dad drinks and does the things that he does. I refuse to blame God,* Julie resigned and went back to reading.

As the weeks passed, each day at school became more and more difficult. Julie had never dreamed that school could be so bad. Things had gone from bad to worse with Lindsey. Julie had never figured out what had caused the problem. All she knew was that not only was Lindsey not talking to her but that none of her classmates, boy or girl, would talk to her either. If anyone was caught talking to her, they were ostracized by Lindsey and the rest of the class. The saddest of all was that it had completely severed the last part of Sarah and her friendship. It was Sarah's friendship that she missed the most. Julie knew that she had brought this onto herself. She was sad that Sarah, like herself, did not realize that she was changing. Julie thought that nothing could have ever been as bad as third grade, but she could never have imagined this. In just a few weeks, Julie had gone from leader to outcast.

Days and then weeks passed by. Day after day, Julie sat alone in the classroom. No one said hi or even asked her a question. It was as if she did not even exist. Julie had reasoned to herself that everything would settle down and blow over after awhile. But it never did.

Julie prayed harder than she had ever prayed. She continued to go to church with Ronnie at evening service and had borrowed Matt's Bible to read before bed. She no longer played with her dolls and had taken to sleeping with the Bible held tightly to her. Maybe her dad would have a hard time pulling the Bible away from her shielding her from the abuse. She continued to feel God's love and presence. She had ceased to ask God why her life was the way it was. It was enough to know that Jesus loved her. It was enough to be able to even feel again. She refused to let the walls of hardness grow around her heart again. The only problem was that by allowing herself to feel love again, it would also mean that she would become vulnerable to feeling the pain also. It seemed that with each mounting day and each passing week that the pain was becoming more than she could bear.

Julie confided with her brothers and her mom about the problems at school. She remembered the words that her mom had spoken to her when she had warned her about Lindsey. She wished that she had listened to her mom. Julie couldn't wait for Tuesday evening and the weekends to visit with her mom. Her mom always took the time to listen. They would sit and talk while playing a game. Julie liked when her mom would tell her stories of her childhood and hardships. She had wished that she could go and live with her mom. Lately however, Bob and her mom had been arguing a lot. She would hear her mom tell Bob, "I don't want to argue while the kids are here." Julie felt sad that they were having troubles. She had thought that it was probably because of them. Everything in life seemed to always be about them.

Julie longed for a new season. The winter that she so loved had been too long. It seemed as if she would never see another spring or smell another flower. Her life had felt the same way. Though she had purposed in her heart to never lose her love for God, somehow no matter how much she had tried, she lost all hope of her life ever changing. She began to fall into a despair that she had never felt before, a despair that seemed to lull her into a desire to want to die.

❀

Julie awoke with a startle. She bolted up in bed with such a thrust that she felt dizzy and lightheaded. Her heart raced within her, and she could feel it pound with great force at every beat against her chest. Julie wiped her brow, which was wet with sweat although the room was cool. The wind howled outside causing her windows to rattle within their frames. She touched her swollen, red eyes with her hand and rubbed them gently.

Tears began to stream down her face—at first, a drop or two, and then into a steady stream. She got up and shut her door so that no one would hear her and then rushed back into her bed. Julie sat on the edge of the bed. She felt sick in her stomach. She reached for the white window blind and gave it a tug and let it go. It spun to the top and continued to spin on its roll. Julie sat as she watched it spin. She turned to look out the window and stared blankly at the night as it turned to an ashen gray and then to blue sky as the sun rose slowly behind the mountaintop.

Nothing seemed to faze Julie. Amid all of her pain and confusion, she felt a strange numbness. As if everything inside of her was shutting down, and she could do nothing to stop it. She buried her head in her hands and turned it back and forth in an effort to find rest for her troubled mind. The memories of the night flooded through her mind. The terror consumed her, and she felt herself shaking. *What had happened? What had happened?*

Julie had suddenly awakened in the night. Fear gripped her heart and terror had filled her as she pushed her dad away. She felt violated but had no memories of what had happened. She jumped out of her bed and ran to the bathroom and locked the door behind her. She didn't know how long she had stayed there. After a long time, she opened the door and slowly listened for any sound in the house. She slowly turned to go back to her bedroom with the idea that she would run back to the bathroom if her dad was still in her room. She laid in the dark the rest of the night and vowed that she would not go to sleep. She knew that her dad had done something terrible to her, the evidence was there, but she didn't know everything that he had done.

Julie took her fists and hit her head as if to pound some memory of what could have happened. But nothing was there except for the terror and fear. Her mind raced. She was due for her period soon. Had he violated her to that extent? How stupid could she have been to have let this happen? How stupid could she have been to not have awakened in time? How could she not remember? But if she was asleep, she'd never know. Her fists were hitting her head harder now, and she stopped as the pain pierced through her. She couldn't concentrate or think.

She lifted her head and wrung her hands nervously together searching for an answer that was not there. Hope seemed to flee from her, and she gritted her teeth as she felt all the years of pain come rushing over her in a wave of despair. She closed her eyes to block out life itself. She clutched her wrists so tightly that her fingernails pierced into her wrists. Julie felt her whole body shake from the inside out. She opened her eyes and looked down at her wrists where her fingernails had pierced them. She saw the purple creases that she had created from the indentations. The blood in these marks appeared as if just waiting to spurt out. She studied them in her hopelessness as a new thought tumbled into her mind, thoughts that she had never entertained as a possible solution. *It would be so easy*, she thought. *The pain would then be over once and for all.* Then it would not matter what her dad had done to her. She would not know, and no one else would know either. The idea seemed worthy of the cost.

Somewhere, from very deep within her soul, Julie felt a loving tug. "No," it said softly but firmly. "No, Julie, this is not the answer. Lo, I am with you always," the loving presence spoke to her heart and drew her to her knees. Julie slid to the floor and lay there limply. She buried her head into her arms and began to sob uncontrollably. She cried and cried until she couldn't cry anymore as she released her pain to the Jesus that she knew still loved her.

Making it together.

CHAPTER

27

The wind blew softly and seemed to caress Julie's face with its tender touch. Julie climbed to the top of the mountain before stopping to rest. She leaned against a tall oak tree and looked up into the deep blue sky. She closed her eyes as the bright sunlight shined down upon her. The warmth of the sun's rays seemed to flow over her and go deep into her soul.

Julie caught her breath and stood looking down at the little white house with the red shutters. It looked so forlorn, its red shutters faded to pink, the porch lost in the overgrowth of the unattended yard. Julie sat down to rest. The bright sunshine warmed the back of her neck. Wisps of her hair blew across her face and tickled her nose.

Julie smiled as she heard the familiar bark. In the distance, Mamie was running to join her. Her ears flopped gaily. Julie noticed that Mamie's gait was much slower these days revealing the years that had crept up on her faithful furry friend. Julie leaned against the oak tree and watched Mamie struggle to climb the hill as it got steeper. "Come on, ole girl. You're almost here!" Julie called out.

Julie felt Mamie's big, red tongue come across her face before she could dodge it. She lost her balance as her back slid off the tree that she was leaning up against when Mamie pounced onto her lap. Julie began to laugh as Mamie flopped down on top of her and licked her feverishly. "Come on, girl. I can't breathe," Julie said in between dodging Mamie's affection. "You got me. You got me!" Julie said laughing out loud.

Mamie gave one last lick and climbed off Julie as if to say, "I win!"

Julie sat up and leaned back against the tree at a slightly different angle. Mamie curled up beside her and rested her wet nose on Julie's lap. Julie sat quietly, looking past the cliff's edge. In the far distance, she could see the whole town of Grantville as if it were a small Christmas village under a Christmas tree. Julie closed her eyes and let her thoughts wander and then opened her eyes.

She patted Mamie's head and stroked her red fur. The weeks had been difficult. Julie could find no peace until she had confronted her dad one morning at breakfast. It had taken all the courage that she had to confront him, but his answer almost destroyed her.

"What did you do to me?" Julie blurted out to him that morning. It caught her dad off guard and startled him to see Julie's austere demeanor. Never had he seen her so bold. He had tried to wave it off with his hand as if it was something as indifferent as the time of day. And then he walked away.

Julie knew that her brothers were still asleep. She was determined to get an answer. "You tell me what you did to me!" she exclaimed and ran to get in front of him. Julie could see that at first, he was shocked. But then to her despair, she saw the cockiness that she had grown so accustomed to, cross his face. With a smirk that Julie could not bear, he looked her in the eyes and said, "You enjoyed it!"

Julie thought that she might faint. She felt the blood leave her face as if it was being drained from her body. She had stared at her dad in brokenness and unbelief before composing herself and running upstairs. She ran into her room and shut and locked the door. She knelt down and prayed until the tears flowed no more.

She waited anxiously during the next weeks not knowing the extent of what had happened to her. She withdrew within herself to the point that her brothers and mom had become worried about her. She wouldn't play any games and would sit and stare into space lost in her own world. And then one day, to her relief, she had her period.

For whatever reason, her dad for at least a few weeks had left her alone. Julie had hoped that maybe in confronting him and continuing with her prayers that the abuse would be coming to an end. But Julie decided that she would try and take more precautions. She decided that she would move her room around in a different position. She deliberately put her bed against the wall nearest the door. From here she would be able to look into her brothers' bedroom. She also talked Ronnie into putting his bed against the wall near his door. This way, he could see her and she could see him since they never shut their doors. Most of the time, their dad wasn't home when they went to bed, so Julie started leaving the hall light on. This dimly lit up her and Ronnie's bedroom. It was enough to start a routine that if the hall light was turned out or her bedroom door was shut, it would have caused her brothers to become suspicious. It began to work. Julie felt that maybe her dad was afraid that either she might finally talk since she was older or that he was afraid that he might get caught by her brothers.

Shortly after that, God answered a prayer in a way that she had never expected. Her dad for the first time in his life was transferred to the midnight shift at work. Because of this, they had a telephone installed. Their dad said that they were now old enough to be left alone at night. Julie thought that she would shout for joy when she found out that her dad would not be coming home at night.

Julie stretched her legs and changed position. Mamie rolled her eyes up at Julie for disturbing her nap. Julie looked down the hill at the little house and then over at Gramma Emma's house. Good memories flooded through her heart. She looked at the old horseshoe pegs where they used to play with trucks and where she remembered happier days. She was now doing better. She knew that she could only take one day at a time. God had given her a new hope, and Julie could feel it growing within her.

Julie petted Mamie's head and said, "We gotta go, girl!" Mamie stood up and shook her fur as she stretched. Julie stood up and took a deep breath of the fresh spring air. She walked down the hillside with Mamie by her side. The forsythias had already bloomed and her favorite, the lilacs, were in full blossom. The smell of lilacs filled the air. She walked down the dirt road past her old home and then past Gramma Emma's house.

As Julie neared the bottom of the hill, she found herself humming a song that they had sung in church the last Sunday. "Many things about tomorrow, I don't seem to understand. But I'll go until tomorrow 'cause I know who holds my hand."

Julie walked slowly with Mamie by her side. She followed the fence that lined their yard and continued to sing the song.

"Hey, Julie!" she heard Jerry call out to her as he sat on the porch rail with Matt beside him. They waved to Julie to hurry and join them. Ronnie was at work. He had started a job over in Grantville at the hospital. Julie took off in a quick trot as Mamie followed closely behind her.

"What's up?" Julie asked as she searched both of her brothers' faces.

"We think that Dad's got a girlfriend," Matt answered.

"You really think so?" Julie asked. She didn't know whether to be excited or scared. Their dad had had a few girlfriends after Rhonda, but no relationships had developed or lasted. Oh, how Julie wished that it would be someone nice—that is, if what her brothers were saying was true.

"What makes you think this?" Julie continued to press her brothers for more information.

"He just seems different, happier than I've seen him for a long time. Kind of like he used to be," Jerry said in a solemn voice.

Julie studied Jerry's face, which was mixed with a hint of joy and a touch of sorrow. She marveled that he also longed to see a dad that they had once known years ago. Julie squeezed between her two brothers and hopped up onto the porch rail and sat with them.

"He also told us to clean the house extra good this weekend and to keep it picked up," Matt added with a grin.

"Wow!" Julie said. "I bet you guys are right."

Just then they heard the front door open, and their dad came out. He was freshly shaven and dressed extra nice.

"I'm going out for a while and then going to work," he said. "I'll see you in the morning before school."

"Come on, Jul!" Matt called out. "Help me finish supper."

"It's your turn to do the dishes, Jerry," Julie said.

"Well, let's get everything done," Jerry added. "Ronnie said that he'd play some ball with us when he got home if there was still daylight."

Spring came and went faster than Julie had ever remembered. Julie was glad when summer finally arrived and they were out of school. Matt and Jerry had been right. Sure enough their dad had a girlfriend. They were all surprised when he brought her to the house to meet them. She quietly welcomed Alice and tried to make her feel comfortable. There was something about her that Julie really liked. Was it possible, that after five years, that maybe their dad had met a nice woman?

As the months passed by, Alice more and more began to become a real part of their family. Julie held her guard up as long as she could. But to her delight, she discovered that it was not necessary.

"What do you think?" she asked her brothers one day as the four of them hung out in her brothers' bedroom.

"She's really nice," Jerry said.

"Yeah, I can't believe it!" Matt added.

"She's a lot younger than dad, but she is really nice," Ronnie said.

"I like her," Julie said with a smile. "And you know what?" Julie asked.

"What?" all three of her brothers asked at the same time. They looked at Julie and the quizzical smile that she had on her face.

"Mom likes her too!" Julie answered.

"You know, you're right," Matt said. "I've seen them talking at the car sometimes."

"Well, if Mom likes her, she's got to be nice," Ronnie assured them.

"I heard that Dad is going to bring her to Gramma's dinner on Sunday," Jerry piped in.

"Really?" Julie asked excitedly. "How do you always find these things out, Jerry?"

Jerry just smiled at his young sister. "I've got my ways, sis."

The more that Alice came around, the more that Julie liked her. There were many reasons, but most of all, Alice was a kind and loving person. Julie couldn't figure out how her dad could have found such a nice woman to be his girlfriend, but for whatever reason, she was so glad. Her dad had not abused her a single time since Alice had come into their lives. Alice began to help them cook the meals, and one Saturday, she even helped them clean the house.

Julie learned from Alice that she was from Michigan and that she didn't have any family here. She had been married once and had divorced. Julie wondered why she had never had children but decided not to ask her. Julie loved the idea of Alice being with them. On several occasions, Julie had awakened to find that Alice had stayed the night. This concerned Julie. Alice was just too nice of a person for her dad to talk into staying there without marrying her. She reminded Julie of being more like a big sister than her dad's girlfriend. Julie began to pray that God would perform another miracle. It seemed hopeless that her dad would ever take the responsibility of marrying Alice, but Julie prayed anyway.

It was a beautiful summer. Everything seemed new and fresh. Alice made new curtains for the kitchen. Together, they cleaned and rearranged the furniture and gave the house a new look. Every night, Alice cooked a home-cooked meal.

Alice didn't seem to have an established church faith, but everything about her was kind and good. One day, when they were cleaning up the dinner dishes together, Julie began to talk to her about how much God loves them. Julie paused to see how Alice would react. Alice reached out and brushed Julie's curls from her eyes. She looked kindly into Julie's searching eyes and smiled a big smile and then said, "Maybe you can help me to understand God more."

Julie smiled back, and her eyes sparkled with a new hope. *Could it be that maybe now things would begin to change in their lives?*

Gramma Emma had asked the family to go on a big picnic out at Hanson's Park. Julie was so excited. She had only the fondest of memories with her family at Hanson's Park. As happy as Julie was about the upcoming picnic, she couldn't help feeling a twinge of sorrow ebb at her heart. She still missed her mom at those picnics. The picnics were never quite the same without her. She decided to share it with her mom when they would meet on Saturday to go school shopping.

It was such a special day for Julie. Her brothers had taken a ride in the old car that Ronnie had bought and was fixing up. Julie felt so happy to share this special time alone with her mom. Julie stopped to look at a pretty dress and asked her mom what she thought of it. Julie thought that it was much too expensive, but her mom took one look at the dress and said, "Julie, it'll look beautiful on you."

"But, Mom, it's a little expensive," Julie said hesitantly.

Ethel took the dress off the rack and held it up to Julie. Tears filled Ethel's eyes unexpectedly. "It's okay, Mom, we don't have to get this one," Julie said quickly. She reached to retrieve the dress from her mom's hand.

"No, honey," Ethel said. "It's not the price. It's just that you are so grown up. You are a young woman now."

"I'll always be your little girl," Julie said as she put her arm around her mom.

They slowly walked to the cash register together and stopped here and there to look at blouses. "Mom, Gramma Emma's having a picnic out at Hanson's Park tomorrow," Julie said a little sadly.

"Well, that's nice, honey," Ethel commented. "It's okay if you go there instead of coming over. You'll have fun."

Julie always marveled at her mom's unselfishness. She knew that her mom had picked up on her sad tone. Julie wanted to explain to her mom what her sadness was all about, so she pressed forward in their conversation. "Mom, Alice is going to come too," Julie started to explain. "Do you like Alice, Mom?"

"Julie, I really like Alice," Ethel answered without hesitation.

"She's really good to us, Mom. She's nothing like Rhonda," Julie continued.

"I know," Ethel answered with a big smile. She gave the clerk the money for the dress, and then they headed out of the store.

"Let's go to Coney Island for some hot dogs," Ethel suggested.

"And a chocolate coke?" Julie hinted.

As they sat and ate, Julie continued the conversation. "Mom, I miss you so much when we go out to Hanson's Park without you."

"It's been a lot of years, Julie," Ethel said in a solemn voice.

"Mom, why don't you come out later and join us?" Julie let the words spill out of her mouth without hesitation.

"Why, Julie, I couldn't do that," Ethel said quickly.

"No, really, Mom. Even Gramma Emma said the other day that she wished that you'd join us sometime."

"Really, your Gramma Emma said that?" Ethel asked surprised.

"Yeah, Mom. And Alice and you are more like friends. And no one would mind. I'm sure. Not even Dad."

"Well, we'll see," Ethel said and then quickly changed the subject.

※

Julie was glad to see Alice in the kitchen when she entered the house. "Hey, you want to help me make some potato salad for the picnic tomorrow?" Alice asked.

Julie ran into the kitchen and grabbed a knife to help peel the potatoes. "When you're dad comes home, we have something we want to talk to you about," Alice said.

Julie glanced quickly to look at Alice's face. *Was there a problem?* she wondered. But to her delight, Alice had a slight smile on her face.

"What?" Julie asked. She thought that maybe she would be able to get Alice to clue her in.

"You'll have to wait," Alice answered with a big smile.

Julie sat at the kitchen table. Her back was against the window as the hot August air blew softly on her neck. Alice hurried to put the corn on the cob on the table with the meatloaf that she had made. Ronnie sat at one end of the table, and Jerry sat at the other end. Matt sat beside Julie, and her dad and Alice sat across the table from them. Everyone passed the food hurriedly and began to eat. Julie took a deep breath to stifle back her emotions. For the first time in so many years, Julie felt like they were beginning to be a real family again. Julie still ached at the thought of her mom not being there, but knowing that her mom liked Alice, as much as she did, seemed to make it okay.

They had all finished eating, and Ronnie started to get up from the table. Alice asked him to wait one minute before leaving. Julie watched Alice's face closely. Alice turned and glanced at their dad. Julie saw their dad give her a faint smile and a nod.

"I wanted to tell you all something before you go," Alice spoke quietly. She paused for a moment and then gave them all a big smile. "I hope this will make you as happy as it has made me," she continued.

Julie glanced at her brothers who looked as puzzled as Julie felt. They all glanced at their dad and then back to Alice.

"Well," Alice said. "Do you remember last week when your dad and I went away for a few days?"

Julie and her brothers all nodded but didn't say a word.

"We got married!" Alice said letting out a big sigh.

"Really?" Julie let out an excited cry and stood up to go over to Alice.

"That's great!" Matt said.

Jerry and Ronnie got up from the table to join Julie. "We're really happy for you, Alice and Dad," Jerry said.

"Yeah," Ronnie added.

"We wanted to tell you first before we tell everyone tomorrow at the picnic," Alice said happily.

Julie lay in bed that night and let the reality of what had happened sink into her heart and mind. She felt a peace flow over her. The little cross that still hung on her wall flickered in the dark night, a reminder that God had seen her desperation and answered her prayers. Julie had many questions that raced through her mind. There were so many what ifs. Julie pushed them all away. *No, for now, it was enough to know that things were happy*, she thought. She would deal with tomorrow's problems tomorrow.

A New Season

CHAPTER

28

Julie rushed past the front door as quickly as she could. They had all hurried back home from Sunday school to get ready for the picnic. Julie ran up the stairs skipping three steps at a time. She slipped and fell flat on the last step.

"You're the only one that I know of, sis, that can fall up the steps," Jerry commented while reaching out to help her up.

"Slow down, Jul!" Matt added.

Ronnie laughed and then said, "You okay?"

"You know it'll be at least a half hour before we leave for the picnic," Jerry told her.

They all darted back and forth getting their things ready. Julie ran downstairs and helped Alice while Matt, Jerry, and Ronnie loaded the car.

Julie couldn't wait to round the last bend in the road that brought them to Hanson's Park. She hopped out of the car and ran to the picnic tables to say hi to her gramma, aunts, and cousins.

"Come on, Jul!" Ronnie called out.

"Yeah, Dad said we have time to take a swim before we eat!" Jerry yelled out.

"Wait until I get some foil," Matt called back to them.

"I'll get the rock," Julie added. She quickly peeled off the clothing that she had put on over her swimsuit.

Julie ran to the river and found a nice round rock. "Here you go, Matt."

Matt took the rock and wrapped the foil around it. Jerry and Ronnie dove into the water head first, followed by Julie, and then Matt, who held the foiled rock in his hand.

"Throw it over here!" Ronnie called out.

"Yeah, it's deeper there," Jerry agreed.

Matt pulled back and gave the rock a quick toss. "One, two, three, go!" Matt yelled out.

Instantly, the water was a mass of splash as all four of them dove into the deep water trying to retrieve the rock. Julie came up first, gasping for air, followed by the others. "Did you get it?" she asked. "I ran out of breath."

"No," all three of her brothers answered.

"It's a little murky at the bottom," Julie said.

They all took a deep breath and then dove again. Finally, Jerry came up with the rock in his hand. "I could barely see the foil," he said.

Julie laughed as she looked at him. His dark hair was matted to his brow, and water ran down his face in streams.

"Gramma's calling us for lunch," Matt said.

They all hurried from the river. Ronnie grabbed Julie's hand, helping her, as they climbed up the slippery clay bank to get to the picnic tables.

After they finished eating, Ronnie suggested that they all take a walk upstream and give their food some time to settle. They climbed down the bank and waded in the more shallow water, which was knee-deep. They then continued down the riverbed, stepping onto the rounded river stones in their bare feet.

"Hey, I wonder if the old swing is still hanging?" Jerry asked.

Julie ran ahead of her brothers to check it out.

"How does she run so fast barefoot on those rocks?" Ronnie asked with a chuckle.

"I don't know," Matt answered back.

"Hey, you guys!" Julie yelled out. "It's still here!"

They sat down on the top of the bank and began to talk.

"Can't we go in yet?" Julie asked.

"No," Ronnie answered. "It's too soon since you ate."

Julie sat back and listened to her brothers talk. She marveled at how grown up they were. She seemingly was unaware of how grown up she, herself, had become. A smile crossed her face as she listened to them talk.

"I graduate this year," Ronnie was saying, "and then as soon as I'm eighteen years old, I'm going to enlist in the Marine Corps."

Julie knew that Ronnie had always said that when he grew up, he was going to be a marine. But the thought of him leaving her was more than she could bear.

"Me too," Jerry said. "As soon as I graduate next year, I'm going to enlist too."

"Not me," Matt says. "I'm going to fall in love, get married, and get a job."

"In that order?" Jerry asked. He gave Matt a quick poke in the arm.

"What about you, Julie?" Ronnie asked.

"Yeah, Jul. What do you want to do when you graduate?" Matt asked.

"I want to go to college," Julie answered in a quiet voice.

"Good for you, Jul," Jerry said with a brotherly confidence. "Good for you."

"I don't know how I'll ever afford to go, but I'd like to go," Julie added.

"Jul, don't worry," Ronnie said. "You'll get scholarships. You'll see."

"You really think so, Ronnie?" Julie asked hopefully.

"Sure you will," Jerry added.

"You're smart, Jul," Matt said matter-of-factly.

Julie thought of the possibility that someday she might go to college. No one in their family had ever gone to college. She stretched out her legs and leaned back on her arms and continued to listen to her brothers talk. The sun bathed her in a warmth that seemed to radiate into her very soul.

Julie stirred upon hearing Ronnie mention the word *Vietnam.* She crossed her legs Indian style and rested her chin in her cupped hands.

"You know they'll send you to Vietnam for sure," Matt stated.

"I know," Ronnie agreed.

"But we have to defend our country," Jerry added.

"Where is Vietnam?" Julie asked. She had heard about it on the television during the evening newscasts. But to Julie, it was a faraway place. How could her brothers be talking about going to a place so very far away?

"Near Asia," Matt answered.

"Yeah, near Cambodia," Jerry added.

Julie had heard enough. It was too wonderful of a day to bring in a cloud of doom. Julie could not bear listening about her brothers going to a place that she had not even studied yet in school. And the thought of them fighting in a war over there and something happening to them was too much for her to think about.

Jerry started to say something, but before he could finish his sentence, Julie had jumped up and pulled his arm from beneath him.

"Hey, whatcha doing, Jul?" Jerry asked as he sat back up.

"Come on, you guys," Julie said. "Let's go swimming!"

"Yeah," said Ronnie.

Matt had already run ahead of them. He grabbed the rope and swung out over the river. He let go, right in the middle of the river, and plunged down into the deep water. Jerry grabbed the rope as it came back and followed quickly after Matt. Ronnie caught the rope on its return and waited a minute for Matt and Jerry to swim out of the way. He took off and let go and landed with a loud splash.

"Good one, Ronnie!" Jerry yelled.

"Your turn, Julie," Matt coaxed his young sister.

Julie caught the rope with both hands. She hesitated upon realizing that the rope was a little shorter than usual and that the drop was a little higher.

"Come on, Jul!" Jerry encouraged. "It's not as far down as it looks."

Julie lifted her feet and the rope took off with her hanging onto it. She swung back, returning to the bank, landing square on her two feet.

"The idea is to let go," Ronnie said teasing her.

"Okay, okay. I'm going," Julie answered. She could hear her brothers chuckling as she took off once again. She swung out swiftly and let go. She felt the water rush past her as she plunged into the deep. When she emerged, she heard her brothers clapping and laughing as she climbed out of the river.

They walked back along the bank of the river to return to their picnic tables. Julie wrapped a towel around her as she followed beside her brothers. She looked at Ronnie's dark, black hair and his round, dark eyes, so expressive as he talked. She looked at Jerry, his lean, tall frame, his dark-brown hair pushed to one side, and his narrow dark-brown eyes, which highlighted his handsome features. She then turned to Matt, with his captivating big, blue eyes being accented by his blond hair. Julie treasured the moment. She walked in silence and enjoyed listening to their conversation. They were all growing up, and their lives were changing faster than Julie could grasp the reality. But for today, they were together. This was their day.

"Look!" Matt said loudly.

"Wow!" Jerry exclaimed.

"It can't be!" Ronnie joined in.

Julie couldn't believe what she was seeing. "It is!" she yelled and then took off running toward her mom's car. Julie couldn't believe it either. Their mom had come to the picnic, and with her, she had brought Gramma Winnie and Pap Pap John.

Julie and her brothers ran up to the car where their mom was standing, talking to Alice. Ethel turned and greeted them as they joined her.

"Mom, you came!" Julie said and gave her a big hug.

Ethel hugged Julie back. They walked to the picnic table where Gramma Emma was uncovering the food and insisting on the new visitors to eat. Julie stepped back and leaned against an old oak tree. She looked up at the massive branches that hung out over the picnic tables providing the much needed shade. Julie watched her family sitting together. Matt and Ronnie and Jerry grabbed some more fried chicken and potato salad and were sitting with their wet suits at the far end of the table where Ethel had joined them. Gramma Winnie had already reached into her big purse and pulled out a deck of cards, shuffling them, ready to get a game of cards going.

Julie saw her dad pop the lid off another can of beer and wobble unsteadily as he sat back down at the picnic table. Alice stood behind him and steadied him with her hand. But nothing could take away the joy that Julie was feeling. Her family was together. Julie never dreamed that there would come a day when they would all be together again at a picnic. Julie listened to the laughter of her cousins playing, her aunts and uncles talking, Gramma Emma's kind voice, and Gramma Winnie's jolly laugh. Julie smiled as she watched all of them. She heard her mom call her name and wave to her to join them. Julie walked to the table and grabbed a cupcake and then sat down beside them. Ethel reached over and took Julie's hand into hers and held it tightly. Julie sat contently and listened to her brothers talk to their mom. There was a sweetness to the moment that Julie wanted to remember forever. "Many things about tomorrow, I don't seem to understand. But I'll go until tomorrow for I know who holds my hand."

Julie at graduation. "Surely goodness and mercy
will follow me all the days of my life."

(circa 1980)

CHAPTER

29

Julie nearly jumped out of her chair as the sound of the door loudly slamming shut startled her back to the present. Her mind was still in a daze. She rubbed her eyes as if to awaken into the reality of her current life.

The wind had picked up, and Julie now realized that the back door had slammed shut. She stood up and ran to check the door and then paused to listen if the noise had awakened the children from their nap. All was quiet. Julie secured the door and then walked over to the stereo. She lifted the lid and, once again, flipped over the records. She pushed the eject button and returned back to sit in the living room.

She paused for a moment and placed her hands onto her hips. "What a mess," she said as she looked at a pile of pictures that were strewn all over the carpet. A gust of wind had blown them all to the floor.

Julie grabbed a box and sat down on the floor to pick up the pictures. She knew that it would take more than a day to sort out a lifetime. But today was the beginning of a process. She knew that God would lead her on this journey to heal.

Quickly, she began to gather the pictures together and put them into the box. When she had picked up the last two packets of pictures, which were separate from the others, she couldn't help noticing the date. She paused and listened once again if the children were stirring from their naps. Slowly, she took the last two packets and opened them. She pulled the pictures from their packets and began to leaf through them.

She held the pictures of her brothers and studied them. Ronnie had gone into the Marine Corps, and Jerry had held true to his promise to follow. Both had served in Vietnam. Julie felt a tear come to her eyes, relieved and thankful that they had both returned home alive. She looked at the picture of Matt and his wife. She drew the pictures closely to her bosom as if to hold them near to her heart.

She then put them down and picked up the rest of the pictures. Julie smiled as she looked at the pictures of her graduation. She leaned back against the chair and closed her eyes and remembered that very special day.

Her heart had pounded as the graduation song had begun and when she and her classmates had marched proudly up the aisle. Julie could still hear her principal's booming voice as he said, "It is with great pleasure that I present to you the graduating class of 1972."

Julie had sat and listened intently to the songs and presentations. Excitement had built as she anticipated receiving her diploma. But she was surprised at the next turn of events. Her principal had stepped up to the podium and announced that at this time he would present the scholarships, awards, and honors. Julie had listened as her classmates received their various rewards. But then to her surprise, she had heard her name being called to come forward.

Julie knew that she had received scholarships, but she did not know that it would be announced at the ceremony. Julie had walked forward as quickly as she could squeeze past her classmates. Her face had turned red as she felt humbled by the attention from her principal, Mr. Jenkins, as he announced the full scholarship that she had received.

Julie smiled as she shook his hand and had turned to leave. The crowd was applauding when to her surprise, Mr. Jenkins continued to hold her hand and continued to talk. "I know of no awards that are available to present to anyone who has gone twelve years of schooling and never missed a single day of school, but it seems worthy to honor her for this dedication."

To Julie's surprise, he had not yet finished his full presentation. He continued to hold her hand and speak. "Julie has represented her classmates on the student council and is also a member of the National Honor Society. She has represented us as Ms. Benson High. And now it is with great pleasure for me to announce that she has been elected by her peers to represent the Benson High School as our representative to the Mineral County Fair to be held in August." Once again, the crowd applauded loudly.

Julie nodded a thank-you and had turned to leave the stage, but her principal continued to hold her hand. "Julie, by the choice of her peers, has also been acknowledged as being chosen for the following honors: Most Likely to Succeed, Best All Around, Friendliest, Most Studious"—and to the thunder of the crowd's clapping—"Most Athletic!" Julie felt her face turn crimson red as she faced the crowd. Her peers clapped, and Julie was touched by the honors they had bestowed upon her. These were the people that she had shared most of her life with, the good and the bad. Julie turned and left the stage and returned to her seat to await the presentation of the diplomas.

"Before we present the diplomas," Mr. Jenkins continued, "Mr. Tindrel has one more award that he would like to present."

Mr. Tindrel stepped up to the podium and began to speak. "On behalf of the Tri-Hi-Y Club, we give an award every year to a member of the senior class. This award is called I'm a Third Award. The Third Award is an award that is given to the senior that has been nominated and elected by our members to possess the following qualities. They must put God first, others second, and themselves third. On behalf of the Tri-Hi-Y Club, we would like to present this award to Ms. Julie Anna Clayton!"

Julie had sat motionless not knowing what to do to accept this great honor. "Ms. Clayton," Mr. Tindrel called out as he motioned with an outstretched arm, "would you come and receive this trophy?"

Julie arose to the thunderous clapping of her friends and family. She climbed the steps slowly and felt her legs shaking nervously with each step. She approached the podium and took the trophy into her hands that Mr. Tindrel had handed her. He gave her a sincere smile as he shook her hand firmly. The award was more than Julie could have ever imagined. She looked out at the audience, and her eyes focused on her family. They were all there, clapping the loudest of all. Her brothers beamed with pride and love for the little sister that was their own. Julie looked deep into her mom's eyes as the tears flowed down her mom's cheeks. The faces of those who loved her were the best award.

Julie felt the tears stream down her face. She opened her eyes and quickly stacked the remaining pictures into the box. As she did, the words to the song playing on the stereo filled her heart.

> Something, beautiful, something good. All of my confusions, He understood. All I had to offer Him was brokenness and strife. But He made something, beautiful out of my life.

A smile crossed Julie's face. She wiped her eyes with her hands. God had kept his every promise to her. He had brought her through and brought her out. He had given her the desires of her heart, a Christian husband and family. Her life had changed, and God had blessed her more than she could have ever known.

Now she would heal. *Oh to honor, you, dear Lord*, she thought. *Oh to honor you!*

Julie felt a slight tug on her blouse. Startled, she then looked down at the tiny face that peered up at her.

"Mommy," the little voice said as he tugged her sleeve again.

Julie looked into the deep blue eyes of her little boy. "Hi, honey. Did you have a nice nap?" Julie put the box of pictures aside on the end table. She took her little boy onto her lap. He laid his head against her shoulder. Julie held him tightly and kissed the top of his head. She gently stroked his blond strands of hair from his sweating brow.

"Mommy!" Mikey whispered in an excited voice as he quickly jerked up his head. "Jenny's awake!" He jumped off Julie's lap and grabbed her hand. "Come on, Mommy," he said and pulled her gently.

Julie motioned with her finger to her mouth for them to be quiet. She knelt slowly down to her son's level and whispered, "Let's peek and see what she's doing."

Mikey let out a low squeal, put his small hand onto his mouth to be quiet, and nodded in agreement. They tiptoed to the bedroom and peeked in. Julie could hear the springs on the baby bed squeaking as Jenny jumped up and down. "She's awake," Julie said out loud.

Mikey ran into the room to greet his sister. Jenny let out a squeal of delight as she saw her brother enter the room. Julie heard the front door open and a familiar voice calling to her.

"Anyone home?"

Julie ran to meet Mike, her husband, at the door. She wrapped her arms around him and gave him a big hug.

"Well, this is a nice surprise," he said as he looked at Julie and gave her a big smile.

Julie could hear the children laughing in the bedroom. She walked beside Mike to the kitchen and started supper.

"Hey, I really like the song that's playing," Mike said.

"Me too," Julie said with a smile. "Me too."

Mike and Julie (Marsha Lynn Barth) and
Michael Jr. and Jenny. *Promises fulfilled.*

EPILOGUE

Many years have passed since the ending of *The Shattering*. There is so much more to tell. How does one heal from the hurt and pain that is experienced from abuse? How do we deal with the broken trust, the shattered innocence and the shattered purity, the crushed hope and the vehement anger? How do we find our identity when it has been shrouded with a cloak of fear and shame, guilt, and blame? It is a journey. A journey of healing that can lead us onto a pathway from Victim to Victor.

I remember when God had tugged at my heart to write this story. I asked God, "Why should I bring all of this up again?" It was in the past and I thought it was better left there. I asked God, "I live in Pennsylvania now—people know me here for who I truly am, why should I speak out and bring all of this shame back onto me?"

Quickly, I heard God speak to my heart with a firmness only surpassed by his love. "First of all, it was never your shame to bear. The cloak of shame was thrown upon you. And secondly, I died on the cross to take this shame from you. Never let anyone ever make you feel ashamed again." A new strength rose within me and I began to write.

The journey of healing leads us from Victim, to Survivor, to Overcomer, to Conqueror, and then to Victor. This is a journey that we are not meant to walk alone. "Behold, I stand at the door and knock, if any will hear my voice and open, I will come in." Jesus beckons us to open our heart to His love. He desires to take us in His bosom and wipe our tears away. He wants to tear down the hardened walls that surround our heart and set us free. Walls that were once built to protect us must now come down so that we can be delivered. Do we let Him tear down those walls? Do we dare open ourselves up to the vulnerability of the cruelty of life? Or do we continue in the denial of abuse and what effect that it had upon us? "Oh, that was in the past. It doesn't affect me now." Doesn't it? Then why are we afraid to deal with it? Satan's greatest defense against us is the shield of silence.

Why do we struggle in our lives, in relationships? Why do we live in denial? Denial of the hurt and pain? Why do we minimize the abuse? "Well it wasn't really that bad." Often, even after we become Christians, we minimize the effect that abuse has had on us. We say, "Well, I've put that under the blood." Have we? So often we have not put it under the blood but under the rug. The issues of life pushed under the rug will only cause us to stumble and fall over the lumpy carpet of life. So what can we do? We need to continue on the journey of healing.

One day through my many years of healing, God spoke to my heart. I was working at a drug rehabilitation hospital. Every day I had typed therapists' notes on dealing with the issues of drug and alcohol abuse. Issues that stemmed from the buried issues of pain and hurt. These were issues that were so similar to my own. God said to my heart once again, "It's time to deal with your past." I wrestled with God over this. "I'm fine, God. I'm doing good. I have a wonderful husband, two beautiful children, and a Christian home. I don't need to deal with anything, all of that is in the past." But He lovingly urged me on, "Am I a God who can only bring you out of your past and not a God who can also heal you from it? Am I not a healer as well as a deliverer?"

I took His hand and continued onward on this beautiful journey. A journey that I had started so very long ago as a child. How could I not trust Him now if he wanted more for me? The journey continued and as the word declares: "And in the process of time," "It came to pass." I continued to heal.

I began to learn more of God's love and grace. I began to know the heart of God—that He is the solution and not the cause. I am always amazed at how much buried hurt and pain will erupt into anger. No matter how much we live in denial and try to suppress the anger that we feel, it will spew forth as an erupting volcano that cannot be held back.

Through my journey, many years later, I can remember one day being very troubled in my heart. I was alone at my home in Pennsylvania. I was busy cleaning, trying to ignore the raging pain in my soul. I couldn't even figure out why I was so bothered. So I pushed aside the pain and hurt. I denied I even felt it, or the anger. I figured if I cleaned like a crazy woman it would just go away. But it didn't. After a while, I felt the familiar tug of God's love on my heart. "Why don't you tell me what's bothering you?" But I continued to push ahead, ignoring the pain, ignoring God's tug. And then again, "Why don't you tell me what's bothering you?" After a little while, I sat down in a chair, perplexed. I could feel His loving presence gently tugging at my heart. Why do we try to push this aside? Why do we quench His loving words? Like so many times on this journey, I began to yield to the One who loved me the most. I opened my heart to His questions.

"You want to know what's bothering me?" I asked. I felt my heart well up within me. I felt the tears begin to fill my eyes. "You want me to tell you what's bothering me?" I asked again out loud. I felt an anger arise in my heart that I did not know existed. As the tears flowed, I continued. "Where were you when all of this was happening to me? Where were the angels? Where were my angels?" I felt a sarcasm erupt out of me bursting through the veil of hurt and pain. "Did I wear my angels out? Was I too much for them to handle? Why didn't they help me? Why didn't you help me?" The tears flowed forth as I sobbed in the pain that I felt afresh. I cried for awhile and then I felt His loving presence engulf me. His peace covered me and I felt as if God Himself had taken me in His arms. I had never known a father's love as a child, never knew how it felt to run into a father's safe arms, or to feel the love of his comforting embrace. But that day, I did. It seemed as if the room filled with His presence, as if angels were in the midst. The anger began to seep away. My heart began to fill with His peace. And then He spoke to me in the stillness. "Every time that you cried, I cried with you. Every time that you cried, your angels cried too. But I cannot change or stop man's power of choice or I would have to rewrite the book. Your dad had a choice but we never left you. We were always there with you." My tears were different tears now. Tears that a God loved me this much. Tears that I mattered and that He had never left me alone. A new realization touched my heart—that truly God is not the cause of man's sins but He is truly the solution for our lives.

Healing is a journey. One that takes time. A journey we are not to walk alone but one that we can take with our Father. We reach to Him and He takes our hand. As we walk with Him, we will find others along this pathway who will walk beside us, side by side. We will help each other and we do heal.

We must deal with the issues of life, to heal from the issues of life, to be able to feel again, and to be made whole. In this book, *The Shattering*, my desire was that the abused and hurting could see the need to deal with these issues.

There is so much more to tell about this journey. So many more questions that need to be addressed and answered. In the sequel that will follow *The Shattering*, I hope to answer many of the questions that you may still have. Questions as to how Julie dealt with these issues. How she dealt with the pain and anger and confusion that had devastated her life. There were many confrontations with her dad in the years that followed. Each step of Julie's healing led her into more bitter conflict with the man that she knew as "Dad." Often she was torn between her own pain and anger and with how she would ever be able to confront her dad over what he had done to her. She knew that if she was ever to heal that she could not sweep it under the rug.

How could she ever forgive him? But if not, then how could she ever heal? How could she care about his very soul being saved when he had raped her own soul? Would she ever be able to forgive him and be delivered from her pain? Would she ever be free from the fear and shame, guilt and blame?

The journey will continue in the sequel that follows. May God's richest love guide you through this process as He walks with you on this healing journey.

Love,
Marty